FEMINISM AND THE POSTMODERN IMPULSE

Post-World War II Fiction

Magali Cornier Michael

STATE UNIVERSITY OF NEW YORK PRESS

Photo on the front cover courtesy of Joanna Foster.

Production by Ruth Fisher
Marketing by Dana E. Yanulavich

Published by
State University of New York Press, Albany

For information, address the State University of New York Press,
State University Plaza, Albany, NY 12246

Library of Congress Cataloging-in-Publication Data

Michael, Magali Cornier.
    Feminism and the postmodern impulse : post-World War II fiction /
Magali Cornier Michael.
        p.   cm.
    Includes bibliographical references (p.   ) and index.
    ISBN 0-7914-3015-4 (hard : alk. paper). — ISBN 0-7914-3016-2
(pbk. : alk. paper)
    1. English fiction—Women authors—History and criticism.
2. Feminism and literature—Great Britian—History—20th century.
3. American fiction—Women authors—History and criticism.
4. American fiction—20th century—History and criticism.
5. English fiction—20th century—History and criticism.
6. Lessing, Doris May, 1919-   Golden notebook.   7. Piercy, Marge.
Woman on the edge of time.   8. Atwood, Margaret Eleanor, 1939-
Handmaid's tale.   9. Carter, Angela, 1940-   Nights at the circus.
10. Postmodernism (Literature)   11. Feminism and literature.
12. Women and literature.   I. Title/
PR888.I45M53   1996
823'.914099287—dc20   95-41406
                                                                      CIP

10 9 8 7 6 5 4 3 2 1

FEMINISM
AND THE
POSTMODERN IMPULSE

෴

For Adrian

CONTENTS

Acknowledgments   ix

Chapter 1   Feminism and the Postmodern Impulse   1
                     The Plural and Constructed Nature of
                         Postmodernism and Feminism   11
                     The Relationship between Feminism
                         and Postmodernism   23
                     Feminism, Postmodernism, and
                         Key Western Concepts   31
                     Feminist and Postmodern Fiction   43

Chapter 2   The Emergence of Disruptive
                     Strategies in Women's Modernist Fiction   47

Chapter 3   Madness and Narrative Disruption in
                     Doris Lessing's *The Golden Notebook*   79

Chapter 4   Worlds in Confrontation:
                     Marge Piercy's *Woman on the Edge of Time*   109

Chapter 5   The Gap between Official History and
                     Women's Histories:
                     Margaret Atwood's *The Handmaid's Tale*   135

Chapter 6   Fantasy and Carnivalization in
                     Angela Carter's *Nights at the Circus*   171

Chapter 7   Feminist-Postmodern Fiction   209

Notes   223

Bibliography   257

Index   269

ACKNOWLEDGMENTS

I wish to thank the people and institutions who helped make this book possible. Emory University's English Department awarded me a fellowship to begin the first version of this project; Saint Louis University provided me with a Mellon Faculty Development Grant to write Chapter 2 during the Summer of 1991; and Duquesne University arranged for some release time as well as awarded me a Presidential Scholarship Grant during the Summer of 1994 to finish the project.

It would be difficult not to acknowledge the value of the two courses I had with Gayatri Spivak as a graduate student, which taught me how to read, think, and write critically from the beginning of my academic career. I thank Elizabeth Fox-Genovese and John Johnston for the many discussions I had with them and for the guidance they provided in the early phases of this project. My colleagues and graduate students at Duquesne University have provided a lively and productive intellectual climate in which to think, teach, and write. Special thanks go out to Linda Kinnahan, who proved to be an invaluable reader and critic of my work, helping me to untangle difficult theoretical ideas and develop more fully the most vital aspects of my arguments. Her intelligent comments and questions energized me, rekindling my enthusiasm each time. I also thank in particular Dan Watkins, Anne Brannen, and Sue Howard for their ongoing encouragement and friendship. I thank Joanna Foster for allowing me to use her artwork, "Tea for Three," on the cover of this book as well as for her friendship. I also want to thank Barbara Mortimer for her friendship and support and for the many useful and engaging discussions in the very early stages of this project.

I cannot even begin to thank Adrian for his never flagging encouragement, support, and love through the years. I am also grateful to Valerie and Brian, who were born in the midst of this project and who have opened to me a whole new realm of life.

Thanks also goes out to my mother, father, sister, and brother, who have always encouraged me and never doubted that I could accomplish whatever I set out to do.

I also thank those who have given me permission to reprint excerpts from previously published material:

From *The Handmaid's Tale* by Margaret Atwood. Copyright (c) 1985 by O.W. Toad, Ltd. First American Edition 1986. Reprinted by permission of Houghton Mifflin Co, all rights reserved; of the Canadian Publishers, McClelland & Stewart, Toronto; and of Random House U.K. Ltd., London.

From *Nights at the Circus* by Angela Carter. Copyright (c) 1984 by Angela Carter. Used by permission of Viking Penguin, a division of Penguin Books USA Inc., and the Estate of Angela Carter, c/o Rogers, Coleridge & White Ltd., 20 Powis Mews, London W11 1JN.

From *The Golden Notebook* by Doris Lessing. Copyright (c) 1962 by Doris Lessing. Reprinted with the permission of Simon & Schuster Inc. and Penguin Books Ltd., London.

From *Woman on the Edge of Time* by Marge Piercy. Copyright (c) 1976 by Marge Piercy. Reprinted by permission of Alfred A. Knopf Inc. and the Wallace Literary Agency, Inc.

From "The Political Paradox within Don DeLillo's *Libra*" by Magali Cornier Michael. *Critique: Studies in Contemporary Fiction.* Volume 35, Number 3, Spring 1994. Reprinted with permission of the Helen Dwight Reid Educational Foundation. Published by Heldref Publications, 1319 18th Street, N.W., Washington, D.C. 20036-1802. Copyright 1994.

From "Angela Carter's *Nights at the Circus:* An Engaged Feminism via Subversive Postmodern Strategies" by Magali Cornier Michael. *Contemporary Literature,* Volume 35, Number 3, Fall 1994. Reprinted by permission of the University of Wisconsin Press. Copyright 1994.

From "Woolf's *Between the Acts* and Lessing's *The Golden Notebook:* From Modern to Postmodern Subjectivity" by Magali Cornier Michael. In *Woolf and Lessing: Breaking the Mold,* edited by Ruth Saxton and Jean Tobin. Copyright (c) 1994 by Ruth O. Saxton and Gloria Jean Tobin. Reprinted by permission of St. Martin's Press.

1. FEMINISM AND THE POSTMODERN IMPULSE

Until very recently, feminist critics tended to distance themselves from postmodernism. Even now, when many of them are actively engaging postmodernism, they remain skeptical and ambivalent about the possibilities of a constructive intersection between feminism and postmodernism. The chief problem stems from questions of politics. Many feminist critics, along with others (such as Marxist critics), criticize postmodernism as apolitical and ahistorical and thus as incompatible with feminism, all varieties of which are concerned with the specific historical oppression of women and seek to redress the ills women have had to bear. However, an active interest in questions of history and politics, rather than a retreat from them, emerges from an analysis of much recent fiction discussed in terms of postmodernism. While charges that this fiction is apolitical and ahistorical do not stand up to close scrutiny, these charges clearly arise from some aspect or impulse within this fiction and within postmodernism that has produced ambivalence in feminist critics. This ambivalence indicates that certain modes of engaging the political may indeed be incompatible with feminism. However, the question remains whether postmodern modes of engaging the political are *necessarily* incompatible with feminism.

Although Don DeLillo's novel *Libra* (1988) raises questions about the assassination of John F. Kennedy, it does not follow the conventions of the thriller in which questions are ultimately resolved. Instead of a neat delineation of a conspiracy with a set scheme, the novel unravels a proliferation of conspiracies whose plots interweave and acquire lives of their own. Nicholas Branch, CIA historian, sums up this position near the end of the novel: "the conspiracy against the President was a rambling affair that succeeded in the short term due mainly to chance. Deft men and fools, ambivalence and fixed will and what the weather was like."[1] In the world of DeLillo's novel, plots rather than conspirators "carry their

1

own logic" (221). Branch is forced to recognize that the overabundance of collected data related to the assassination is all "marked by ambiguity and error, by political bias, systematic fantasy" (15), and that there is no such thing as "simple facts" (300). But, rather than use Branch's recognition as a step toward a new but still constructive political reading of the assassination, the novel proposes that all that can be derived from the masses of data are various patterns of coincidences.

Another strand of *Libra*'s narrative depicts the harsh material conditions of Lee Oswald's life, primarily through his mother's defense of him. Marguerite Oswald's incessant bid to connect her son's problems to his economically deprived childhood exists in tension with the novel's presentation of Lee Oswald as little more than "a quirk of history," "a coincidence" (330). While the novel treats Marguerite Oswald as a victim of sociohistorical forces, it presents Lee Oswald as a man trying to make himself into an active subject with a self-fabricated role in history; in the end, however, history sucks him in. *Libra* thus simultaneously uses and problematizes the conventions of realism and the humanist notion of the subject in the depiction of its characters. The core of the novel displays a split between relations based on cause and effect and on patterns of coincidences, as well as between individual and corporate agency. Lee Oswald simultaneously constructs himself as the President's assassin and fits into a role of the imagined gunman scripted by one of the CIA-linked conspirators: "Mackey would find a model for the character Everett was in the process of creating" so as "to extend their fiction into the world" (50).

Libra's emphasis on coincidence and patterns of coincidences typifies many novels that have been discussed in terms of postmodernism—including Thomas Pynchon's highly acclaimed *Gravity's Rainbow* (1973)—but raises serious problems for the feminist reader and critic. Feminism in all its variants is an active political stance; it critiques the dominant male-centered culture from a particular position and viewpoint, which takes into consideration the complex of power relations—particularly gender/sex relations—between people, institutions, ideologies, languages, and other systems that function within culture at large, and aims in various ways (depending on the type of feminism) to end women's oppression. Feminism is thus inherently an activist oppositional politics that seeks specific social and cultural changes within the context of everyday material existence.[2] As such, feminism is engaged in both deconstruction *and* reconstruction. The problem for feminists with a novel like *Libra* is that to endorse coincidence as the ruling force behind events is effectively to deny individual agency and to diminish the possibility of direct, constructive, responsible political action. If "Secrets build their own networks" (22), then there are no clear origins or originators. Responsibility becomes diluted in a way that leaves open the door to various types of fascism or anarchy, to reactionary and/or potentially destructive politics.

As Fredric Jameson points out, "everything is 'in the last analysis' political,"[3] in the sense that everything is a product of and engages in culture and the power relations that create and are perpetuated by the various systems (such as institutions, ideologies, languages) that make up a culture. There are no neutral positions; everything is situated vis-à-vis specific positions within the complex of power relations that is culture. While the claim that everything is political is a useful and radical formulation in its unveiling of the illusion of neutrality, it can also work to dilute the term *political* into near meaninglessness. One means of preventing such a dilution is to differentiate specific politics—that have political agendas with an "acknowledged commitment to a point of view"[4] and to certain aims—from the broad general notion of the political. As I have suggested, feminism in its various forms is a specific oppositional politics whose aims are ultimately revolutionary—to eradicate women's oppression. Novels like *Libra* are problematic for feminists precisely because they are ultimately political in an abstract general way with no clear politics or means of engaging issues of activism and constructive change. Although *Libra* moves toward a specific politics in its suggestion that the CIA was actively involved in the President's assassination, the novel reduces its implied possibility of political action to farce as plots break down, transform themselves, and diffuse responsibility. *Libra* offers a new way of thinking about John F. Kennedy's assassination and presents a gripping picture of the events and characters surrounding the assassination, but it finally frustrates its own depictions by setting chance and coincidence against sociopolitical forces in complex patterns of interference.

Postmodern fiction's tendency to reduce individual agency to corporate agency and sociopolitical forces to chance and patterns of coincidences has understandably drawn sharp criticism from feminist literary critics and, unfortunately, has also led many to a wholesale rejection of postmodernism. But postmodern fiction is not inherently apolitical. DeLillo's *Libra* is a striking case in point, since its subject matter is a specific and highly charged event that has always been associated with the realm of the political. Rather than being apolitical, the novel demonstrates the pervasiveness of the political and of all types of politics; yet, paradoxically, it also blunts the more subversive implications of the specific politics that surface within its pages in an excess of overdetermined data linked to the assassination. Linda Hutcheon acknowledges that the "unresolved tensions of postmodern aesthetic practice remain paradoxes, or perhaps more accurately, contradictions," but argues that this "may be the only non-totalizing response possible"[5]; however, actually retaining unresolved tensions may be impossible, given that postmodernism underscores the illusion of any possibility of neutrality and objectivity within the dynamics of relations of power—especially within Western thought and culture, in which relations of power are structured on a model of hierarchical oppositions. In *Libra,* the tensions between relations of cause and effect and patterns of coincidences do not stay unresolved; the latter clearly dominate by the end of the novel.

With its depiction of the chaos ruled by chance and coincidence that ensues once the logic of cause and effect is challenged, *Libra* makes no attempt to address the possibility of radical social and metaphysical transformation and effectively mutes potential reconstructive impulses. Instead, the novel considers only the breakdown of the Western tradition and its version of political agenda and individual agency. *Libra* does not perform or move toward the reconfiguration that its challenge to Western tradition inherently implies.[6] Pynchon's *Gravity's Rainbow,* with its looming figure of the rocket, its chaotic Zone, and its despotic and overstructured "they-system," offers an even more striking example of the way in which postmodern fiction has tended to internalize the contemporary destabilization of Western metaphysics and the subsequent descent into overdetermination (obsessive structures) or underdetermination (chance and coincidence), without offering any clear visions of a way out.[7] Clearly not apolitical, these novels nonetheless fail to go beyond the chaos or obsessive structures brought on by their disruptions of the status quo.

However, many recent novels *do* consider the range of possibilities that open up once Western metaphysics is problematized at the
same time as they use a variety of disruptive aesthetic strategies—
that have been associated with postmodernism—to challenge the
Western tradition.[8] New forms of specific political engagement
emerge as these novels seek constructive transformations beyond
the chaos or obsessive structures created by their subversions of the
status quo. Little attention has been given to this more positive or
utopian trend within postmodern fiction, the leading examples of
which are novels with feminist impulses that have only very recently
begun to be discussed in terms of postmodernism. I refer here to
novels with *feminist impulses* rather than to feminist novels, to
avoid hypostatizing a collection of plural and dynamic practices.
Furthermore, this formulation underscores the variety of strategies
or elements located in most fiction (a variety that traditionally is
effaced), even when certain ones dominate, and allows for the presence
of differing degrees of any given strategy or element. This avoids
rigid category markers and the exclusions that result and instead
highlights the hybrid nature of fiction with respect to formal
conventions. Rather than labeling a text as feminist or not feminist,
I am suggesting that it is far more constructive to examine a text's
feminist elements (to whatever degree they exist) and their relationship to other elements in the text. Likewise, it is more productive to
speak of fiction with *postmodern impulses* rather than of postmodern
fiction.[9] For the sake of convenience and less convoluted sentence
structures, I will often use the terms feminist and postmodern fiction;
however, these terms will denote certain clusters of practices rather
than fixed categories. I am thus proposing that a range of recent
fiction demonstrates *both* feminist *and* postmodern impulses, even
if the former dominate and have often been examined to the
exclusion of the latter.

Aesthetic strategies that radically subvert Western metaphysics and are commonly associated with postmodern fiction are
indeed prevalent in feminist fiction since the 1960s, even though
these texts have for the most part been overlooked by literary critics
who discuss postmodern fiction. These strategies include disruptions
of traditional notions of subjectivity, character development, representation, language, interpretation, narrative, history, and binary
logic in general (strategies that will be discussed in greater depth
later in this chapter), which take a variety of aesthetic forms such

as the juxtaposition or collage of various types of texts or discourses, the dislocation of traditional temporal and spatial matrices, the active and self-conscious refusal to provide narrative authority or closure, and the appropriation and reworking of popular forms. The use of postmodern features often gives thrust or power to feminist elements, so that the postmodern features become in themselves feminist. As an active oppositional politics, feminism transforms or translates the strategies it co-opts so as to satisfy its political aims. If certain postmodern aesthetic strategies can and do serve a feminist agenda, then locating the points at which feminism and postmodernism intersect becomes a potentially advantageous project for feminists. Literary examples of a fruitful intersection between feminism and postmodernism are surprisingly widespread; they can be found not only in radically experimental fiction with a very limited readership—like the novels of Kathy Acker and Christine Brooke-Rose[10]—but also in the novels of widely read and acclaimed writers whose texts contain feminist elements.

Recent fiction that uses postmodern strategies to further feminist aims is distinct from much postmodern fiction, however, precisely because feminist fiction is linked to a specific politics that cannot sever its ties to the material situation or to its activist goals. Although feminist fiction is not reducible to political tract or propaganda, it nevertheless cannot totally separate aesthetics from political practice. For feminists, literature has a "social function" to effect "changes in the cultural and ideological spheres."[11] The problem with extreme forms of aesthetic experimentation (including ones often associated with postmodernism) is that they necessarily entail a small elite audience of those willing to engage in the unfamiliar and thus limit the wide dissemination of a text's political implications. Furthermore, radical experimentation can be so deconstructive as to leave no grounds on which to effect reconstructions. Indeed, much recent feminist fiction uses the conventions of realism side by side with disruptive postmodern strategies, thereby transforming rather than completely eradicating traditional representation. This fiction performs a balancing act to ensure a large reading public and remain anchored to material conditions while simultaneously engaging in a subversive critique of the Western tradition in order to create a space for reconstruction. That much feminist fiction engages in such a balancing act is inextricably connected to its need to find means by which to retain an active link to political practice in the material world.

Feminists cannot allow all struggle to be relegated to the realm of ideological struggle or of discourse, since this positioning of struggle tends to lose sight of women's physical daily oppression. Feminists must remain aware of what Michele Barrett refers to as "the integral connection between ideology and the relations of production" without collapsing the two spheres: "Ideology is embedded historically in material practice but it does not follow *either* that ideology is theoretically indistinguishable from material practices *or* that it bears any direct relationship to them."[12] Barrett's formulation is crucial in that it helps to explain why new aesthetic forms that subvert binary logic, including the classic oppositions between men and women and between male and female, do not necessarily entail a parallel subversion within material existence. In other words, aesthetic practices do not always either effect or reflect changes in material conditions. As Rita Felski asserts, "there exists no obvious relation between the subversion of language structures and the processes of social struggle and change," which leads her to posit that there is no "necessary connection between feminism and experimental form."[13] While Felski's point is well taken, she seems to set up an opposition between experimental forms and realism that is artificial and does not account for much recent fiction. Indeed, much popular feminist fiction since the 1960s blends together postmodern (which is in many ways experimental) and realist forms.

One of the crucial intersections between feminism and postmodernism rests in their ties to material cultural practices and their "insistence on the link between the textual and the social."[14] As I will argue in greater detail later in this chapter, postmodern aesthetics and theories cannot be divorced from the contemporary postmodern culture, condition, or social formation even if their relationship is often oppositional. In their concern "with a critical deconstruction of tradition," their questioning of "cultural codes," and their exploration of "social and political affiliations,"[15] most postmodern theories and aesthetics directly engage cultural practices. Although some forms of postmodern fiction seem to sever ties to the material situation, this is not the case with much of postmodern fiction. Postmodern theories and aesthetics are very much interested in material existence but insist that access to it is highly problematic, since that access is always mediated and therefore always plural and provisional. Indeed, much postmodern fiction both engages and problematizes the material and social, often by examining its construction into history.

The primary problem with postmodern fiction for feminism lies not with its severing ties to the material situation but rather with its tendency to move toward overdetermination or underdetermination. In contrast, recent feminist fiction tends to explore what lies in between those two extremes as it actively seeks possibilities for change. This utopian impulse derives from the specific political agenda of fiction with feminist impulses. As has often been the case with politically engaged literature, feminist fiction relies heavily on the conventions of realism even when it uses postmodern strategies that challenge those very conventions. Even though its politics are Marxist rather than feminist, the Frankfurt School's *Realism versus Modernism* debate is a useful starting point in the attempt to designate the features that distinguish fiction with both feminist and postmodern impulses from other postmodern fiction.[16] Although Bertolt Brecht argues that "the realistic mode of writing" bears "the stamp of the way it was employed, when and by which class, down to its smallest details," he nevertheless calls for a new form of realism that would be "wide and political, sovereign over all conventions" and would "not bind the artist to too rigidly defined modes of narrative."[17] As Jameson suggests, Brecht brings together "'realistic' and experimental attitudes" and rejects both "a naive mimetic position" and "purely formal experimentation."[18] In much the same way, some recent writers are using subversive postmodern strategies to challenge the conventions of realism at the same time as they are attempting to forge new means of representing reality.

Theodor Adorno is a better bridge to a discussion of postmodernism and feminism, however, since he suggests that all art is both connected to and distanced from reality. He argues that the posited antithesis between "committed" and "autonomous" art that characterizes the *Realism versus Modernism* debate is precarious at best, since all creation originates in empirical or surface reality and yet is always at one remove from reality (representation as distinct from reality). Adorno's posited dialectic, which both preserves and negates the concepts of committed and autonomous art, is helpful in accounting for the postmodern process of difference and deferral and the feminist political commitment found in fiction that has both feminist and postmodern tendencies.[19] Although feminist texts that use postmodern strategies acknowledge that reality is always mediated by representations, they nevertheless stress the connection between representation and the material historical situation. In order to retain that connection, much recent feminist fiction does not totally jettison the conventions of realism, even as it questions and undermines those conventions.

As Catherine Belsey explains, "realism" reflects not the world but rather "the world constructed in language," "out of what is (discursively) familiar." While fiction that uses postmodern strategies to propel its feminist aims demonstrates its awareness that "what is intelligible as realism is the conventional and therefore familiar"[20] and, indeed, challenges the conventions of realism, much of this fiction also makes use of these conventions as a means of communicating with readers for whom the conventions of realism are the only, or at least the most familiar, codes by which they read/interpret texts. As Janet Wolff argues, "realism may be the only possible language of communication for a particular audience," so that a "subversion of realism" may create a "real problem of accessibility to popular audiences."[21] Since this fiction's use of the conventions of realism is self-conscious, however, it forces its readers to recognize the constructed and artificial quality of traditional realism with its claims to mimesis and truth. Although Belsey is correct in her assessment of realism as "a predominantly conservative form" that confirms "the patterns of the world we seem to know" and effaces its "own textuality,"[22] writers as diverse as Margaret Atwood, Angela Carter, Maxine Hong Kingston, Doris Lessing, Else Morante, Toni Morrison, Marge Piercy, Marilynne Robinson, Alice Walker, Fay Weldon, and Christa Wolf have appropriated the conventions of realism for more subversive feminist aims. By juxtaposing realist and postmodern strategies, these writers offer a representation of the world that is familiar and thus both accessible and plausible to the reader while, simultaneously, disrupting the conventions of realism by foregrounding their contradictions and links to a Western metaphysics implicated in material oppression. This strategy is politically effective in that it invites a large readership with its recognizable realist elements and yet challenges those conventions through disruptive strategies that allow for the creation of a space for constructing something new. After all, fiction can be politically effective only in so far as it affects or transforms the consciousness of readers and therefore depends on some sort of convergence between reader and text.[23] These texts with feminist impulses may be an instance of what Belsey calls the "interrogative text," which employs "devices to undermine the [realist] illusion, to draw attention to its own textuality" and "enlists the reader in contradiction." [24] Unlike a writer like Brecht, however, these novelists do not distance their audience as a means of foregrounding contradiction; instead, they draw their readers into the text through their use of the conventions of realism and then use strategies that disrupt the status quo to force their readers to question those very conventions.

Recent writers whose works exhibit feminist tendencies are faced with the same crisis of representation that all contemporary authors face, a crisis brought on by the theoretical and philosophical undermining of the subject, reality, language, interpretation, representation, history (which I will discuss in greater detail later in this chapter); and many feminist novels are engaging postmodern aesthetic strategies as a means of meeting this crisis. At the same time, however, their political agenda makes them retain stronger ties to realism. For instance, they do not engage in as radical a dispersion of the subject even though they question the humanist subject, because their feminist commitment necessitates that they highlight the connection between subject positions and the human beings that inhabit them, that they retain some kind of notion of individual agency, and that they reach as large a readership as possible.

Before investigating the ways in which specific literary texts since the 1960s have made use of strategies that disrupt the status quo to further feminist aims and how these strategies might point toward radically new forms of feminist aesthetics,[25] it is necessary to examine certain issues surrounding feminism and postmodernism more specifically: the plural and constructed nature as well as the cultural context of both postmodernism and feminism; the relationship between feminism and postmodernism, including how feminist critics have responded to postmodernism and why the intersection between feminism and postmodernism has not been overwhelmingly embraced by feminist critics; a broad outline of what the area of intersection between postmodernism and feminism consists of and how it might be useful to feminism.

The Plural and Constructed Nature of
Postmodernism and Feminism

To counter limited and misleading definitions of postmodernism, it is essential to recognize postmodernism as a plural rather than a singular entity. The same can be said of feminism. It would thus be more accurate to speak of feminisms and postmodernisms.[26] Feminism and postmodernism in fact defy not only definition but also categorization: they cannot be labeled or reduced merely to a period, historical cultural condition, sociopolitical movement, philosophy, critical approach, or aesthetics, but rather encompass all of these. Ihab Hassan's claim that postmodernism must be viewed as both "an artistic tendency" and "a social phenomenon" is, for instance, also an apt formulation of feminism.[27] Linda Hutcheon takes a different tack by differentiating between "the cultural notion of postmodern*ism*" and "postmodern*ity* as the designation of a social and philosophical period or 'condition'."[28] While it is potentially useful to differentiate between the postmodern condition or social formation and postmodern cultural practices, especially since the latter are often critical of the former, postmodern cultural practices can also be separated into aesthetic and theoretical/philosophical practices—practices that are related but not equivalents—and, furthermore, each of these broad categories encompasses sets of plural, heterogeneous, dynamic practices.[29] Although postmodern aesthetics draws on postmodern theory/philosophy's critical deconstruction of Western metaphysics and cultural norms, it is for the most part less esoteric, more accessible, and more intricately connected to the material world than the theory/philosophy. For example, postmodern theory's rejection of the hierarchical opposition between high art and mass culture is actively enacted within postmodern fiction through a variety of aesthetic strategies, such as the co-optation of popular literary forms like science fiction, detective stories, thrillers, ghost stories, tall tales. Discussions of postmodernism must take into consideration its various designation as cultural condition, theory/philosophy, and aesthetic practices, all of which are interconnected and yet distinct and all of which are always plural and in flux or in process.

In addition, both postmodernism and feminism are terms that have been constructed. Their constructed nature is important to consider not only because these terms cover a broad spectrum of interrelated but distinct practices but also because these terms are constructed strategically. The dominant contemporary versions of postmodernism in its various guises as cultural dominant, theory, and aesthetics have been formulated within a highly specific Western and chiefly academic cultural context that remains very much male-centered. This tendency by critics (particularly male critics) to construct male-centered paradigms is widespread and points to the difficulties of escaping a male-centered Western metaphysics that continues to dominate even as it is being challenged. For instance, in *Constructing Postmodernism* (1992), Brian McHale makes the useful observation that postmodernism is not "some kind of identifiable object 'out there' in the world" but rather is constructed: "postmodernism exists discursively, in the discourses we produce *about* it and *using* it." He further argues (again usefully) that "constructions ... are *strategic* in nature, that is, designed with particular purposes in view," so that "the issue of *how* such objects [as postmodernism] are constructed ... becomes crucial." However, McHale does not question who the "we" producing these discourses consists of and thus overlooks the essentially male character of this "we" (something I will explore more fully later in this chapter). Although he posits postmodernism as "a plurality of constructions," his assumption of an unexamined and undefined "we" limits the variety of constructions of postmodern fiction that he outlines and the specific literary texts that he investigates.[30] As a result, his only extensive analysis of fiction written by a woman is that of Christine Brooke-Rose's work, which he treats with no references to gender, sex, or feminism. What I am suggesting is that, like many other critics focusing on postmodernism, McHale does not question the male-centered aspect of the various constructions of postmodern fiction he explores and helps to create, even though he asserts and purports to understand that constructions are always strategic and therefore political. If, according to McHale's own theoretical discussion, literary critics construct/define what postmodern fiction is, then I am proposing to critique existing constructions as male-centered and to revise/reconstruct established versions of postmodern fiction so as to take into consideration recent fiction with feminist impulses that have been barred from the discussions because they do not quite fit the models/constructions established by mostly male critics. Indeed, many feminist texts are not discussed as postmodern fiction precisely because they engage conventions of realism; however, upon close analysis, I have found that much recent feminist fiction simultaneously uses and undermines realism using strategies that are both feminist and postmodern, indicating the existence of politically specific forms of postmodern aesthetic strategies.

The tendency to use the term postmodernism without questioning its chiefly male constructions is widespread and certainly not limited to literary studies. Recently, a good number of feminist critics in various fields have begun to investigate the constructed character of postmodern theory. As Meaghan Morris argues, "in spite of its heavy (if lightly acknowledged) borrowings from feminist theory, its frequent celebrations of 'difference' and 'specificity', and its critique of 'Enlightenment' paternalism, postmodernism as a publishing phenomenon has pulled off the peculiar feat of reconstituting an overwhelmingly male pantheon of proper names to function as ritual objects of academic exegesis and commentary"—she lists "Habermas, Lyotard, Rorty, Jameson, Huyssen, Foster, Owens, and so on." Furthermore, "Participants in a postmodernism debate are 'constrained' to refer back to previous input, and to take sides in familiar battles on a marked-out, well-trodden terrain."[31] In much the same vein, Chantal Mouffe asserts that "Too often a critique of a specific thesis of Lyotard or Baudrillard leads to sweeping conclusions about 'the postmoderns',"[32] and Judith Butler points out that grouping "together a set of positions under the postmodern" enacts a "gesture of conceptual mastery" and a "ruse of power."[33] Again, the problem for feminist critics and feminist aesthetics is that in practice the term postmodernism already is marked as a given— notwithstanding theoretical arguments to the contrary. To construct postmodern theories or aesthetics that include and account for feminist work requires a critical rereading of established constructions to establish their blind spots (including but not limited to a blindness to feminist practice) as well as a creative rereading of feminist texts that pays close attention to the strategies that exist alongside feminist strategies and/or propel forward specific feminist aims.

Similarly, feminism is not only plural but also strategically constructed. Although the postmodern debates have to a certain extent excluded feminists through their specific ways of constructing postmodernism, feminists have tended to construct feminism in monolithic terms and in opposition to equally monolithic versions of poststructuralism and postmodernism (which are often collapsed). Recently, however, many feminist critics have begun the task of re-evaluating the relationship and possible intersections between feminist and postmodern theories. As Mouffe argues, to explore the relevance of the postmodern "critique of essentialism" for "feminist politics" entails engaging "all its modalities and implications and not quickly dismiss it on the basis of some of its versions."[34] Linda Singer also warns against "what is often offered as a facile distinction between feminism's political engagement and postmodernism's aestheticized self-absorption."[35] Indeed, as I will argue, postmodernism is neither essentially or necessarily apolitical nor aestheticist. An argument can also be made for certain forms of feminist practice that become examples of "aestheticized self-absorption" (see my discussion of Brophy's novel later in this chapter).

Although the contemporary phases of both feminism and postmodernism are plural and constructed, they do have one basic thing in common: they are products of and, simultaneously, contribute to the present global climate. They are shaped, among other things, by the recent history of two world wars and mass racially and ethnically motivated genocides, the threat of atomic annihilation, the cold war (until very recently) and the wars it created and supported (particularly the Vietnam War), the growing gap between first and third world nations, multinational corporations, the proliferation of mass media, and the recurrent clashes between right- and left-wing thought and policies. Furthermore, the philosophical shifts that these historical events and transformations have engendered, particularly the questioning of the Western metaphysics which underlies them, also affect recent forms of feminism and postmodernism. In addition, contemporary forms of feminism and postmodernism are situated in the public domain as well as in private elitist institutions such as universities and museums. This public presence results in part from the very public eruptions of "cultural and ideological conflicts" such as "the student and civil rights movements of the sixties," "the growth of the women's movement in the seventies," and the gay movement and the abortion rights campaigns in the eighties and into the nineties: movements directed at "prevailing cultural modes" and highlighting the "multiplicity of arenas of oppression within [existing] social and personal life."[36]

At the same time as they are products of the post-World War II cultural and intellectual climate, recent forms of feminism and postmodernism also contribute to that climate. They participate within cultural practices and in the theoretical assault on Western metaphysics that has increasingly characterized much of intellectual life and activist campaigns in the decades since the 1960s.[37] As Hassan suggests, the only pattern that can be discerned in postmodernism is its "revisionary will in the Western world, unsettling/resettling codes, canons, procedures, beliefs" as it reaches "for something other, which some call posthumanism,"[38] something it has in common with recent feminism. Indeed, Singer asserts that the recurrent practice in both feminism and postmodernism is "an explicit discursive strategy of challenging the terms, conventions, and symbols of hegemonic authority in ways that foreground the explicitly transgressive character of this enterprise"[39]; and Wolff echoes Singer's words, adding that this challenge "is the promise of postmodernism for feminist politics."[40] Although these formulations might seem too abstract and overarching, they point to a prevailing impulse that underlies most postmodern theoretical and aesthetic practices (but perhaps not necessarily postmodern culture itself) and that is echoed in feminist practices. A more detailed examination of both postmodernism and feminism may provide a means of better understanding why the relationship between the two trends has remained tenuous and of delineating a space in which they might coexist and, more importantly, benefit each other.

The problems exhibited by some critics in their approaches to postmodernism derives in part from a failure to address the plural and constructed nature of postmodernism. Although the notion of an institutionalized postmodernism seems like a contradiction in terms given Hassan's description/definition, many critics (feminists in particular) assume a fairly standardized version of postmodernism as ahistorical, as apolitical, as relativistic, as doing away with the subject and with notions of individual agency. However, at least theoretically, most critics specifically engaged in the postmodernist debate reject such rigid definitions and acknowledge postmodernism as a plural or heterogeneous phenomenon. For example, they account for the distinct notions of postmodernism exhibited within different disciplines, nationalities, and periods of time.[41] Although Hassan, an influential postmodern critic, has repeatedly

insisted that postmodernism is not monolithic and varies from field
to field, his 1982 list of postmodernist traits, which he differentiates
from modernist traits, has become the standard means of delineating postmodernism for many critics. More specifically, critics tend to
focus on his inclusion of *deconstructive* traits such as "Play,"
"Chance," "Exhaustion/Silence," "Indeterminacy," "Decreation/
Deconstruction," "Schizophrenia," "Dispersal," "Difference-
Differance/Trace," while ignoring potentially *reconstructive* traits
such as "Desire," "Process/Performance/Happening," "Participation,"
"Text/Intertext," "Irony," "Immanence."[42] Indeed, in a 1986 essay,
Hassan explicitly states that postmodernism contains both "deconstructive" *and* "reconstructive" tendencies. Nevertheless, his inclusion of *"self-less-ness"* as a deconstructive characteristic of postmodernism has helped to secure the often-cited notion that postmodernism does away with the subject.[43]

Within the literary establishment, a similar disjunction is
apparent between the version of postmodern fiction that is assumed
by those critics directly engaged in the postmodern debate and the
tendency of many critics to conflate postmodern and contemporary
fiction. As Hans Bertens demonstrates in his 1984 survey of postmodern fiction, the range of fiction discussed in terms of postmodernism includes the works of such disparate authors as Sukenick,
Malamud, Federman, Bellow, Mailer, Brautigan, and Pynchon.[44] I
would argue, however, that the works of novelists such as Bellow
appear under the rubric of postmodernism through the mis-associa-
tion of postmodern and contemporary fiction. Postmodernism is not,
however, a synonym for contemporary, even though it certainly is
present in the contemporary context. Much fiction produced in
recent years contains no or few subversive strategies that could be
linked to postmodern aesthetics and instead holds on uncritically to
realist, Victorian, or gothic conventions, an assertion that is reinforced by a quick examination of the paperbacks lining the shelves
of airport newsstands and chain bookstores. Attempts to define
postmodernism have also led critics to engage in misguided arguments aimed at establishing whether recent postmodern fiction differs from modernist fiction in degree or in kind. It is more apt, however, to view postmodernism as simultaneously a continuation of
and a reaction against modernism. As Hutcheon suggests, postmodernism's relation to modernism is complex, in that it involves both a

"retention of modernism's initial oppositional impulses, both ideological and aesthetic" and an "equally strong rejection of its founding notion of formalist autonomy."[45] Moreover, Andreas Huyssen convincingly argues that postmodernism is a reaction against an institutionalized version of high modernism, which has "domesticated" modernism by "burying the political and aesthetic critiques of certain forms of modernism."[46]

Anti-postmodern literary critics, including many feminists, generally associate postmodern fiction specifically with extreme forms of experimentation of the early 1970s, such as the novels of Sukenick and Federman. Generally referred to as surfiction, these texts are characterized by formal innovations and anti-referential tendencies.[47] They intentionally avoid stable subject positions as the focus of the text becomes aimed increasingly at language or writing itself, reinforcing many critics' fear that postmodernism spells the death of the subject. Self-reflexivity dominates in many of these novels, to the extent that satiric or parodic force and political resonance are reduced or muted, since satire, parody, and engaged politics require some kind of at least temporary grounds or matrix of shared values; as a result, opponents of postmodernism have declared these novels apolitical. While challenging referentiality is certainly not an apolitical move, surfiction is political in a theoretical sense that remains distanced from engaged politics. By effectively disallowing (rather than problematizing) referentiality, these texts tend to sever language and representation from the material historical situation to such a degree that they disallow any exploration of the ways in which they are interrelated and are both functions of complex relations of power. Furthermore, these novels presuppose a highly educated audience and are consequently read by a very small elite, which severely limits any wide communication of their disruptions of the status quo. Although these texts have been the target of anti-postmodern criticism, they in fact constitute only one small strand of the great variety of novels that have been termed postmodern.

Writers of the late 1970s and of the 1980s have moved away from such a direct concentration on formal innovations and anti-referential stances and are more overtly addressing history and politics; yet many detractors of postmodernism are still equating postmodern fiction with this handful of early works of surfiction. As

Larry McCaffery suggests, it may be that certain formal "experiments proved to be dead ends or were rapidly exhausted and then discarded," which supports the notion that postmodern fiction is neither homogeneous nor static.[48] In addition, the public oppositional movements grounded in specific politics that developed in the 1970s and 1980s, and that help to shape the current cultural climate, have necessarily affected the production of fiction; after all, fiction, as a cultural product, cannot be divorced from its material and ideological conditions. In a related vein, Huyssen discusses postmodernism in terms of recent historical development, delineating a series of "phases and directions" since the 1960s that emphasize "some of the historical contingencies and pressures that have shaped recent aesthetic and cultural debates." While Huyssen acknowledges a certain "affirmative" strand of postmodernism during the 1970s and early 1980s that "had abandoned any claim to critique, transgression or negation," he emphasizes its coexistence with an "alternative postmodernism in which resistance, critique, and negation of the status quo were redefined in non-modernist and non-avantgardist terms." Moreover, he suggests that this latter movement's critical edge was a product particularly of "the art, writing, film-making and criticism of women and minority artists."[49] I would argue that this "alternative" strand of postmodernism surfaces within much recent fiction but has not been explored thoroughly enough because of the rather limited notions of postmodern fiction that (mostly white male) critics have developed as a result of their almost exclusive focus on the texts of white male writers.[50]

Any discussion of fiction with postmodern impulses is necessarily complex, since postmodern aesthetics are neither singular nor static. Although tendencies toward anti-referentiality and formal innovations persist, they cannot be equated with all postmodern fiction. Indeed, I am suggesting that much recent fiction with postmodern impulses emphasizes resistance, transgression, and critique of cultural institutional and ideological structures; it is this "alternative" strand of postmodernism (as Huyssen calls it) on which I will focus my discussion. Such acclaimed novels as Robert Coover's *The Public Burning,* Don DeLillo's *Libra,* E.L. Doctorow's *Ragtime,* John Fowles's *The French Lieutenant's Woman,* Thomas Pynchon's *Gravity's Rainbow,* D.M. Thomas's *The White Hotel,* and Kurt Vonnegut's *Slaughterhouse-Five,* all of which have been discussed in terms of postmodernism, overtly engage history and politics at the same time as they problematize the notions of history and politics as well as the possibility of representing them. Although some of these novels in the end dilute their own political edges by seemingly rejecting any forms of individual agency, as in the case of *Libra,* others, such as *The French Lieutenant's Woman,* insist on individual agency as a tool of political action: Sarah's deliberate decision falsely to claim herself as the French lieutenant's mistress is an active strategic, and therefore political, move. Not only do these particular novels participate in an alternative radical critique of the status quo, using subversive aesthetic strategies associated with postmodernism, but many other novels not currently discussed in terms of postmodernism also do so—particularly recent fiction with feminist impulses.

Although in many ways a strong and engaging critical study of feminist fiction and its modes of experimentation, Molly Hite's *The Other Side of the Story: Structures and Strategies of Contemporary Feminist Narrative* (1989) severs feminist fiction from postmodern fiction precisely because the book does not engage postmodernism as a plural and constructed entity with wide ranging and sometimes contradictory tendencies. Hite's book presumes, without exploring, the disjunction of feminist and postmodern fiction, as indicated in the question that launches the discussion: "Why don't women writers produce postmodern fiction?" Hite assumes a singular and exclusively *deconstructive* postmodernism when she argues that "experimental fictions by women seem to share the decentering and disseminating strategies of postmodernist narratives, but they also seem to arrive at these by an entirely different route, which involves emphasizing conventionally marginal characters and themes, in this way *re*-centering the value structure of narrative." However, Hite's notion that "the context for the innovation [of feminist fiction] is a critique of culture and a literary tradition apprehended as profoundly masculinist"[51] can also be applied to much fiction that has been associated with postmodernism—for example, Thomas's *The White Hotel* and Fowles's *The French Lieutenant's Woman.* Acknowledging that postmodernism is plural and dynamic, encompassing a wide range of subversive tendencies, that postmodern theories have been constructed in ways that have tended to exclude feminism in practice if not in theory, and that post-World War II postmodern and feminist fiction are (at least in part) products of the same cultural condition, leads to a recognition that recent experimental fiction with feminist impulses cannot be totally disassociated from fiction with postmodern impulses. Indeed, I am suggesting that it is more apt and potentially more productive to view certain trends within some recent feminist fiction as signaling a more engaged version of postmodern fiction, which might conceivably influence the direction of fiction in general by opening up the category of postmodern fiction to include other previously ignored practices and thus acknowledge and promote those practices.

As in the case of postmodernism, feminism's plural nature must be accounted for before an intersection between feminism and postmodernism can be posited. Although many different types of feminisms are collected under the generalized heading of feminism, they can be divided loosely into two broad trends with distinct philosophical approaches: 1) feminisms that primarily aim for women to achieve equal status with men within existing social structures; and 2) feminisms that reject the possibility of women's achieving total emancipation under existing social structures and, therefore, seek to dismantle and restructure the social system. It must be noted, however, that these two types of feminisms are not polar opposites and do not exist in binary opposition to each other. Both strands of feminisms are grounded in the same basic drive to expose and counter the traditional oppression of women; the difference between them lies in their philosophical underpinnings, specific aims, and strategies for achieving those aims.

The first type of feminism's adherence to existing social structures necessarily entails a certain degree of allegiance to and collusion with the system of thought from which those structures are derived: the thought systems of today's Western cultures are still firmly grounded in Renaissance humanism and Enlightenment ideals, which were developed primarily by and for white bourgeois males. The inherent contradiction in the stand of these feminists is that they embrace certain humanist and Enlightenment notions that lie at the heart of a deeply male-centered Western metaphysics. They have had a difficult time coming to terms with contemporary theory—demonstrating discomfort with and even hostility toward it, especially during the 1970s—which is indicative of an unyielding adherence to a humanism that a variety of recent theoretical approaches (especially poststructuralism) question and challenge. These feminists initially were reluctant to recognize that theoretical assumptions of some kind underlie all criticism and writing, whether or not those assumptions are acknowledged, and that all theoretical paradigms are political in nature: there are no neutral positions.

Within literary studies, feminists working within a liberal humanist tradition get caught in a bind when they attempt to use an aesthetics that is grounded in male-centered humanist assumptions in the pursuit of feminist political goals. Toril Moi convincingly argues that, within literature, the often unquestioned use of realism to depict the various inequities faced daily by women gives rise to a "radical contradiction" between "feminist politics and patriarchal aesthetics." She explains that realism is anchored on a mimetic theory of art that views the humanist self as the *"sole author"* of the literary text, so that the text becomes the expression of this unique and traditionally male creator.[52] As Moi suggests, many feminist literary critics have been slow to rigorously question the assumptions or political basis of the realist aesthetics they appropriate. During the 1970s, feminist critics worked fruitfully to give women a voice in order to redress the historical suppression of women's experiences and stories; however, these critics tended to uncritically take up the position of authorial authority in relation to other women that they criticized men for taking. Their attempts to pinpoint some kind of definitive representation of women's oppression led them to treat literature written by women as a direct reflection of women's experiences. This "appeal to experience as uncontestable evidence" is problematic, according to Joan Scott, in that it posits "individuals who have experience" rather than "subjects who are constituted through experience" and thus makes unnecessary the exploration of "how difference is established, how it operates, how and in what ways it constitutes subjects who see and act in the world"; in short, it "reproduces rather than contests given ideological systems."[53] As Hite notes, "the notion that women are in this sense 'natural' or 'straight' writers, who manage to get reality—particularly their own experiences—onto the page with a minimum of art or decision making, has informed a whole practice of feminist criticism, so that some of the most important examples of this criticism have fostered the association between women's writing and aesthetic conservatism." [54] Although the foothold gained by critical theory within academia has forced all critics to reassess their relation to theory and to examine their own interpretive strategies, a humanist tendency nevertheless prevails in some feminist literary criticism. While theoretically informed in many ways, for example, the work of Sandra Gilbert and Susan Gubar remains based on the assumption that literature reflects almost unproblematically the struggles being waged in the real world.[55]

The notion of art as a direct reflection of reality not only assumes that a fixed objective reality exists and can be recuperated but also veils the ways in which a work of art is an artificial construction that can never exactly mirror what it is attempting to represent. Literary texts are clearly shaped, among other things, by the intention of its author, by the perspective and interpretation of its reader, by the socio-historical context of its production and of its readership, and by the language and discourses in which it is written. As Barrett suggests, a literary text can offer at best "an indication of the bounds within which particular meanings are constructed and negotiated in a given social formation."[56] Indeed, feminist scholarship as a whole has developed a much more incisive analysis of its own critical methods and theories during the 1980s and into the 1990s.

As soon as feminists begin to unveil and challenge the theoretical assumptions of the dominant systems of thought that have traditionally oppressed women, they belong to the second strand of feminism—which seeks to change social and metaphysical structures themselves. Exposing and analyzing the underlying assumptions of a culture that has always been male-centered is the first step toward challenging that culture's social and ideological structures. Thus, this type of feminism contains points of intersection with postmodern theories and aesthetics, and the discussion of feminism from this point on will refer to this strand of feminism unless otherwise noted. A brief and general working definition of this type of feminism, which envelops without erasing the differences between the various feminisms it encompasses, will suffice as a basis for this discussion: it is a political and critical stance that focuses on the sexual and gender biases inherent in society and its cultural products and on the social construction of gendered beings and of sexuality. It aims to expose the ways in which Western male-centered culture works in order to retain its power, to subvert those means and challenge the very structure of society, and ultimately to offer blueprints for a restructured and new society.

The Relationship between Feminism and Postmodernism

Many of postmodern theories' and aesthetics' aims are in fact similar to those of feminism—to expose and subvert Western metaphysics and its cultural products—although they do not focus primarily on the construction and role of gender and sexuality. The challenge to the Western notion of the subject, however, leads directly to issues of gender and biology, since Western culture has traditionally associated the subject or self with man, while woman has been relegated to the position of object or other.[57] Furthermore, postmodern theories' energetic critiques of the system of hierarchical binary oppositions that undergirds Western thought destabilize the classic dichotomies between man and woman, male and female, masculine and feminine. Since these hierarchically charged oppositions have ensured the dominance of both men and Western metaphysics, challenges to them have the potential of being in concert with feminist aims.[58] Although the positions of postmodern and feminist theories and aesthetics with respect to the culture they are criticizing are not equivalent, since feminist theories and aesthetics are grounded in an activist political stance that seeks to end women's oppression while postmodern theories and aesthetics merely have political potential in their tendency to problematize Western metaphysics and the ways it is encoded within cultural and ideological structures, it appears that some of their ultimate aims are to a certain extent compatible.[59] Indeed, feminist and postmodern theories and aesthetics may mutually stand to benefit from a *rapprochement,* given that the former have been criticized for lacking both stringent critical modes and radical aesthetic strategies, while the latter have been criticized for lacking a clear political direction and possessing an ambivalent sense of social criticism.[60] The possibility of using postmodern critical and aesthetic strategies to counter the criticism aimed at feminism is of particular interest, since feminism is widely regarded as a politics with liberatory potential and yet at the same time has demonstrated conservative or traditional tendencies.

However, many feminists have rejected postmodernism outright (along with poststructuralism, to which it is often mistakenly equated, as I will discuss later in this chapter), regarding it as just another masculinist conspiracy. The major obstacle seems to be postmodernism's questioning of the humanist notion of the subject. These feminist critics reject the idea that, just when women have finally attained the position of being able to define themselves as subjects, the subject is in their view being eradicated. As Felski has succinctly argued, "In the earliest feminist writings on literature ... female subjectivity provided the central category around which a feminist aesthetic was defined, and feminist critical response was validated on experiential rather than theoretical grounds."[61] Indeed, various feminist critics such as Rita Felski, Elizabeth Fox-Genovese, Nancy Hartsock, and Patricia Waugh (among others) have worked recently to distance feminism and postmodernism. For instance, Hartsock's rejection of postmodern theories as useful for feminism is apparent in her reiteration of the question, "Why is it that just at the moment when so many of us who have been silenced begin to demand the right to name ourselves, to act as subjects rather than object of history, that just then the concept of subjecthood becomes problematic."[62] Within literary studies, feminist critics like Waugh and Felski argue that, while they share some concerns, feminist fiction and postmodern fiction are fundamentally at odds with each other and have moved in different directions. Waugh asserts that, while postmodern fiction articulates "the exhaustion of the existential belief in self-presence and self-fulfillment" and "the dispersal of the universal subject of liberalism," women writers are beginning "to construct an identity out of the recognition that women need to discover, and must fight for, a sense of unified selfhood, a rational, coherent, effective identity."[63] Although Felski notes that "Feminism can in fact be understood as an example of a 'postmodern' worldview which is fundamentally pluralistic," she warns against "a postmodern relativism" that is incompatible with feminism and chooses to focus her analysis of "feminist literature" on "autobiographical realist narrative." Felski acknowledges "the value and importance of contemporary experimental writing by women," but she seems to set up an opposition between esoteric experimental and popular realist fiction.[64] What I am suggesting, however, is that such an opposition is false, that much popular feminist fiction combines realist and experimental modes.

Postmodern theories' vigorous challenges to traditional hierarchical binary oppositions, especially the opposition between man and woman, further accentuate many feminists' discomfort with what they see as a subversion of women's attempt to define their own subjecthood. Representative of this tendency is the early writing (1977) of Elaine Showalter, in which she misreads post-structuralist theory and rejects what she inaccurately terms "theories of the transcendence of sexual identity" as "evasions of reality," an accusation that retains credibility among some critics.[65] The problem with this criticism is that it does not examine rigorously enough identity, gender, and reality as socially constructed notions. Since Western society has been and still is inherently male-centered, its established conceptual norms should be highly problematic for feminists. Furthermore, calling into question the traditional humanist notion of the subject does not necessarily eliminate the subject. It is only the *concept* of the subject as it currently exists that postmodern theories examine and problematize. As Showalter has herself recently argued (1989), feminists must/can retain "the idea of female subjectivity, even if we accept it as a constructed or metaphysical one."[66] The feminist fear of dismantling the opposition between man and woman is firmly grounded in binary thought. However, challenging biological and gendered identity does not necessarily entail doing away with difference. Differences between men and women can exist outside of Western binary oppositions, which are inherently hierarchical and within which one term has always dominated. Women and men differ biologically, for example, but it does not follow that they must exist in opposition to one another; the existing opposition has been created to establish hierarchy within the relations between the sexes, so as to secure male dominance. Male dominance and the Western system of binary oppositions are thus inextricably linked. But, without the need for dominance, differences need not be polarized into oppositions and need not be reified and homogenized to serve as grounds for identity. The postmodern destabilization of binary logic can be the site of a political intersection with feminism, since feminism seeks to eradicate men's dominance over women as well as revalue women's differences from men and (the more recent move among feminists) women's differences from each other.

In the 1980s, many feminists joined in questioning the humanist concept of the subject, but most often via poststructuralism rather than postmodernism. French feminists like Julia Kristeva and Luce Irigaray have participated energetically in the poststructuralist debates from their inception, as have a good number of Anglo-American feminists, notably Catherine Belsey, Jane Gallop, Alice Jardine, Toril Moi, Gayatri Spivak, and Chris Weedon, among others. This poststructuralist tendency within feminism has been criticized, however, for exacerbating the growing rift between academic feminism and feminism as a mass political movement focused on material changes. Although Kristeva and Jardine have also engaged the possibility of linking feminism and postmodernism, Kristeva is interested primarily in semiotics and male modernist writers, and Jardine poses excellent questions which remain unanswered.[67] Both of these critics, moreover, tend to collapse post-modernism and poststructuralism.

Postmodernism and poststructuralism are not equivalents, even if the distinction between the two is fluid rather than rigid: the former is an umbrella term which encompasses a variety of sociohistorical, theoretical, and aesthetic phenomena (see earlier discussion), while poststructuralism refers to a historically specific set of philosophical discourses. Postmodernism focuses on culture at large and thus penetrates a variety of discourses.[68] As Hassan aptly summarizes, postmodernism and poststructuralism "finally resist conflation" because "Postmodernism appears larger, is international, in scope. Art, politics, technology, all of culture, fall within its compass, as do trends from Japanese architecture to Columbian magic realism."[69] However, postmodern and poststructuralist *theories* do have overt points of intersection, most notably in their aims to challenge key Western concepts like the subject, truth, reality, representation; to demystify the notion of language as stable; and to problematize the system of binary hierarchical oppositions that undergirds Western thought. But, while poststructuralism encompasses a plurality of strategies, it nevertheless tends to be dominated by abstract philosophical discourses that remain distanced from material conditions. While postmodern theories are also philosophical discourses, they tend to focus their critiques more specifically on the present historical social formation and the interrelations of social formation, relations of power, aesthetics, and theories/philosophies. Postmodern theories are distinct from and yet intricately linked to the postmodern condition and the variety of postmodern cultural products and aesthetics, such as postmodern fiction, poetry, drama, performance art, painting, sculpture, photography, architecture. The difference between postmodern and poststructuralist theories is particularly evident in their distinct approaches to the issue of subjectivity, which is crucial to my discussion of the link between feminism and postmodernism. While poststructuralist theories have been accused by critics (especially feminist critics) of doing away with the subject, postmodern theories and aesthetics tend not only to challenge established notions of the subject but also to seek new ways of reconceptualizing the subject that challenge and de-universalize the presuppositions of Western culture. In other words, poststructuralist theories tends to focus on deconstruction, while postmodern theories and aesthetics emphasize *both* deconstruction *and* reconstruction.

Although feminists sympathetic to poststructuralism see the value of questioning concepts constructed within a male-centered culture, they have tended to be ambivalent about poststructuralism's deconstructive tendency, especially with respect to the subject. Huyssen blames poststructuralism for "jettison[ing] the chance of challenging the *ideology of the subject* (as male, white, and middle-class) by developing alternative and different notions of subjectivity." He argues that "The postmoderns," on the other hand, seem to have "recognized this dilemma" and to be "working toward new theories and practices of speaking, writing and acting subjects."[70] Feminism appears to share with postmodern theories and aesthetics similar impulses to find new ways of conceptualizing the subject, although feminism does not engage in as radical a dispersal of the subject and, in fact, adamantly retains its primacy. As an engaged and specific political stance that aims to expose and challenge existing relations of power, feminism cannot disengage itself from the material historical situation or from some kind of model of individual agency. However, many feminist critics are now actively rethinking this still vital subject as necessarily constructed. Consequently, the forms of postmodernism that are compatible with feminism are ones that question and problematize Western metaphysical concepts but also engage in reconstructive practices and retain close ties to material conditions.

Although feminists have tended to be wary of embracing post-

modernism, a surprising number of proponents of postmodernism—
who are almost all men—have discussed feminism as a potentially
powerful but as yet untapped voice in the postmodern debate.[71]
Huyssen, who sees postmodernism as having a "critical potential,"
asserts that "women's art, literature and criticism are an important
part of the postmodern culture of the 1970s and 1980s and indeed a
measure of the vitality and energy of that culture" and finds it "baf-
fling that feminist criticism has so far largely stayed away from the
postmodernism debate which is considered not to be pertinent to
feminist concerns."[72] In a similar vein, Craig Owens refers to "feminist
practice" as "one of the most significant developments of the past
decade" and proposes "that women's insistence on difference and
incommensurability may not only be compatible with, but also an
instance of postmodern thought."[73] Although other critics mention
and hint at a connection between feminism and postmodernism,
these two strong examples adequately demonstrate the extent to
which male critics engaged in the debates about postmodernism
have from the beginning asserted feminism as compatible with
postmodernism.[74] In spite of these examples and the increasing
participation of feminist critics in the postmodernist debate, many
feminists have tended and still tend to view the debate as existing
within a masculinist enclave.

Indeed, the postmodernist debate has until very recently been
conducted almost exclusively by male critics, especially within literary studies. In discussions of fiction, (mostly male) literary critics
have primarily used novels by male writers as examples of postmodern
texts, and their analyses of postmodern elements usually dominate
to the point that other stances, such as feminism, never enter the
critical inquiry.[75] Indeed, postmodern elements or topoi seem to be
discussed/constructed in ways that disallow the entry of feminism
into the discussion. Brian McHale's *Postmodernist Fiction* (1987),
the first book-length study of postmodern fiction, fails to address
feminism altogether. The terms "feminism" or "feminist" are absent
from the 235 pages of McHale's critical book; the closest he comes to
addressing feminism is in a brief paraphrase of Gunter Grass's
notion that "official history" is the history "of the male sex."[76] Out of
the multitude of examples of postmodern writers that McHale gives
to illustrate his various points, only six women writers are cited:
Monique Wittig, Christine Brooke-Rose, Brigid Brophy, Angela

Carter, Maggie Gee, and Muriel Spark—with the addition of Gertrude Stein as a strong pre-postmodern. Texts written by these women writers are for the most part cited in lists of examples but are given no lengthy analyses. It is also revealing that most of the woman-authored texts mentioned by McHale are rather esoteric, are not particularly feminist, and are neither popular nor well-known novels—with the exception of Wittig's *Les Guérillères*.[77]

It is necessary to distinguish between texts written by women and feminist texts. Since women necessarily write from a culturally constructed position that is gendered, women's writing is likely to contain insight into the specific and shared experiences of women in a culture that has relegated them to a position inferior to that of men. Feminist fiction is written from a specific position assumed in relation to gender and sexuality as cultural constructions; it actively seeks to disrupt conventions by revealing and subverting the ways in which Western male-centered culture seeks to maintain men's position of dominance. In this sense, feminist and postmodern impulses intersect, so that postmodern fictional strategies that subvert a binary logic that is deeply male-centered, and literary conventions grounded in that logic, might serve as vehicles for the specific politics of feminist fiction. To return to the distinction between feminist and woman-authored texts, the feminist stance has no one-to-one relationship with gender or biological sex, so that theoretically a feminist could be either female or male. Since Western culture remains highly male-centered, however, a man is still inherently always in a position of authority; and a man's position of authority comes into conflict with the feminist stance, which challenges that very authority. Women are therefore more likely to be feminists today, precisely because they are not in a position of authority and are as a result more aware of the oppression under which women have been forced to live. It is also difficult and often problematic to label an entire text feminist since, as Mikhail Bakhtin suggests, novels are inherently multivoiced (even when that multiplicity is suppressed), which is why I have argued that it is more useful to discuss feminist elements or impulses within a given text.

McHale's silence about feminism and his use of few texts by women as examples of postmodern fiction epitomizes the lack of engagement by postmodern literary critics with feminism and with women writers as utilizing postmodern strategies and again points

to the terms in which postmodernism has been constructed, which
seem to leave out feminism.[78] Although some of the texts written by
women that McHale cites do contain feminist elements, even if he
does not note them, their tendency to drastically subvert and play
with language and other cultural signs overshadows and limits
their radical transformative potential by distancing themselves
from the material situation to the point of severing rather than
exploring the interconnections between language and the material
conditions—in addition, these texts sever themselves from a wide
readership. Brigid Brophy's *In Transit* (1969), for example, calls
into question the dichotomies between man and woman and
between masculine and feminine by presenting a protagonist who
does not know if he/she is a man or a woman and who spends most
of the novel seeking to resolve this indeterminacy but is ultimately
unsuccessful. Although the gesture is initially feminist in stance, it
loses its specific political impetus through its excess of play with the
variety of culturally constructed signs that normally work to position
individuals. Ultimately, it is inconceivable, from a feminist perspective, that any one in the present world could remain very long in
doubt as to his/her position as man or woman, since these culturally
determined positions have traditionally been attached to biological
sex. The novel's interest in problematizing the binary opposition
between man and woman is supplanted by its impulse toward play
and anarchy, so that not only is the dichotomy undermined but
difference itself is lost. As the novel is increasingly seduced by
indeterminacy and its characters and plot collapse, stable meaning
is no longer possible and the specific feminist politics are buried in
the ensuing chaos. While exploring the ways in which culture
constructs and assigns gender is clearly a feminist endeavor, the
novel's subsequent muting of the inescapable gender categories that
name and constrain women veers away from an engagement with
existing structures of power and in effect erases women's specific
oppression as well as women's anatomical and sexual difference
from men. Although the narrative's move toward anarchy suggests
a political stance, its simultaneous move toward an abstract
theoretical level no longer anchored in the material situation renders
its political effectiveness questionable at best.

Brophy's novel helps to situate in a more concrete fashion the
objections many feminists have had to postmodern theories and

aesthetics; but the example also supports the claim that certain theoretical impulses within postmodern aesthetics, rather than postmodern aesthetics in general, are incompatible with feminism. Such theoretical impulses include tendencies toward endless anarchic play, overdetermination, underdetermination, indeterminacy, dispersal—what Hassan has termed the deconstructive traits of postmodern theory and aesthetics. However, there exists a whole reconstructive strand of postmodern aesthetics that clearly contains points of intersection with feminism, and thus invites analysis, but has remained relatively unexplored within the scope of recent fiction by the (mostly male) critics who have constructed/defined postmodern fiction.[79] Feminism's relationship with postmodernism can be defined, at least partially, in the terms Fredric Jameson uses to discuss postmodernism's relationship with Marxism. Jameson rejects both a "facile repudiation" of postmodernism "as some final symptom of decadence" *and* an "equally facile celebration" of "the new forms as the harbingers of a new technological and technocratic Utopia." His call for an assessment rather than either a rejection or an unqualified embracing of postmodernism is an appropriate challenge to offer feminists, since feminism stands to benefit from certain postmodern strategies and yet must reject others in order to retain its political edge. A specifically feminist assessment of postmodernism must be performed, however, instead of Jameson's Marxist proposal, which views postmodernism as a sign of "cultural mutation" within late capitalism.[80] Indeed, feminist critics in various fields are actively engaged in such a reassessment.

Feminism, Postmodernism, and Key Western Concepts

As a first step toward delineating an area of intersection between certain forms of feminism and postmodernism, the elements and sets of concerns that they have in common need to be examined in more detail. Although from a different angle, Alice Jardine's *Gynesis* (1985) has begun this task by locating three relevant intersections between the feminist gesture and French critical modes: 1) "the word 'author,' and more generally the complex question of the speaking subject"; 2) "the status and stakes of representation"; and 3) "the radical requestioning of the status of *fiction* and (intrinsically) of *truth*."[81] The three focal points Jardine presents beg further analysis and seem relevant to the topic of the affinities between feminism and postmodernism, especially since she does not elaborate the points and is focusing most specifically on French poststructuralism. Although postmodernism and poststructuralism are not equivalents (see earlier discussion), they do share the impulse to call into question key Western concepts such as the ones pinpointed by Jardine: subject, representation, fiction, truth. The primary area of intersection between feminist and postmodern critical practices, in fact, lies in their common aim to question, expose, and subvert Western male-centered tradition, culture, and thought, an agenda that begins by challenging the concepts central to upholding Western thought and male dominance.

It must be conceded to those critics who deride postmodern aesthetics for not being anything new that humanist concepts have been under fire from their inception. Arnold Hauser's *Mannerism* testifies to the radical departure from "aesthetic doctrines based on the principle of order, proportion, balance, of economy of means, and of rationalism and naturalism in the rendering of reality" taken by art in response to the crisis of the High Renaissance. But, while mannerist art saw a "fusion of semblance and reality" and brought together "different levels of reality" in order "to cast doubt on the validity of any objectivity," mannerism is situated in a specific historical moment and cannot be equated with later aesthetic trends even if they have common elements. For instance, Hauser argues that, in spite of the parallels between modernism and mannerism, modernist art was "more radical than mannerism, in that it not only discards natural reality, not only distorts it, but to an extent replaces it by completely imaginary or abstract forms."[82] Much the same argument can be advanced to discuss postmodern fiction, many of whose radical elements have precursors and yet differ significantly from those precursors. Although mannerism thematizes the blurring of the boundary between reality and appearance, particularly through the masquerading of identity, postmodern aesthetics goes much further in its presentation of reality as always already represented—there is no *fusion* between reality and appearance—and of identity as nothing more than a dynamic set of subject positions. Postmodern fiction is not new, in the sense that nothing is created out of nothing; yet the ways in which it uses/co-opts characteristics that parallel those of other radical aesthetics are specific and historically situated.

Of interest to contemporary feminism are the strategies by which postmodern theories and aesthetics question and subvert the artificial system of binary hierarchical oppositions that grounds and reinforces both Western thought and male dominance. Indeed, the masculinist bias inherent in this system of oppositions demonstrates the degree to which binary thought is male-centered. Each set of oppositions has a dominant term associated with man, authority, and privilege and a subordinate term associated with woman: man and woman, male and female, masculine and feminine, subject and object, self and other, sanity and madness, reason and irrationality, active and passive, presence and absence, truth and falsehood, fact and fiction.[83] Irigaray has argued that within Western thought woman is "theoretically subordinated to the concept of masculinity" and "is viewed by the man as *his* opposite, that is to say, as *his* other, the negative of the positive."[84] Since the subordination of woman within the very structure of Western thought is at the root of and reinforces daily the physical and psychological oppression of women and the continued dominance of men, challenges to the system that perpetuates these inequitable positions are potentially compatible with feminist aims.

The Subject

Since many feminists reject postmodern theories on the grounds that they supposedly deny the subject, it is necessary to investigate how these theories in fact challenge the traditional conception of the subject. The term *subject* must first be differentiated from a living human being; a subject is always a socially and culturally constructed position. Rather than denying the subject outright, postmodern theories call into question the traditional humanist notion of the centered rational self-determining subject by situating the subject within culture and as a construction of culture.[85] Jacques Derrida, who has often been accused of doing away with the subject, in fact stresses that the "subject is indispensable" but "is a function, not a being," and that his aim is not to "destroy the subject" but to "situate it" by attempting to discover "where" the notion of the subject "comes from and how it functions."[86] In a similar vein, feminist critics like Catherine Belsey, Judith Butler, Theresa De Lauretis, Diana Fuss, E. Ann Kaplan, Chantal Mouffe, Joan Scott, Patricia Waugh, Chris Weedon, and Janet Wolff have recently argued that the subject is "socially constructed in discursive practices"[87] and "clearly *is* historically determined and situated,"[88] although they also emphasize the importance of exploring the connections between theoretically defined subject positions and the human beings who fill those positions.[89]

If the subject is a socio-cultural function, then notions of the subject are open to transformation. Therefore, it is more apt to discuss subjectivities rather than subjects, since the subject is not a static object but rather is always in process as it continuously moves toward a "becoming-other" than itself.[90] Michael Wood and Louis Zurcher, Jr. suggest that the shift from a humanist to a postmodern notion of subjectivity can be viewed as a shift from a self thought of as either or both an essential core—the soul, in its original Christian formulation—and "an object built up through cumulative effort to a present-oriented self realized, discovered, and actualized in a continual process."[91] The postmodern subject is not set in opposition to the classic centered subject but rather is situated as a function of various historical and socio-cultural forces and power relations.

It is thus not anti-postmodern to argue, as E. Ann Kaplan does, that feminists "need to continue to construct strategic subjectivities" from which to work toward change, as long as those subject positions are understood as artificial rather than natural.[92] Postmodern theories implicitly offer the possibility of self-construction through their rejection of an essential or transcendent self. Although Weedon suggests that there exists a limited "range of subjectivity immediately open to any individual" at any given time, individual agency is still possible within that range.[93] Human beings can and do engage in political actions within the scope of the subject positions available to them, which include subject positions that are marginalized—often as "mad or criminal"—because they threaten the dominant order.[94] Positing the subject as a function does not inherently deny the material and historical existence of human beings, nor does it deny forms of identity and agency. Rather, post-modern theories insists that human beings constantly take up and give up various sociocultural subject positions, so that human beings have no essential, singular, unified, and stable subjecthood or selfhood. Postmodern identity can be viewed as "an ensemble of 'subject positions' that can never be totally fixed in a closed system" and as "always contingent and precarious, temporarily fixed at the intersection of those subject positions"—at "nodal points, partial fixations." But these nodal points can serve as "precarious forms of identification" to construct "forms of unity and common action" that do not depend on centered subjects or on preexisting identities or unities.[95] Although these identities are not essential and thus are subject to change, they nevertheless serve the function of grounds from which to organize coalitions and collaborative political action.

Within recent fiction, the postmodern challenge to the humanist subject results in characters depicted as lacking control, as not distinctly separated from the outer world and from each other, as fragmented, as de-centered, and as detached from any one given position or point of view. Postmodern theories and aesthetics expose the gaps within subjectivity that have most recently been covered over by a bourgeois version of individualism and by high modernism's alienated subject and individual ego-self. No longer locked within the rigid oppositions between subject and object and between self and world, postmodern subjectivity encompasses both and neither terms of these dichotomies: a continuous process of difference and deferral is at work. Through its detachment from any one given position, postmodern subjectivity unveils notions of hierarchy and opposition as artificial constructions used by the dominant order to retain its position of power. Since women have traditionally been relegated to the negative or subordinate positions within binary hierarchical oppositions, feminism stands to benefit from certain attempts to break down these dichotomies.

Many feminists have been reluctant, however, to challenge this system of binary oppositions even though it undergirds a male-centered metaphysics. Although these primarily liberal feminists reject the hierarchy inherent in the dichotomies, and in some cases even try to reverse the hierarchy, they nevertheless seem to want to hold on to the oppositions themselves in some sort of neutral balance. This fear of letting go of traditional oppositions is grounded in a belief that rejecting the opposition between man and woman would result in an erasure of the differences between men and women, which they view as a negative consequence.[96] However, notions of difference and of binary opposition cannot be equated: difference can be defined as *not the same* in a neutral sense, while a binary opposition involves placing differences in polarized and hierarchical positions and is therefore always politicized. Rejecting the hierarchy but not the oppositions themselves seems doomed, since the two are inherently linked; it is a halfway rejection that remains in collusion with the oppressing system.

Only by questioning the whole system of oppositions on which Western metaphysics is based can feminists radically challenge the dominant system under which women have always been oppressed. Some feminists are in fact actively searching for entirely new notions of the subject and self, which do not exist in oppositional relation to any object or other, rather than for some sort of universalized female or feminine subject in the traditional humanist style. In *Housekeeping* (1980), for example, Marilynne Robinson constructs a new female subject that has no basis in binarisms and inherently criticizes the established order. By making her central character, Sylvie, a transient woman with no fixed home, Robinson can posit a subject grounded in difference but not in the accepted distinctions between inside and outside or feminine and masculine or in the standard notion of time. Margaret Atwood's *The Robber Bride* (1993) also engages in a radical reconceptualization of the subject, particularly in its presentation of Zenia, who is continuously constructed and reconstructed through the narratives of three women whose lives Zenia has drastically affected. The three narratives point not only to their own constructions of Zenia but also to Zenia both as constructed by sociocultural forces and discourses and as self-constructed. By the end of the novel, Zenia functions as a powerful metaphor for the possibility of challenging the traditional male-centered order. Repeatedly constructing her own versions of herself gives Zenia power to survive in a hostile world that pushes to construct women in oppressive ways. Postmodern theories and aesthetics have similarly sought to challenge and replace the humanist version of the subject and self and, as such, have something to offer feminists: a radical reconceptualization of the subject and self.

Representation

Since any discussion of the notion of the subject is in effect a discussion of representations of the notion of the subject, the means by which representation has been grounded and legitimized must be examined. Within Western metaphysics, the categories of reality, life, fact, and truth have traditionally been set in opposition to representation, art, fiction, and falsehood. The basis of these oppositions lies in the notion that a stable objective reality exists outside of representation. Realist aesthetics assumes that this objective reality can be represented directly, while high modernist aesthetics insists that reality is always skewed by perspective or point of view so that every individual perceives her or his own version of reality. Both realism and modernism depend on their own accepted version and particular representation of reality, which Roland Barthes argues is "far from being neutral" and is "on the contrary loaded with the most spectacular signs of fabrication."[97] Postmodern aesthetics go beyond realism and modernism, however, not by denying that reality exists but rather by insisting that concrete reality is *always* mediated by culturally constructed representations. The notion that things and events are always already represented problematizes the conventional distinctions between reality and representation, life and art, fact and fiction, truth and falsehood. Although postmodern aesthetics does not collapse these dichotomies, it undermines their rigidity and significance. Within much postmodern fiction, for example, the sharp distinction between what is real and what is fictional becomes radically blurred to the extent that the opposition loses its force or legitimizing power. If both real and fictional things and events are understood to be mediated by representation, then both are constructions even though they exist on different fictional levels. Delegitimizing the established hierarchical opposition between reality and fiction becomes politically effective from a feminist standpoint, by encouraging examinations of the ways cultural norms and codes have strategically created this opposition as a means of achieving power and by revealing the artificial bases of existing relations of power and thus the possibilities for change.

Furthermore, the assertion that mediated representations are the only means of access to reality transforms art into a valid and potentially active space for political engagement. As Waugh suggests, fiction that "lays bare the conventions of realism" can help "us to understand how the reality we live day by day is similarly constructed, similarly 'written'."[98] As Brian Wallis argues, art becomes a realm with the power to unveil "cultural codes" as "arbitrary and historically determined" and therefore as constructed and open to change. Moreover, if "all institutionalized forms of representation certify corresponding institutions of power," then analyzing modes of representation becomes a vital and powerful feminist strategy.[99] Subverting the traditional distinction between art and reality challenges Western binary logic and the power relations constructed upon that logic. By undermining the verities or truths that have grounded Western aesthetics, postmodern aesthetics in effect undermines the verities or truths that have grounded the dominant systems that have produced those aesthetics. As Wolff argues, "aesthetic strategies that subvert the rule of logic, reason, and realism can release the repressed voice of those who are silenced." [100] Relatively few feminists, however, have acknowledged the possibility of a link between the political potential of postmodern aesthetics and feminism's own specific political agenda, which seeks to analyze and restructure relations of power. Instead, some feminist fiction and criticism unquestioningly hold on to the conventions of realism—fiction as a reflection of women's lives—and, as a result, remain effectively caught within a metaphysics that is inherently male-centered. But the postmodern claim that any notion of reality is always already a function of representation suggests that no system of thought can legitimately claim to be grounded in preexisting neutral truths or reality. Postmodern aesthetics exposes processes of construction and opens up the door for the manufacturing of new sets of provisional truths—or fictions—to replace the old ones. Theoretically, these truths would remain unfixed and always in process of being challenged, revised, replaced and, as such, would evade being reified permanently into preexisting grounds for institutions of power. Furthermore, since "representation participates actively in the *construction*" of "social values and ideologies,"[101] constructing specifically feminist forms of representation becomes a necessary feminist practice. If the goal of feminism is not only to question and unveil the workings of existing systems of power but also to offer possibilities for a restructuring of social and thought systems, undermining the opposition between reality and fiction gives feminism a strong base from which to work.

Many feminists do challenge accepted notions of reality, by exposing representations of reality as versions of reality that have traditionally been male-centered. As Kate Linker suggests, representation "acts to regulate and define the subjects it addresses, positioning them by class or by sex, in active or passive relations to meaning."[102] Analyses of politically engaged feminist fiction demonstrate that representations that highlight their own fictionality can nevertheless serve as illustrations of women's lives; and the politics of these texts are effective precisely because they are not obfuscated by the neutrality claims of realism. In *The Life and Loves of a She-Devil* (1983), for example, Fay Weldon challenges the conventions of realism with her central character's outrageous self-transformation from an ugly six feet two inches tall woman into an attractive woman of five feet six and a half inches. At the same time, however, Weldon uses this absurd, unrealistic transformation to illustrate the desperation of women trapped within subordinate positions and by damaging culturally constructed notions of femininity.

Language and Interpretation

The postmodern problematization of representation is accompanied by a rigorous interrogation of the notion and role of language and of interpretation. If objective reality is accessible only through representations, then the notion of language as a stable system of signs in which meaning exists in a one-to-one relationship with a given object or idea collapses. Postmodern theories conceive of language as a network of signs whose meanings are always in the process of sliding and shifting. Meaning is always being constructed and reconstructed rather than being fixed; however, this does not negate meaning. In the case of most postmodern fiction, texts are characterized not by anti-referentiality but rather by an overabundance of references that destabilizes meaning (see my earlier discussion of *Libra*), even if meaning is often recuperated. The unstable nature of this conception of language exposes language as potentially malleable. Interpretation becomes a continuous process: with each fluctuation in meaning, interpretations are subverted and must be reworked.

The reconceptualization of interpretation as an ongoing process allows for, and in fact makes necessary, the rereading and reinterpretation of texts and thus calls into question notions of correct readings. Since interpretations of texts have tended to be male-centered, the postmodern move to open texts to reinterpretations offers feminism ways to rethink questions of language and interpretation. The recognition that language is unstable, and that meaning and interpretation are constructed and strategic political processes, provides a grounds for feminist attempts to expose the complex of power relations that ground and are infused within cultural practices. Feminists have repeatedly been denigrated for bringing politics into everything; but this charge loses credibility when it surfaces that all readings, interpretations, and language itself are inherently political. In *Cassandra* (1983), for instance, Christa Wolf rereads, reinterprets, and rewrites the Trojan war story from the perspective of both Cassandra and a contemporary woman narrator. Wolf implicitly highlights the male-centeredness of the story in its traditional form through her retelling of "Homer's historical epic of men and their politics and wars in terms of the untold story of women and everyday life."[103]

Narrative in Fiction and History

The postmodern problematization of representation also leads to a questioning of narrative, the traditional means by which a story is told. How can a story be told if there is no stable basis, if both language and representation are suspect? Narrative is a verbal communication process that is generally acknowledged to involve three aspects: story (events to be narrated), text (spoken or written discourse), and narration (act or process of the text's production).[104] But current notions of narrative have been shaped by and within a specifically male-centered cultural context and may thus need to be questioned by feminists who seek to expose and subvert masculinist biases within cultural structures and discourses. Postmodern strategies that both challenge traditional notions of narrative and create new ways of telling a story are thus potentially useful for feminists. Postmodern fiction, for example, tends to shatter notions of beginning and ending and to adapt new forms to shape new contents and vice versa. These strategies challenge the conventional distinction between aesthetic form and content, which has traditionally been reflected within narrative. The postmodern notion of identity as decentered, dispersed, and unstable extends to postmodern narratives, which tend to be fractured into a mixture of various forms-contents. Thomas's *The White Hotel* (1981), for instance, is dispersed into various narrative fragments—poem, letters, dreams,

postcards, Freudian case study, journal, documentary—that undermine each other and challenge a single all-embracing narrative. At
the same time, however, Thomas's novel uses its fragmented narratives to communicate forcefully to its reader the ways in which
male-centered Western discourses (in this case Freudian psychoanalysis) are implicated in the violence and misogyny that surface
in concrete material situations like the Nazi extermination of Jews.

Narrative is also prevalent in discourses other than fiction,
particularly within history. Traditionally understood as an account
of facts and real events, history nevertheless requires narrative to
present these facts and events in ordered sequences. Like fiction,
history consists of a narrative with story, text, and narration; but,
unlike fiction, history has been relegated to the realm of truth
within Western culture. The postmodern challenge to the notion of
history as truth leans toward a confrontation of both history and
historicity—historical actuality or fact. Through such strategies as
inserting historical figures and events into fictional texts (and thus
overtly fictionalizing them) and emphasizing the lack of access to
past figures and events, postmodern fiction problematizes the
classic oppositions between fact and fiction, truth and falsehood,
and further undermines any rigid distinction between historical and
fictional facts, events, or narrative. History and fiction are not
collapsed, however; they are designated as narratives distinguished
by their frames rather than by universalized notions of truth and
falsehood. Postmodern theories and aesthetics do not deny that
events occurred in the past but rather question how events are
recounted. It is the accessibility of the past rather than the past
itself that is being challenged, since history is "inaccessible to us
except in textual form."[105] Without denying that history is a vital
structuring and stabilizing element within culture, postmodern
theories and aesthetics demonstrate that history is a constructed
institutionalized truth within a specific cultural context and is
therefore provisional and plural in nature.

Postmodern fiction often incorporates historical events and
characters, regardless of the accuracy of the context, as a radical
means of illustrating history as a culturally constructed narrative
rather than a series of raw unbiased facts or events. DeLillo's *Libra*,
for example, acknowledges the past by making the John F. Kennedy
assassination its topic and using historical figures as its characters;

but, at the same time, the novel demonstrates the inaccessibility of that past except through fragments of multiple narratives. In a different vein, Fowles's *The French Lieutenant's Woman* both engages history, by locating its action in the Victorian period and making Victorian mores a central concern, and questions the accessibility of this specific past, by grounding its narrator's commentary in a contemporary context. Although some postmodern fiction that is more pervasively anti-referential has a tendency towards ahistoricism, much postmodern fiction both engages and problematizes history to some degree.[106] Indeed, by highlighting history, postmodern fiction demonstrates its inextricability from sociocultural discourses and the specific power relations inherent in the continuous reproduction of those discourses. In its direct engagement of its readers through a common received history, which it both co-opts and subverts, postmodern fiction reveals itself as culturally responsive and belies the charges of aestheticism often levelled against it.

Since history has been constructed from a primarily male-centered perspective, feminists have also worked to challenge existing notions of history. Feminists have been active in bringing previously ignored women into mainstream history and in constructing a history of women parallel to mainstream history. While these activities are valuable, in that they call attention to the work and actions of women who have traditionally been marginalized from a male-centered culture, such revisionist work fails to challenge the accepted notion of history itself. The postmodern problematization of historicity, however, offers feminists a means by which and a basis from which to perform a radical rethinking of the Western conception of history. Writers whose works demonstrate feminist impulses have in fact used many of the strategies usually associated with postmodern fiction to simultaneously engage and problematize history. In *Beloved* (1987), for example, Toni Morrison uses elements of the supernatural or the uncanny to represent the unrepresentable and the marginalized of history. Morrison engages the postmodern tendency to move toward the limits of representation, toward what Hassan calls *"The Unpresentable, Unrepresentable,"*[107] as a means of narrativizing the history that has been denied her black women characters and of recapturing the history they have suffered. In a different vein, Elsa Morante's *History: A Novel* (1974) offers a narrative of twentieth-century history that challenges official history by flaunting its own idiosyncrasies and overtly blurring the distinction between history and fiction. Morante replaces the supposed objective narrative voice traditionally used to recount history with a highly individualized subjective voice and conjoins lists of chronologically ordered world events with personal histories. The novel fulfills the feminist aim of challenging the authority and dominant position of official history and of exposing the value of personal histories or stories.

Feminist and Postmodern Fiction

Recent challenges to notions of the subject, of reality, of language, and of narrative have brought about a crisis in representation. How can anything, most importantly the subject, be represented if reality is not accessible outside of representation and language is inherently unstable? Postmodern fiction has engaged this dilemma by highlighting its own fictional status as well as its manipulation of language. Within postmodern fiction, for example, the subject is illustrated or intuited through the text's language; characters no longer impersonate *real* people but rather are overtly presented as constructions. For example, Wolf's *Cassandra* presents Cassandra as a contemporary narrator's construction. Characters have not disappeared from all postmodernist fiction, however, which indicates that in many instances traditional representation has been transformed rather than totally eradicated. While postmodern fiction challenges mimetic representation, it also offers a new, more overtly textual and self-reflexive form of representation that exposes its own filtered or biased quality. Moreover, the impulse to challenge Western metaphysics opens up a space for the possible construction of new versions of traditional concepts (like subjectivity) that would no longer be grounded in Western forms of binarism and universals—a space that some feminist fiction has exploited for its more radical political aims.

By actively extending postmodern disruptive strategies into material cultural practices and domains, feminism becomes potentially more powerful politically in its criticism of received knowledge than postmodern theories and aesthetics; yet, at the same time, feminism often retains conservative tendencies that blunt that potential. Postmodern theories and aesthetics, on the other hand, have a tendency to blunt their own political edge by overdestabilizing received knowledge to the extent that even temporary grounds for criticism are lost, as exemplified by my earlier discussion of DeLillo's *Libra*. Postmodern critical and subversive strategies acknowledge their position within the culture they challenge, however, which demonstrates that the postmodern impulse is not inherently divorced from the material sociohistorical situation even if certain overly esoteric or theoretical tendencies can and do surface. Not only do postmodern theories and aesthetics offer criticism of established culture, but they also generate forms of internal criticism that expose previously covered-over gaps within culture. In fact, many recent writers acknowledge the political potential of certain postmodern strategies and enlist these strategies to fulfill radical feminist aims.

In the chapters that follow, the dynamic intersection between feminist and postmodern impulses within recent fiction will be more thoroughly demonstrated through the analyses of four already distinguished novels published since World War II by acclaimed anglophone novelists of varied national, intellectual, and social backgrounds: Doris Lessing's *The Golden Notebook* (1962), Marge Piercy's *Woman on the Edge of Time* (1976), Margaret Atwood's *The Handmaid's Tale* (1985), and Angela Carter's *Nights at the Circus* (1984). I chose these particular novels (out of a large number of possibilities) for three reasons: they are already widely read, acclaimed, and respected; they engage specifically feminist politics; and they are representative of various and distinct ways in which feminist aims have been furthered through the use of strategies that disrupt Western metaphysics and are associated with postmodernism.[108] These novels have until very recently been discussed primarily as feminist fiction, but the following analyses demonstrate that their feminist thrust is strengthened by the use of postmodern elements that undermine the status quo but that critics have for the most part overlooked. The aim of this study is to examine how specific texts with feminist impulses use a variety of postmodern disruptive strategies, how the use of these strategies as vehicles for feminist aims differs from their use in non-feminist texts, and what new possibilities are created for new forms of feminist aesthetics through the use of these strategies. I will particularly emphasize the ways in which feminist fiction always retains sight of the material situation, even as it engages subversive aesthetic strategies, and engages in deconstruction as a means of creating a space for reconstruction. Before examining the novels by Lessing, Piercy, Atwood, and Carter, however, an examination of women writers' versions of modernist fiction is in order, since recent fiction with feminist impulses can be argued to be a product of both its contemporary cultural climate and its literary precursors.

2. The Emergence of Disruptive Strategies in Women's Modernist Fiction

Insofar as postmodernism is both a reaction against and a continuation of modernism, the impulses disruptive of Western metaphysics used for feminist purposes in recent fiction have their roots not only in contemporary existence, theory, and thought patterns but also in women writers' versions of modernism in the first half of the twentieth-century. As Andreas Huyssen suggests, postmodernism's reaction against modernism is in effect a reaction against an institutionalized "austere image of 'high modernism,' as advanced by the New Critics and other custodians of modernist culture."[1] Indeed, a domesticated highly ideological version of modernism developed during the 1940s and 1950s, characterized by an "(ostensibly) apolitical formalism."[2] This apolitical stance results at least in part from high modernism's adherence to binary logic in its hierarchical positioning of aesthetics in opposition to politics, of high art in opposition to mass culture, of the artist in opposition to the average person. Moreover, literary high modernism centers around specific male writers and thereby reinforces the classic male/female dichotomy; within the Anglo-American tradition, these writers include T.S. Eliot, Ezra Pound, and James Joyce, among others. The canon of literary high modernism conspicuously leaves out the writings of women, precisely because such work does not exactly fit the categories used to delimit high modernism. While in many respects reacting against canonized modernism, contemporary writers with feminist aims arguably build from, rather than react against, subversive strategies within the work of women modernists. I am suggesting that the novels by Lessing, Piercy, Atwood, and Carter that I have chosen to analyze exist within a specific *literary* history and context that may help to explain how and why these novels differ from those of their male contemporaries that also demonstrate postmodern impulses.

I am not claiming, however, that the fiction of women modernists necessarily contains overt feminist or postmodern impulses. Following in the wake of critics such as Ann Ardis, Carolyn Burke, Marianne DeKoven, Rachel Blau DuPlessis, Ellen Friedman, Susan Stanford Friedman, and Sydney Janet Kaplan (among others), I am simply acknowledging that the first half of the twentieth-century was the site of a convergence of literary experimentation, commonly referred to as modernism, and women's struggle for independence, most visible in the active and eventually successful suffrage movements but also evident in the very public New Woman debates raging during the last two decades of the nineteenth-century.[3] Although the term *feminist* can be and is often applied to some of the modernist fiction written by women, the feminism that dominates women modernists' texts is generally more in the liberal feminist tradition, which seeks equality for women rather than a restructuring of society. However, certain more disruptive strategies emerge from some of the modernist texts written by women that prefigure and anticipate contemporary fiction's challenges to Western modes of thought, particularly recent fiction with feminist impulses. Many of the women modernists experiment with narrative expressly to find a means of depicting *women's* material lives and thought processes, for which they feel traditional narrative does not allow. The resulting subversions of traditional narrative begin the task of undermining the white, bourgeois, male assumptions on which conventional narrative modes are based. As Ellen Friedman argues, "the rupturing of traditional forms becomes a political act" that is "allied to the feminist project."[4] In other words, the disruption of Western tradition challenges a mode of thought that is deeply male-centered and therefore can potentially be harnessed to propel forward feminism's specific oppositional politics (see Chapter 1).[5]

Although high modernism in theory transcends the political through its engagement in a purely aesthetic realm, in actuality high modernism suppresses turn-of-the-century politics: most notably the suffrage, socialist, and New Woman debates. For instance, by severing the radical present from a vilified conservative Victorian past (and thereby creating a binary opposition), the writers canonized by high modernism also erase the "anti-bourgeois energy" and the "socioliterary radicalism" evident in the debates surrounding the New Woman and New Woman novels. As Ann Ardis argues, many of the New Woman novels of the 1880s and 1890s "anticipate the reappraisal of realism" usually credited to modernist writers by "demystify[ing] the ideology of 'womanliness'," questioning "the epistemology of representation," and "figur[ing] desires that have never been realized before." Not only do these novels challenge "the bourgeois Victorian social order's prescriptive definition of 'correct' female behavior but also the pattern of thinking in hierarchically organized binary oppositions."[6] All of these experimental strategies, which involve disrupting the dominant binary mode of thought, also characterize much fiction by women modernists and might help to explain why the high modernist canon has marginalized these texts. If in some ways women modernists continue to write versions of New Woman novels at the same time as they participate in aspects of high modernism, then their connection with and interest in the political debates of the cultural moment threaten the binary logic on which high modernism depends to define itself and distance itself from the material situation.

The fiction of writers such as Dorothy Richardson, Gertrude Stein (early fiction), May Sinclair, H.D., Djuna Barnes, Mina Loy, and Virginia Woolf is firmly anchored within certain aspects that have traditionally been associated with high modernism in its attempts to efface the author; its emphasis on identity, especially locating or recovering an essential self, and on the split between the inner and outer self; its adherence to the notion that objective reality exists but is always distorted by subjectivity; and its attempts to find a more accurate form of realism through the depiction of individual consciousness.[7] However, women modernists' experimentation with form and style is intricately linked to their attempts to delineate a specifically *female* subject. These writers' particular focus on women's material lives and thought patterns results in certain disruptions of traditional narrative and of Western conceptual modes that differ from those of their male contemporaries and that demonstrate the germs of a movement toward the more radical subversions created by more recent fiction with feminist impulses. As they wrestle with the notion of female subjectivity, women modernists employ a variety of strategies that move beyond reactions against Victorianism and turn-of-the-century Realism to challenge traditional narrative and Western metaphysics itself. These strategies range from Richardson's construction of the stream-of-consciousness technique and repudiation of grammatical conventions; to Stein's focus on female desire and use of rhythmic repetition; to Sinclair's unveiling of madness as an arbitrary but gendered social construction; to H.D.'s breaking down of the conventional hierarchical oppositions between sanity and madness, inner and outer self, heterosexuality and homosexuality; to Barnes's creation of a disjointed and fantastic narrative to subvert gender boundaries; to Loy's depiction of the role of relations of power in the construction of subjectivities and aesthetics; to Woolf's manipulation of fantasy, parody, and metafiction to destabilize gender boundaries and emphasize the realm of the *in between*.[8]

The link between women modernists' fiction and both the sociopolitical debates of the times and radical stylistic innovations (associated with modernism) is most evident in the work of Dorothy Richardson. In many ways, Richardson's thirteen volume *Pilgrimage* (1915–57) is a New Woman novel, whose heroine challenges the conventions of women's role by distancing herself from her family both physically and economically, by experimenting with sex and romantic love but rejecting marriage, by pursuing a career as journalist and writer, and by creating new roles for herself. At the same time, while Richardson's firm adherence to the opposition between men and women and between masculine and feminine is conservative in impulse, her development of a stream-of-consciousness technique to depict the workings of a woman's mind is revolutionary.[9] Since conventional narrative tends to focus on the outer or social self, and since women's social selves have traditionally been produced in accordance with the norms of a male-centered status quo, Richardson's experimental narrative technique allows her to depict the division between the inner and outer self, between women's social roles and individual consciousnesses. The narrative of *Pilgrimage* consists of the fragmented but continuous flow of the central character's, Miriam's, thoughts and impressions, written in the first and third person with little punctuation. Linear temporality is dropped in favor of an order based on the workings of memory. Richardson's new narrative technique enables her to represent the conflict between Miriam's sense of multiple social roles or selves, "of being a collection of persons," and her emphatic assertion of an essential core self, "that self within herself who was more than her momentary self," "her authentic being," "the changeless central zone of her being."[10]

While Richardson's technique and aims fall squarely within modernism, particularly in the emphasis on the recovery of an essential self, certain elements sprinkled throughout her novel— even if sparingly—hint at more radical disruptions. Moreover, these elements are tied to her specific interest in depicting a woman's consciousness and life. The novel offers in Miriam a character who is aware that language shapes the world and that a new mode of writing has revolutionary potential, especially since language has consistently been shaped by what Miriam refers to as a "male-centered and -structured" culture: Miriam does not want to write "like a man," using men's language.[11] Richardson's own writing technique flagrantly violates traditional rules of English punctuation and syntax, has no set form or linearity, and is shaped according to "psychological veracity" rather than "technical conformity." On one level, Richardson's subversion of conventional writing is an attempt to break from traditional male-centered language and narrative rules in order to represent a woman's mind at work.[12] Her experimentation remains anchored in the material situation, reacting against women's containment by cultural structures at large (especially the norms limiting women to the positions of wife and mother) and, more specifically, by male-centered aesthetic forms such as Realism. By offering new aesthetic forms, Richardson implicitly reveals that dominant codes and structures are constructed, and therefore open to change, and that there is a vital link between dominant aesthetic forms and relations of power.

Although Richardson remains caught within mimetic aesthetics in her own innovative attempt to represent faithfully a woman's consciousness, on a thematic level the novel begins to question the possibility of mimetic representation when Miriam asserts that "nothing can ever be communicated,"[13] fears "misrepresentation" when telling anecdotes, and recognizes "the gulf between life and the expression of it": "It isn't true. It's words. Nothing can ever be expressed in words." These comments all point to an awareness of a gap between words and meaning, between signifier and signified. Furthermore, even if Miriam remains trapped within oppositional thought, especially in her inability to overcome the division between her identification with what she views as male-centered thought and knowledge and her female body and sexuality, she occasionally rejects on an intellectual level "the drawing of lines and setting up of oppositions," which she attributes to male-structured logic: "Men are either-or, all the time."[14] Even if Richardson does not pursue, and at times overtly frustrates, the implications of her revolutionary impulses, and even if she remains firmly anchored within a modernist aesthetics, her novel nevertheless anticipates things to come. More specifically, the recognition that language is an imperfect medium of expression, which surfaces both thematically and formally in *Pilgrimage*, and the uneasy beginnings of a questioning of mimetic representation and oppositional thought on a thematic level prefigure the contemporary emphasis on the instability of language and thus its reactionary or revolutionary potential, the impossibility of mimetic representation, and the oppressive nature of binary logic. While many modernist writers explored the problems with realist mimesis, what is particularly noteworthy here is that all of the elements in Richardson's novel that push toward more radical disruptions of Western metaphysics stem from an identification of traditional language, aesthetics, and logic with men, or at least with a male-centered culture, and an attempt to repudiate or frustrate that identification.

Gertrude Stein's early novel *Three Lives* (1909) also manipulates language and narrative as it addresses the notion of the female self and of women's oppression within a male-centered culture both thematically and stylistically, but in very different ways from Richardson.[15] The book is divided into three distinct stories—"The Good Anna," "Melanctha," "The Gentle Lena"—that work together to depict the lives of working class women and the limited possibilities open to them. Whether women are presented as conforming to and even helping to sustain culturally imposed norms actively or passively, as in the cases of Anna and Lena respectively, or as deviating from those norms, as in the case of Melanctha, they are all eventually sapped of their strengths by a culture that expects women to give of themselves to the exclusion of fulfilling their own needs. Anna works incessantly serving others until she dies "with her strong, strained, worn-out body" (82); Melanctha feels lost and eventually dies alone of consumption after both Rose and Jem reject her and leave her alone and unable "to feel safe inside her" (233–34); and Lena becomes unable to "feel very much now about anything that happened to her," as she becomes "more and more lifeless" and finally dies in childbirth (278–79). Although friendship, love, and even passion between women help to sustain Anna, Melanctha, and

Lena, society's privileging of heterosexual relations intrudes into these relationships between women and dissolves them. Anna's relationship with "Mrs. Lehntman was the only romance Anna ever knew," but there soon "loomed up to Anna's sight a man, a new doctor that Mrs. Lehntman knew," who breaks up the women's close ties (55–56); Melanctha's friendship with Rose comes to an end when Rose feels threatened by her husband's increasingly "good and gentle" disposition toward Melanctha (228); and Lena's arranged marriage to a man who cares little for her makes her unable to spend time with the other servant girls, with whom she feels a bond and who "made a gentle stir within her" (247). Indeed, the stories demonstrate how the desires of women in general have no place in western societal norms for women.

Of the three title characters, Melanctha is the only one who does not suppress her desires and who rejects the notion of the self prescribed by the culture in which she lives. "Melanctha" is the longest and most fully developed of the three stories. It creates a vision of the female self as shifting and as grounded in material physical experience and experience-based thought. The conflicted relationship between Melanctha and Dr. Jeff Campbell emphasizes the female subject as different from the traditional Western humanist—and very much male—subject produced within the model of rational thought. In contrast to Melanctha's unbounded yearning for "real experience," for "feel[ing] things way down in you" (122) (which Jeff interprets as irrational), Jeff believes "you ought to love your father and your mother and to be regular in all your life, and not to be always wanting new things and excitement, and to always know where you were, and what you wanted, and to always tell everything just as you meant it" (116–17). Jeff's adherence to the humanist notion of the whole stable essential self surfaces in his unsuccessful attempts to pin down Melanctha: "Tell me honest, Melanctha, which is the way that is you really, when you are alone, and real, and all honest" (139). But Melanctha resists attempts to position and delimit her; rather than suppress her desires, as her culture demands, she allows her desires to guide her: she is "complex with desire." Because she loves "too hard and too often," she disrupts the cultural standards that define women as passive and asexual and prescribe for women a "proper" monogamous heterosexual relationship resulting in marriage and children (87–89).

Melanctha defies these cultural scripts by "wandering," by acknowledging and using the "power" that her sexuality gives her (95), and
by actively desiring "real, strong, hot love" (122). Although questioning
identity is central to most modernist fiction, "Melanctha" moves
beyond modernism in its presentation of a protagonist whose self
remains in a continuous process of becoming as she seeks to satisfy
her desires. Melanctha is not interested in recovering an essential
self covered over by an increasingly mechanized and violent world;
rather, she seeks to develop an uncontained self free to become.

Another means by which Melanctha counters Jeff's, and society's,
endeavors to confine and name her is to question language's ability
to express and contain the realm of desire and emotions: "You see,
Jeff, it ain't much use to talk about what a woman is really feeling
in her. You see all that, Jeff, better, by and by, when you get to really
feeling" (135). She rejects Jeff's "always wanting to have it all clear
out in words always, what everybody is always feeling" (171) as
deceptive and misguided, since their language has been constructed
within a culture that has traditionally privileged a model of rational
thought over feeling. Melanctha further undermines binary logic
through her refusal to view the world in terms of right and wrong,
good and bad. Unlike Jeff and her friend Rose, Melanctha does not
conform to the socially established norms of behavior, "the right way
she should do" (207), because she does not view life in rigid binary
terms. Although others are attracted to Melanctha precisely because
she is not contained by cultural norms, the indeterminate nature of
her self and her refusal to play by the rules leads them eventually to
distance themselves from her, from that which is threatening to the
status quo.

In a typical modernist move, Stein's writing style in *Three
Lives* calls into question the expressive function of language by
engaging in rhythmic repetition and thereby subverting traditional
linear narrative. Certain phrases within a given passage or even
story are repeated with slight variations to create the effect that
words can at best approximate meaning. In the following passage,
repetition enacts the inability of language to explain rationally the
relationship between Melanctha and Rose. It remains unclear why
Melanctha clings to the "simple, sullen, selfish" Rose; however, the
narrative creates an impression of Melanctha's attachment to Rose
even if it remains unfixed, unstable:

And Melanctha Herbert clung to Rose in the hope that Rose could save her. Melanctha felt the power of Rose's selfish, decent kind of nature. It was so solid, simple, certain to her. Melanctha clung to Rose, she loved to have her scold her, she always wanted to be with her. She always felt a solid safety in her. Rose always was, in her way, very good to let Melanctha be loving to her ... Melanctha needed badly to have Rose always willing to let Melanctha cling to her. Rose was a simple, sullen, selfish, black girl, but she had a solid power in her. (210)

The variations in word choice and sentence structure work to build a web of meanings that does not represent so much as rhythmically create a sense of the relationship between the two women. Stein demonstrates through her writing style that language is malleable and can be manipulated in ways that counter the traditional association of language and mimesis and the use of language as a mechanism of containment. The narrative of "Melanctha" refuses to name and contain Melanctha, choosing instead to approximate her through a physical enactment through repetition of the unstable nature of language. Stein's use of repetition in *Three Lives* differs from (and, indeed, predates) the experimentation with language of male modernists, however, in that it is a function of a specific attempt to represent women—their selves, their lives, and their relationships to each other and to men. The repetition opens up language and narrative by freeing meaning from male-centered definitions and rules of grammar and syntax, which delimit women and representations of women by emphasizing a linear, cause and effect logic that has little relevance to women's lives and psyches. At the same time, however, Stein's writing retains a firm grounding in its women characters' material existence, focusing for instance on their relationships with men and women and the function of economics and social norms within those relationships. Stein's experimentation attempts specifically to render women's lives and selves outside of the male-centered forms and paradigms (such as the conventions of literary Realism) that have traditionally named and objectified women. The specific political agenda of Stein's experimentation highlights the potential link between fictional strategies and changes in material conditions, which are always also necessarily ideological. Since cultural norms and institutions construct subjectivities, challenges to those norms create a space for constructing new subjectivities.

May Sinclair coined the term "stream-of-consciousness" to describe Richardson's technique in a praising review and adopted the technique in her own writing. While her work is not as overtly experimental as that of Richardson or Stein, in *Mary Olivier: A Life* (1919) Sinclair represents the flow of her main character's thoughts as a means of depicting the deep split that exists between women's expected social roles and their inner or essential selves. Moreover, the sympathetic portrait of Mary Olivier's Aunt Charlotte, who is pronounced mad by her family, anticipates contemporary feminists' analyses of how the label of madness has historically been attributed to women who do not conform to the status quo. The novel hints at the precariousness of identity as well as the role of cultural forces in creating and imposing identities. Charlotte is gradually marginalized from society by her own family as a result of her illusion that every man is a potential husband for her and of the overt flirting in which she indulges in her attempts to secure a husband. Finally, she is literally imprisoned at the top of the house; a young Mary notes "The doors and the partitions, the nursery and its bars, the big cupboard across the window, to keep her from getting away." Eventually Charlotte is institutionalized against her will: "They were holding her up by her arm-pits, half leading, half pushing her before them. Her feet made a brushing noise on the flag stones." A subsequent discussion between Mary and her brother Mark suggests that they recognize the politically motivated use of the term *madness* to support socially established standards:

"Poor Charlotte's the sanest of the lot, and she's the only one that's got shut up." [Mark]

"Why do you say she's the sanest?" [Mary]

"Because she knew what she wanted." [Mark]

"Yes. She knew what she wanted. She spent her whole life trying to get it [marriage]. She went straight for that one thing. Didn't care a hang what anybody thought of her." [Mary]

"So they said poor Charlotte was mad." [Mark]

"She was only mad because she didn't get it." [Mary][16]

Mary's last comment underscores her understanding of the fine line between acceptable and unacceptable behavior for women in a male-structured culture. Women are urged to marry, but they must submit to rules of courtship in which women remain ostensibly passive. Sinclair's novel disrupts the traditional hierarchical opposition between sanity and madness by highlighting its existence as an arbitrary but gendered social construction: Charlotte would not have been labelled mad if she had managed to snag a husband, since that is the chief aim society instills into women. In its focus on women's material lives and their oppression by societal norms and language, the novel demonstrates the destructive aspects of male-centered binary logic. However, the novel also points to the artificiality of that logic and the norms based upon it (Charlotte would not be labeled mad if she had married) and thus implicitly points to the possibility of challenging them.

H.D.'s subversion of the conventional association of madness with a negative state in *HERmione* (1927)[17] is more radical. Unlike Charlotte, who is crushed by the label of madness, Hermione is rejuvenated by her bout with madness. H.D.'s novel thus anticipates contemporary novels such as Doris Lessing's *The Golden Notebook* (1962) and *The Four-Gated City* (1969), in which madness functions as a potentially positive experience—as a means of rejecting the status quo, indulging in unbridled introspection, and creating a new decentered multiple sense of self. Unlike Lessing's novels, however, *HERmione* retains a strong adherence to the notion of a unified essential or core self. The novel's grounding in modernism is exhibited in the great gap or distance Hermione feels between her inner and outer self; in fact, she refers to herself alternately as Her and as Hermione: "Hermione Gart hugged HER to Hermione Gart. I am HER" and "I am Hermione" (94–95). Hermione's split self is in part a result of her struggle with her bisexuality, which is not accepted, and indeed is silenced, by the society in which she lives and with which she herself has difficulties coming to terms.[18] She views her outer self as a set of roles, "repeating words that had been written" (33) for her, while her inner self remains for the most part hidden. It is only after having descended to and then emerged from a delirious breakdown, during which she no longer has to struggle between her social roles and her inner self, that she is able to assert her true self and sexual identity and to break from her familial surroundings by leaving for Europe. The novel ends with Her feeling "Practical and at one with herself, with the world, with all outer circumstance" (234). This reconciliation of her inner and outer self, even if temporary, points to the novel's modernist valuation of an essential self; yet the novel's use of madness as a positive process to bring about this reconciliation is more subversive of Western conceptual modes, in that it implicitly challenges the negative association of madness and pushes toward a questioning of the traditional hierarchical opposition between sanity and madness—as well as between inner and outer self and between heterosexuality and homosexuality—and of male-structured binary logic in general.

While *HERmione* is composed of an emotional stream-of-consciousness narrative, its subversion of narrative also includes occasional treatment of language as tangible object and as potentially malleable. Hermione is aware of "the stark rigidity of words, words that were coin; save, spend": "I have tasted words, I have seen them" (75). The narrative itself emphasizes this materiality of language through its use of repetition, of words and phrases as building blocks toward some potential but far from stable meaning: "She saw it now. She saw it now. She would always be seeing what she saw now in a flash" (105)[19]. H.D.'s emphasis on the materiality of words and her frequent use of repetition point to an implicit uncertainty over the traditional notions that a one-to-one relationship exists between word and meaning and that mimetic representation is possible. Unlike the male modernists, however, her exploration of language is grounded in an attempt to posit a female subject that remains in process, rather than fixed, and therefore evades containment.

In *Nights* (1935),[20] H.D. introduces a metafictional twist that further questions the possibility of mimetic representation and interpretation. The novel posits an author figure, John Helforth, whose lengthy prologue comments on and inevitably interprets the manuscript he is introducing, which destabilizes the truth value—on which he insists—of the events that he discusses and that are recorded in the manuscript's narrative. Helforth's suggestion that the names of the novel's author and characters are pseudonyms further challenges the notion of a single stable reality or truth: "I can not [sic] do better than use the names in this manuscript, as Natalia Saunderson used them. Her name is not Natalia nor

Saunderson, neither is her sister-in-law called Renne, nor her husband, Neil" (3). In addition, *Nights* is the novel H.D. writes, the novel "Natalia" leaves behind when she commits suicide, and the novel Helforth edits and introduces. This multiplicity of authors challenges the notion of authorship by refusing the traditional one-to-one correspondence of author and text and thus pushing toward the contemporary assertion of intertextuality. *Nights'* challenges to traditional narrative, mimetic representation, and authorship occur in the service of the development of a woman, the author-character Natalia, as complex and multifaceted, as possessing an inner or core self that men like Helforth cannot understand or represent. While the novel remains anchored in the modernist tradition, it nonetheless begins to challenge certain Western conceptual norms—such as the distinction between truth and non-truth and the attribution of meaning to authorial intent. By producing a slippery text in which all meanings and names remain open, unfixed, H.D. refuses to contain, name, and thus objectify Natalia.

Djuna Barnes's *Nightwood* (1936) moves toward even more radical disruptions of Western metaphysics with its disjointed and fantastic narrative and with its more overt subversions of gender boundaries, binary logic, notions of identity and an essential self, language, and possibilities of mimetic representation. As Friedman suggests, *Nightwood* is a "Denunciation of Western patriarchy, of its sexual mores and sociocultural expectations, as well as its forms of narrative"[21]; and, as such, the novel's various disruptions are explicitly linked to its aim of subverting the male-centered status quo. The fragmented nonlinear narrative, depicting a civilization "in decay, an aristocracy in disarray, a people estranged from a sense of identity,"[22] is only loosely connected by Dr. Matthew O'Connor's soliloquies, which are themselves fairly disjointed; and the narrative and various characters remain distanced.

Barnes flagrantly violates conventional notions of identity and gender boundaries in her creation of Dr. O'Connor as a character. Introduced as a "middle-aged 'medical student'" and an "Irishman," O'Connor admits that he is a "charlatan" and that this gives him power, since it makes his identity indefinite or indeterminate.[23] He even goes so far as to suggest that he has "become anonymous" (82). The novel also frustrates the notion of identity as fixed by depicting O'Connor solely through his fantastic rambling storytelling, so that his identity remains a question mark; within the scope of the novel, he has little existence outside of the stories he tells. His identity is further complicated by his being biologically male and yet having a less easily defined gender. Other characters observe him at various points "snatching a few drops from a perfume bottle," "dusting his darkly bristled chin with a puff, and drawing a line of rouge across his lips" (36), wearing "a woman's flannel nightgown" and "a wig with long pendent curls," and being "heavily rouged and his lashes painted" (79). O'Connor explicitly affirms his ambiguous gender when he refers to himself as "the last woman left in this world, though I am the bearded lady" (100). His use of the feminine pronoun "she" to designate God further demonstrates his unconventional notions of gender: "Personally I call her 'she' because of the way she made me" (150). Barnes's creation of O'Connor's unstable gender and identity challenges the notion of a fixed essential self and the association of gender traits with biological sex and begins to undermine key conceptual pillars of male-centered Western culture. However, the novel does not totally escape the modernist insistence on the core self, as is evidenced when O'Connor is hailed by an acquaintance and "instantly the doctor threw off his unobserved self, as one hides, hastily, a secret life" (110)—this "unobserved self" suggests some kind of essential self.

Nightwood also demonstrates a suspicion of language, and of the possibility of using language to depict the world mimetically, in its destabilization of notions of reality or truth. Since the novel includes no authorial or narrator's commentary, no yardstick against which to measure, the truth value of O'Connor's stories remains suspended, emphasizing the fictionality of any narrative. At one point, O'Connor even explicitly refers to "history" as nothing more than culturally constructed "stories," no more real than the stories he tells: "'but think of the stories that do not amount to much! That is, that are forgotten in spite of all man remembers (unless he remembers himself) merely because they befell him without distinction of office or title—that's what we call legend and it's the best a poor man may do with his fate; the other'—he waved an arm—'we call history, the best the high and mighty can do with theirs'" (15). A prime example of the fictionality of any story or history is Felix Volkbein's barony and ancestry, which proves to be totally fabricated by his Jewish father, complete with "a coat of arms that he had no right to and a list of progenitors (including their Christian names) who had never existed" (3). Not surprisingly, Felix feels most at home in the world of the theater and circus, where he can become "a part of their splendid and reeking falsifications" (11). The novel implicitly acknowledges that the reality or falsity of the world and that of the circus or theater are only a matter of degree and not of substance, anticipating the more drastic challenges to the traditional Western notion of reality in contemporary novels such as Angela Carter's *Nights at the Circus* (1984). The fantastic and disjointed quality of Barnes's entire narrative further suggests that reality is impossible to locate or to represent. By highlighting the impossibility of accurate mimetic representation, the novel opens up a space for new means of creative representation. Indeed, the novel uses its disjointed form to highlight both the artificiality of rational thought and its inability to depict a world in which gender boundaries are fluid and culturally constructed rather than natural or essential.

Nightwood ends inconclusively with Robin Vote, who has remained distanced and resisted definition throughout the novel. Failing in her undefined quest to find her self, she descends to animal status, literally on all fours, barking at or with a dog: "Then she began to bark also, crawling after him—barking in a fit of laughter, obscene and touching" (170). This final scene belies the traditional notion of an essential self and undermines the established dichotomy between humanity and nature. What is most disturbing about Vote's breakdown is that it ends the novel and offers no hint of a reconstruction to follow. The novel itself, however, does not equate (even if it establishes a link in the case of Robin) the lack of a centered humanist subject with a descent into animalism or chaos. After all, O'Connor is able to continue functioning within society even though his identity remains indeterminate. Barnes's novel thus begins to push beyond its modernist assumptions and techniques, particularly in its undermining of gender boundaries, which implicitly challenges male-structured binary logic in general as well as the language and concepts in which that binarism is inscribed.

Mina Loy's *Insel* also experiments with narrative to produce a surrealist text, as she addresses the issue of the woman artist.[24] The unnamed narrator is both attracted to and repulsed by Insel, a surrealist painter, and surrealism as an aesthetic movement. She is drawn by surrealism's shattering of the traditional distinction between reality and fiction, which allows for new possibilities of representation. However, as a woman artist, she is excluded from an aesthetics that is inherently misogynist and practiced almost exclusively by male artists. Even Insel marginalizes himself from surrealism, precisely because, as an aesthetic movement engaged in an art system involving critics, galleries, and monetary exchange, surrealism functions within rather than against the dominant culture. Indeed, the narrator is drawn to Insel in part for his successful attempts to evade institutions such as the art system, the economic system, and heterosexual relationships. However, the narrator slowly recognizes that, although Insel functions to a certain extent as her alter ego, she and Insel occupy very different positions with respect to the dominant culture. While Insel willfully marginalizes himself from cultural institutions by constructing himself as a starving self-abased artist, the narrator is marginalized by those institutions. As a man within a culture that privileges men over women, Insel necessarily occupies a position of power whether he wishes to do so or not. As the narrator notes, "There was a way of speaking that word ["power"] peculiar to those alone who have wielded it—that way was his" (42). The novel also demonstrates the ways in which Insel uses the narrator in a very traditional sense, as a mirror in which to recognize and validate himself. Without an other, he remains "non-existent," for "alone his magnetism had no one to contact" (49–50). He crushes the narrator as a woman not only psychically, by taking away her sense of self, but also physically. She has difficulties understanding "why this fantastically beautiful creature should have both hands round my throat" but is forced to recognize his dominant position as a man in a male-dominated culture: "myriads of distraught women were being strangled in my esophagus" (158). The novel thus reveals the ways in which Insel remains a part of the relations of power his life style and paintings work to subvert.

Unlike Insel, the narrator cannot construct herself as an artist without addressing the issue of sex and gender. As much as she regards Insel as an alter ego, as the kind of artist she wishes to be, the narrator notes that his creativity contains a "male difference." To become a woman artist, she must break away from conventional male-constructed forms: "I felt, if I were to go back, begin a universe all over again, forget all form I am familiar with, evoking a chaos from which I could draw forth incipient form, that at last the female brain might achieve an act of creation" (37). Surrealism, however, disrupts traditional form without negating the hierarchical binary oppositions between man and woman, male and female. The novel highlights the problem inherent in trying to be a woman surrealist through its depiction of the narrator stuffing her "scribbles" into "a long painting overall," whose "neck and sleeves" she sews up to construct a "corpse-like sack" (40): she hides her writing in order to protect her artist self and figuratively kills herself in the process.   By the end of the novel, however, she recognizes that she must distance herself from Insel and surrealism in order to create. Unlike Insel, she cannot retreat from the physical and psychic boundaries that confine and oppress her but instead must find ways to attack those boundaries that structure the material situation. Although her connection with Insel, an "inexpressible communion" (63) outside of language, provides her with new paradigms and visions that shatter cultural and aesthetic norms, she must nevertheless say "Good-bye" to Insel's illusory realm of no boundaries (which in actuality retains certain boundaries, as evidenced in his physical abuse of women) in order to create forms that undermine the whole binary system that undergirds existing power relation. By demonstrating the ways in which culture and relations of power construct subjectivities and aesthetics, the novel undermines notions of an essential self and of neutral aesthetics as it works to delineate a space for the woman artist. The tension between the narrator's attraction to surrealism and her exclusion from it in many ways parallels the position of many recent writers (such as the writers who demonstrate feminist impulses and whose fiction I have chosen to explore) who engage postmodern aesthetic strategies but are excluded from discussions of postmodern fiction because they have their own versions of postmodern aesthetics.

Even an admittedly brief examination of a few examples of women's modernist fiction provides ample evidence to support my contention that disruptive strategies, which push beyond modernism and begin to challenge male-centered Western metaphysics itself rather than merely Victorianism and turn-of-the-century Realism, emerge from the fiction of women modernist writers as they attempt to portray women's lives and consciousnesses. To more fully justify this claim, however, I find it both necessary and productive to analyze in greater depth Virginia Woolf's writing. After all, she is arguably the most prominent literary predecessor of contemporary Anglo-American women writers. Woolf's access to the Hogarth Press, which she and her husband, Leonard Woolf, operated, meant that her books were published as soon as they were written and in a respected press. Furthermore, her central position within what became known as the Bloomsbury circle has given her a stature and recognizability that many of her contemporaries lack. I do not mean to take away from the undeniably high quality of her writing by focusing on the material basis of the high visibility of Woolf's work but rather to help explain more fully why it has been more difficult for critics to ignore her work and why she is often the only woman writer to be included—if any are included at all—among the major modernist writers of fiction.

From the perspective of this discussion, it is noteworthy that those of Woolf's novels that most radically disrupt key elements of Western thought—*Orlando* (1928) and *Between the Acts* (1941)— have received less critical attention than many of her other texts. Since they are harder to fit within the established framework of high modernism, they are generally left out of critical discussions or course syllabi as oddities, as less serious, or as inferior.[25] While both of these novels remain grounded in modernist aesthetics, they also contain impulses and strategies that overtly push beyond modernism. The two novels highlight Woolf's sometimes contradictory conceptions of the subject and of representation. Moreover, they demonstrate more explicitly than some of her other texts the tension between the modernism and the movement beyond modernism that emerges from her writing in general and that is explicitly tied to feminist impulses.

As early as 1924, in her essay "Mr. Bennett and Mrs. Brown," Woolf focuses specifically on the problem of the subject and its novelistic representation. Her view of the writer's task as an attempt to represent an elusive subject underscores her adherence to traditional notions of the subject as possessing an essential core and of art as mimetic, even if she questions the means by which representation can be achieved. Rejecting the notion that subjects or characters can be represented adequately in terms of their particular social and material contexts, Woolf insists that the goal of the modernists is to capture the essence of the subject. Yet her warning to readers not to "allow the writers to palm off upon you a version of all this, an image of Mrs. Brown, which has no likeness to that surprising apparition whatsoever," implicitly acknowledges the difficulties of mimetic representation and of pinpointing an essential core within human beings.[26] A tension surfaces within the essay: on the one hand, she seeks new ways of achieving mimesis, while, on the other hand, she seems to discredit the possibility of mimesis. Although Woolf's discussion centers around a neutral or genderless subject, her representative subject is a woman, and Woolf criticizes the means by which the Edwardian male novelists—Bennett, Wells, and Galsworthy—would have depicted Mrs. Brown. Woolf's call for new ways of representing the subject thus seems to contain a more specific but as yet not verbalized call for new ways of representing a female subject, a challenge that she takes up in her own writing.

In her book-length essays *A Room of One's Own* (1929) and *Three Guineas* (1938), Woolf specifically addresses the notion of the gendered subject and, to do so, begins to undermine the binary logic that forms the basis of Western culture. Although she does not use the term *gender,* she describes the distinct but socially constructed positions that situate men and women. In *A Room of One's Own,* she articulates the connection between art and economics, and its implications for women, with her now famous assertion that "a woman must have money and a room of her own if she is to write fiction."[27] She explains the scarcity of women-authored works of genius by arguing that such texts "are not spun in midair by incorporeal creatures, but are the work of suffering human beings, and are attached to grossly material things, like health and money and the houses we live in" (43–44), and that the difficulties with material circumstances have been "infinitely more formidable" (54) for women, who have been too busy bearing children and raising families to make money and who were long denied by law the right to possess money (22–23). Woolf asserts that the position of artist has been gendered in Western culture, since only men have had "the power and the money and the security" (34) necessary for the production of art. Her argument implicitly parallels the more recent theoretical arguments that explore how all subject positions are culturally constructed, and therefore always gendered, in a culture that posits men and women, male and female, as hierarchically opposed.

In her attempts to justify the absence of women writers in the past and to delineate a new female subject who would be able to write works of genius, Woolf depends on a notion of the subject as culturally constructed, and thus open to change, rather than as an essential static entity. Since women and men have been constructed differently, Woolf suggests that their respective "creative force[s]" (91) differ and indeed are complementary. Although she suggests that "a great mind is androgynous," in the sense that "the mind is fully fertilised" only when it fuses the male and female creative forces, Woolf nonetheless recognizes that culturally constructed differences between women and men are so great that, while a woman "must have intercourse with the man in her," "the woman predominates over the man" (102). Consequently, a woman writer needs to find a "sentence proper for her own use," since the traditional shapes of sentences and books have "been made by men out of their own needs for their own use" (80). Woolf defends her delineation of a specifically female subject by undermining the hierarchy implicit in the traditional opposition between man and woman, male and female, but retaining a non-hierarchical notion of difference. Moreover, her assertion that women writers need to develop their own aesthetic strategies recognizes the connection between aesthetic forms and relations of power, between aesthetics and the material situation—both of which are male-centered in Western culture.

In *Three Guineas,* Woolf again argues that men and women have different perspectives because of the differences in their educations, ownership of property, physical activity, and travel: "the result is that though we look at the same things, we see them differently."[28] Her insistent call for "Men and women working together for the same cause" (102), to restructure society, indicates that she is challenging Western male-centered culture and its constructed hierarchical opposition between man and woman.[29] Woolf concedes, however, that men and women will have different methods of working toward that common goal, since women's methods will reflect a perspective based on their culturally imposed background of "poverty, chastity, derision, and freedom from unreal loyalties" (80). She also warns that women may become corrupted by the male-dominated system if they join societies and professions or enter universities, since all these institutions exist within the very system that needs to be challenged. Although Woolf emphasizes the culturally imposed differences between men and women, she nevertheless rejects the traditional hierarchical opposition in which men dominate; she argues that "A common interest unites us; it is one world, one life" (142).

Three Guineas also undermines the classic opposition between the public and private realms, an opposition that is intimately associated with the dichotomy between man and woman. Traditionally, Western culture has positioned men as active participants in the public arena, which includes politics and professional involvements, while relegating women to the private or domestic side of life. Woolf argues that this false and artificial separation promotes the subjugation of women and works against a free and just society. She maintains that "the public and the private worlds are inseparably connected" and that "the tyrannies and servilities of the one are the tyrannies and servilities of the other" (141), rejecting any sharp distinction between what is public and private. The hierarchy inherent within the opposition also crumbles under Woolf's insistence that the two spheres are interdependent, that "without private there can be no public freedom" (120). Woolf is clearly responding to the rise of fascism and militarism on the eve of a devastating second world war, which she links to a male-centered Western culture. Her call for a restructured society begins to chip away at Western binary logic while being allied with, and in fact becoming indistinguishable from, the text's assertion of a female subject.

While the notion of the female subject is central to most of Woolf's writing, *Orlando* and *Between the Acts* depict female subjectivity using strategies that pose more overt challenges to Western metaphysics and prefigure similar disruptive strategies associated with postmodern fiction. In order to destabilize accepted norms of sex and gender, *Orlando* undermines conventional narrative and representation. At the novel's start, Orlando is a sixteen-year-old boy in sixteenth-century England, and by the novel's end Orlando is a thirty-six-year-old woman living in the early twentieth-century, thus shattering gender, sex, and temporal boundaries. Woolf rejects realism in her attempt to create a character who experiences everything, choosing instead fantasy as a vehicle for the novel's various disruptions. Through its use of non-realist modes to depict fantastic occurrences, *Orlando* deliberately disengages itself from the conventions of realism and creates a space for change, for the new.[30]

For example, Woolf uses the masque, an artificial spectacle that is allegorical and unreal, as a vehicle for the revelation of Orlando's fantastic sex change.

Although Orlando undergoes a sex change, Orlando's gender remains ambiguous throughout the novel; the sex change merely concretizes the marriage of the feminine and masculine in the figure of Orlando. Orlando appears as "a mixture" of "man and woman, one being uppermost and then the other."[31] The novel also presents other characters having ambiguous gender and sex: Sasha is first described as a "person, whatever the name or sex," who possesses an "extraordinary seductiveness" (37); the Archduchess turns out to be "a man and always had been one" (179); and Shelmerdine is "a man as strange and subtle as a woman" (258). Woolf's emphasis on androgyny—on the erasure of the opposition between masculine and feminine—is both utopian and problematic. It is utopian in its refusal to equate sex with gender or with identity and yet problematic in its failure to account for biological differences between the sexes and to take on the whole system of hierarchical oppositions created by Western culture to uphold the dominance of white bourgeois males.[32] Moreover, although Orlando's transformation undermines the equation of sex with identity, it retains the notion of an essential self. Orlando is fragmented but still centered around an essential core: Orlando possesses "a great variety of [surface] selves to call upon" (309), as well as a "true self" (310), "a single self, a real self" (314). Orlando remains "undoubtedly one and the same person" (188), regardless of the sex change and the inevitable changes in behavior and emotions that follow. The sex change thus results in an uneasy tension between elements that disrupt and reinforce traditional concepts.

The novel disrupts established notions of gender by depicting gender as a cultural construction that is learned, rather than natural to a given biological sex: Orlando must adapt to her sex change. Once in the possession of a female body, Orlando is consciously forced to adopt feminine gender traits approved by convention: "women are not (judging by my short experience of the sex) obedient, chaste, scented, and exquisitely apparelled by nature. They can only attain these graces, without which they may enjoy none of the delights of life, by the most tedious discipline" (156–57). Orlando is sharply aware of the means by which society keeps women in an inferior position: restrictive clothing, such as "the weight of the crinoline" (244); lack of legal rights, which make it necessary that Orlando's estates "descend and are tailed and entailed upon the heirs male of my body, or in default of marriage" (255); lives that are little more than "a succession of childbirths" (229). While Orlando begins to conform to societal expectations of women, at times she rebels against the restraints placed on women: "she seemed to vacillate; she was man; she was woman; she knew the secrets, shared the weaknesses of each" (158). For instance, Orlando indulges in cross-dressing and bisexual experiences, confounding established gender distinctions and sexual norms: "From the probity of breeches she turned to the seductiveness of petticoats and enjoyed the love of both sexes equally" (221). The novel thus destabilizes the conventional binary oppositions between man and woman, masculine and femi-nine, while still acknowledging biological differences and the cultur-ally imposed gender traits that derive from sexual differences and are used to create hierarchical oppositions. However, there remains a certain tension between the novel's impulses to celebrate androgyny and to subvert the dominant male-centered culture (see earlier discussion).

Orlando's challenge to dominant culture is also evident in its playful disruptions of narrative and representation. The novel offers itself as a mock-biography written by a self-conscious, intrusive, and comically unreliable narrator-biographer. On one level the novel is a parody of serious biography—complete with preface, footnotes, and scholarly index to substantiate the biographer's claims and authority—that breaks down the sharp distinction between fact and fiction and begins to question the possibility of mimetic representation. The novel undermines the official evidence and facts used by biogra-phers or historians, through its presentation of a narrator who mourns the lack of written records and admits that much of his story is "dark, mysterious, and undocumented" (65) and that he has been forced "to speculate, to surmise, and even to make use of the imagination" (119). His conclusion that "truth does not exist" (192) further unsettles the accepted boundary between biography-fact and fiction. Moreover, the novel incorporates historical figures, like Shakespeare, Marlowe, Jonson, Browne, Donne, Addison, Dryden, Pope, into its pages, alongside completely fabricated characters, to more overtly blur the distinction between fact and fiction. Indeed, the "fictional" poet Nick Greene is a far more developed character and a more tangible presence than the *real* literary figures. Orlando also engages in an implicit questioning of the possibility of mimetic representation: "Life? Literature? One to be made into the other? But how monstrously difficult!" (285) For example, Orlando despairs at being able to capture in words the colors of nature, such as "The sky is blue" and "the grass is green," and concludes that "I don't see that one's more true than another. Both are utterly false" (102). The novel not only destabilizes the distinction between reality and fiction but also deprivileges reality in moves that anticipate more recent fiction. Indeed, although in some respects *Orlando* remains anchored in modernism, particularly in its presentation of Orlando's essential self, the novel also encompasses strategies that move toward the postmodern. As Woolf's novel works to destabilize the hierarchical oppositions that structure notions of sex and gender in Western culture, using fantasy and parody, it implicitly undermines other norms and conventions of the dominant male-centered system, such as temporal boundaries, notions of mimetic representation, and the dichotomy between fact, or truth, and fiction.

Woolf's last published novel, *Between the Acts,* is another example of a text that is anchored in and yet clearly pushes beyond modernism, although it does so in very different ways than in the case of *Orlando. Between the Acts* is torn between a modernist conception of the fragmented subject, as possessing an essential self distinct from the social or surface self and from the outside world, and a (postmodern) notion of the fragmented subject as unstable, centerless, and dispersed.[33] Miss La Trobe is the epitome of the modernist alienated artist, presented as an isolated, lonely, and eccentric figure—"She was an outcast"—with a strong central core that allows her to create.[34] Her modernist aesthetics surface in her belief that she can represent the essence of characters or subjects and that she can create a sense of unity. She is intent on finding new methods of representation but does not question the possibility of representation itself. Miss La Trobe's experimental play is a pageant of history that aims to bring together the members of the audience and make them "see" (98) historical events in their political and social contexts and thus assumes that a real or true history can be represented.

The modernism inherent in the depiction of Miss La Trobe as

alienated artist, and of her play as an effort to find a new way of representing reality, is juxtaposed with a vision of the subject that pushes toward the postmodern in the depiction of the audience and its reactions to the ending of the performance. In the last scene of the play, "The Present Time. Ourselves" (178), all the actors come out on stage with mirrors and other reflecting surfaces, which they point at the audience. This scene, which forces the audience to look at itself while "the looking-glasses darted, flashed, exposed" (183), steps decisively beyond modernism. The mirroring effect breaks down the barrier between audience and stage, audience and actors, and thus undermines the traditional distinctions between reality and fiction, life and art. The distorted and fragmented reflections of themselves, which the members of the audience are forced to view, visually emphasize the subject as fragmented, centerless, and dispersed and also blur the distinction between individuals: "Now old Bart ... he was caught. Now Manresa. Here a nose ... There a skirt ... Then trousers only ... Now perhaps a face ... Ourselves? But that's cruel. To snap us as we are, before we've had time to assume ... And only, too, in parts ... That's what's so distorting and upsetting and utterly unfair" (184). The audience itself becomes a character in the play and in the novel, as individuals are revealed to lack unity, wholeness, separateness. The play's last scene thus creates the image of a fragmented subject with no distinct limits or center. The individuals in the audience are unable to evade their own distorted reflections; they are trapped in front of the spectacle of their own decentered and dispersed subjecthood.

The fragmentation and distortion that results from the mirrors in this scene of Woolf's novel differs from the modernist fragmentation and distortion evident in something like Picasso's canvases. When a Picasso painting distorts the human body by presenting various perspectives of body parts simultaneously, the human figure nevertheless remains: no dispersion of the subject occurs, and the subject retains a center. However, the multiple mirrors in Woolf's scene create a plethora of disconnected body parts, pointing to a subject that has no distinct limits or center. In addition, a Picasso painting retains the status of aesthetic object separate from its viewers. In contrast, the mirror scene in Woolf's novel breaks down the distinctions between audience and actors, life and art, reality and fiction. Although, on the one hand, the play attempts to bring the audience together, on the other hand, its depiction of the present through the use of mirrors denies the audience any sense of unity or wholeness: "The audience saw themselves, not whole" (185). Miss La Trobe's play thus both embraces and surpasses high modernism.

The play not only challenges the notion of a centered essential self with its mirror scene but also accentuates the precariousness of any sharp distinction between life and art. Its beginning and ending remain indeterminate. After "God Save the King" plays, neither the audience nor the now silent actors seem to know whether or not the play is finished—"Was that the end?" (195). Furthermore, the novel presents the actions both on and off the stage without giving priority to either, which effectively blurs the line between reality and representation and prefigures recent fictional strategies highlighting the ways in which everything is always already represented. The exchanges between the novel's various characters during the play's official "Interval" (95) do not differ much from the skits within the play itself. In both instances, the action revolves around the tensions between the sexes, around love, hate, flirtation, jealousy. There is a sense in which the play seems to be life with the stage play occurring between life's acts, and yet the reverse is also true; the opposition between life and art, between reality and fiction, no longer has any firm basis. The most overt breakdown of the dichotomy between reality and fiction occurs at the novel's end, which enacts the age-old conventional plot of the opposition between man and woman. Significantly, this scene appears in two contexts or on two different levels: it is simultaneously Miss La Trobe's vision of her next play *and* a confrontation between two of the novel's characters, Isa and Giles: "Before they slept, they must fight; after they had fought, they would embrace...Then the curtain rose. They spoke" (219). The two images blur into one, creating an image of life as an old plot that has not changed over time and that is neither or both fiction and reality. The conflation of various narrative levels further problematizes the dichotomy between reality and fiction.

Isa is another modernist alienated artist figure, although she keeps her poetry secret from those around her; but her depiction at times steps beyond modernism. It is not clear, for instance, that she has an essential or core self, since she is so divided between her various roles as wife, mother, poet, romantic, lover. William Dodge notes the multiple selves she takes up and discards: "he saw her face change, as if she had got out of one dress and put on another" when her little boy appears, and minutes later "again she changed her dress" (105) to address the nurse. Isa feels trapped within marriage, within the old love-hate oppositional plot, and yearns for a new relationship between the sexes: "Surely it was time someone invented a new plot" (215). This acknowledgment of the need for structural changes is a feminist move with radical implications, which suggests that Isa is keenly aware of sexual politics and its role in subject formation. However, she lacks the strength to step out of the old plot even though she glimpses possibilities for change. She is unable to escape "the burden ... laid on me in the cradle" (155) of being a woman in a male-dominated world. For example, she is powerless in the face of the double standard that allows married men but not their wives to philander: "It made no difference; his infidelity—but hers did" (110). The novel's movement toward a notion of the subject as a set of constructed roles rather than an essential core is further demonstrated in the presentation of Isa's acute awareness of the sexual politics that affect her life in asides, in thoughts, in between the actions of the novel. To highlight the realm of the *in between* is a potentially radical move, in that it disrupts a Western metaphysics that is grounded in binary thought, which attempts to negate all that lies in between polar opposites. This focus on the realm of the *in between,* which the novel's title highlights, calls attention to the ways in which Western culture masks and silences the working of sexual politics in the construction of subjectivity, in order to create the illusion of an essential central self.

On the level of language, the dynamic narrative emphasizes the gaps, pauses, or silences that are part of the communication process, and therefore part of material existence, and yet are not allowed and cannot be recorded with words. The novel depicts language as unable to represent the inner thoughts and emotions of individuals or the relations between characters: "We haven't the words" (55). The novel stresses, for instance, the loaded silences that occur between individuals, especially between the sexes, and the pauses in group conversations that seem to serve as forms of non-verbal communication.[35] Isa reads "mystery" in Rupert Haines' "ravaged face" and "in his silence, passion," while Mrs. Haines is "aware of the emotion circling them, excluding her" (5–6). Although

Isa and Giles exchange no words within the novel, they communicate incessantly through powerful silences:

> Giles then did what to Isa was his little trick; shut his lips; frowned; and took up the pose of one who bears the burden of the world's woe, making money for her to spend.
>
> "No," said Isa, as plainly as words could say it. "I don't admire you," and looked, not at his face, but at his feet. "Silly little boy, with blood on his boots."
>
> Giles shifted his feet. Whom then did she admire? Not Dodge. That he could take for certain. Who else? Some man he knew. Some man, he was sure, in the Barn. Which man? He looked around him. (111)

Woolf highlights silence as a means of depicting desire, a "preverbal desire" that "is all feeling and image, a storage of sensations."[36] The novel's fluid and poetic style records the nonverbal sensory world through language, manipulating language to represent that which the dominant order attempts to suppress from and with language.

The novel's focus on silence—on what lies in between actions, words, and thoughts—functions as a politically charged device, emphasizing the cultural silencing of that which threatens the status quo. The material physical world enters the novel only as disconnected intrusions occurring in between events or thoughts. Although World War II is raging at the time the novel is set, 1939, war only surfaces through isolated instances, such as when "twelve aeroplanes in perfect formation" (193) fly over the audience in between the halting attempts of Reverend Streatfield to explain the "meaning" of the play once it has come to a close. Sexual violence also enters the novel in spurts; images of the gang-rape Isa has read about in the *Times* intrude into the gaps of her thoughts throughout the day. The juxtaposition of this picture of rape, which was "so real" (20), and the pastoral and traditional setting of the novel highlights the sexual politics implicit in the act of rape, and its being silenced, and in the male-centered English family and culture: "Every summer, for seven summers now, Isa had heard the same words; about the hammer and the nails; the pageant and the weather. Every year they said, would it be wet or fine; and every year it was one or the other. The same chime followed the same chime, only this year beneath the chime she heard: 'The girl screamed and hit him about the face with a hammer'" (22). The short flashes of the rape scene take on at least as much importance as the events being dutifully recorded at length by the narrative, so that the realm of the *in between* becomes a locus of attention. The novel's interest in silences or gaps exhibits a feminist impulse by placing emphasis on the sexual violence that remains unspoken and yet is powerfully present in traditional settings and narratives. The novel implicitly connects war/fascism and rape/sexism by presenting them as the unspeakable silenced elements within the traditional English family setting.[37] Moreover, the novel demonstrates the ways in which the sexual violence that Isa's culture silences in effect constructs her subjectivity: she remains unable to act outside of the roles prescribed to her even though she acknowledges how these roles limit and subdue her.

The novel's treatment of the issue of gender also demonstrates a movement away from notions of an essential self. *Between the Acts* highlights and inherently criticizes the way in which gender is constructed and gender traits assigned within a male-centered culture through sympathetic depictions of characters derided for not fitting within accepted gender boundaries. Mr. Oliver calls his grandson "a cry-baby" (13) and "a coward" (19) for being frightened by a paper beak, embracing the conventional notion that boys must be courageous and never cry. The characters view Miss La Trobe as an oddity and an outcast because she breaks the set standards for women. She is neither delicate nor demure; instead, she is "swarthy, sturdy and thick set," she is sometimes seen "with a cigarette in her mouth," she uses "rather strong language" (58), and she has lived with an "actress who had shared her bed" (211). But it is the character of William Dodge who calls the most attention to the workings of social convention in the construction of gender. Again, the novel uses silence as emphasis. Giles angrily denounces Dodge's failures as a man but leaves out the crucial condemnation: "A toady; a lickspittle not a downright plain man of his senses; but a teaser and twitcher; a fingerer of sensations; picking and choosing; dillying and dallying; not a man to have straightforward love for a woman—his head was close to Isa's head—but simply a——At this word, which he could not speak in public, he pursed his lips" (60). Homosexuality is taboo, since it threatens the neatly established association of specific gender traits and roles with each of the sexes. Even Dodge views himself as "a half-man," as a "mind-divided little snake in the grass" (73), highlighting the extent to which individuals internalize the prescriptions of conventions and to which subjectivity is shaped by cultural norms.

Nevertheless, with the exceptions of the scene in which the audience is forced to watch its own reflection, the presentation of Isa as a conglomeration of various roles or selves, and the depiction of gender as a cultural construction, the novel retains a modernist notion of the subject as possessing an essential core beneath the surface fragmentation. Through its depiction of characters possessing some kind of individual essence that makes them autonomous and privileged, the novel separates the subject as essence from any type of social, cultural, historical, or political context. Furthermore, the rare intrusions of the politics of material existence help to create a subject that is divorced from the world, thus upholding the dichotomy between the inner self and the outer world. Woolf's attempt to capture the female subject by depicting the sensory world becomes so narrowly focused on the individual experience of daily life as to almost totally exclude the larger cultural movements and institutions that necessarily structure individual experience. On the other hand, the rare intrusions of the politics of material existence in between scenes, words, and thoughts call attention to all that is suppressed in order to enforce the status quo and implicitly challenge the dominant order and its binary mode of thought that results in oppression and violence—particularly against women.

As my brief analyses demonstrate, the fiction of women modernists contains a variety of features that anchor it firmly to the established canonized high modernism and yet contains a number of elements that begin to disrupt traditional Western metaphysics, to the extent that women's modernist fiction does not comfortably fit within the institutionalized version of modernism, which itself remains a function of binary logic. While the writing of women in the early part of the twentieth-century remains more modern than postmodern, particularly in its emphasis on locating or recovering some sort of core self, it clearly pushes against the limits of high modernism. As they endeavor to depict a specifically female subject and experiment with new means by which to do so, women modernists tend to disrupt traditional narrative, as well as accepted notions of gender and sexuality, in ways that begin to challenge the binarism inherent in Western thought. The result is often a tension between modernist notions and the germs of a movement toward a more radical challenge to Western conceptual modes, a tension that may explain in part why women's fiction has been almost totally excluded from the modernist canon.

Women modernists such as Dorothy Richardson, Gertrude Stein, May Sinclair, H.D., Djuna Barnes, Mina Loy, and Virginia Woolf construct an array of innovative formal strategies in their attempts to represent a specifically female subject. At the same time, these strategies challenge Western metaphysics, particularly the humanist notion of the subject as centered and whole, notions of language as stable and expressive, conventional linear narrative, and binary logic in general. Striving to depict a woman's subjectivity, Richardson creates a stream-of-consciousness technique that defies linearity as well as conventional grammatical rules. Stein's use of rhythmic repetition enacts the inability of language to explain or capture women and their desires—which have been silenced by Western culture—and presents language as a mean of approximating rather than containing women. As Stein works to connect women's desires to their subjecthood, a notion of the subject evolves that is in process rather than static. Sinclair unveils madness as an arbitrary but gendered social construction and as a means of delimiting women's subjectivity. In her attempt to capture a woman struggling to define her subjectivity within a culture that suppresses bisexuality, H.D. breaks down the distinctions and hierarchy between sanity and madness, the inner and outer self, and heterosexuality and homosexuality. Barnes constructs a disjointed nonlinear fantastic narrative to subvert conventional gender boundaries that attempt to fix the subject. Loy highlights the tension inherent in a woman's attempts to become an artist within the context of male-centered experimental aesthetic movements. Woolf manipulates fantasy, parody, and metafiction to emphasize the realm of the *in between* and to destabilize gender boundaries in her quest to depict a female subject.

The analysis of even a limited number of texts written by women modernists demonstrates that contemporary women writers whose work exhibits feminist and postmodern tendencies do have a strong literary tradition of experimental feminist-oriented writing from which to build. Although recent women's fiction draws heavily on its own historical and intellectual context, its roots in modernism cannot be overlooked. Rather than high modernism, however, the literary tradition to which these contemporary writers are connected is a version of modernism that has been excluded from the canon, a modernism that includes women writers and their specific forms of experimentation. The women modernists experiment with narrative and language specifically to create new modes of representation that defy the traditional containment of women, their material experiences, and their experience-based modes of thought. The strategies disruptive of the status quo that emerge from the texts of women modernists as they strive to depict *women's* consciousnesses and lives in effect prefigure or anticipate the more radical challenges to Western metaphysics found in the works of many contemporary women writers. The fiction of these more recent writers steps decisively beyond modernism, without stepping back to social realism, as it boldly co-opts disruptive postmodern strategies to propel its radical feminist aims.

3. MADNESS AND NARRATIVE DISRUPTION IN DORIS LESSING'S *THE GOLDEN NOTEBOOK*

Doris Lessing's *The Golden Notebook* uses, challenges, and pushes beyond the conventions and conceptual underpinnings of both high modernism and the social realism against which modernists reacted. In her 1957 essay, "A Small Personal Voice," Lessing asserts that "the realist novel, the realist story, is the highest form of prose writing," but her own writing and views on the novel undergo a shift away from realist modes by the time she writes *The Golden Notebook* (1962).[1] Lessing's novel is located within the context of the massive questioning of Western ideology that has dominated intellectual life since World War II. Like other literature of the period, *The Golden Notebook* responds to a new world of violence, terror, and chaos: the atomic bombing of Hiroshima and Nagasaki, Stalin's purges, South African apartheid, the instability of newly independent Third World nations. Within this disturbing context, *The Golden Notebook* attempts to situate and define a new female subject, to re-analyze the relationship between reality and literature, and to construct a new novel form. Such a project of redefinition necessarily disrupts the existing Western system of thought and values, particularly the binary logic that underlies Western metaphysics and shapes human consciousness as well as social structures and norms.

In order to depict a woman's attempt to define herself as a subject and as a writer, the novel co-opts a number of postmodern aesthetic strategies. More specifically, it radically decenters and fragments subjectivity and narrative, and it undermines the binary logic that has traditionally reinforced the oppression of women and the erasure of women's stories-histories within Western culture, through hierarchical oppositions such as those between man and woman, subject and object, self and other, sanity and insanity, reality and fiction.[2] However, these disruptive tendencies coexist with certain modernist and realist elements, as *The Golden Notebook* blends together and attempts to negotiate between a variety of aesthetic and conceptual modes to fulfill aims that are feminist in impulse.[3] The novel is experimental and yet recognizable; indeed, it has enjoyed a wide audience from its publication to the present. Although the novel's existence as a conglomeration of various texts testifies to the impossibility of encompassing a contemporary human being's life within traditional narrative, its very existence as a novel also proclaims the possibility of new modes of representation that challenge without completely exploding narrative. Narrative remains a vital means of communicating human experience and history, even if traditional forms have tended to silence those who threaten the position of power held by white, bourgeois males in Western culture. Lessing's novel also holds on to a traditional notion of subjectivity and self and grounds subjectivity in the historical material situation, at the same time as it moves toward a postmodern decentered fluid notion of subjectivity. The novel simultaneously disrupts traditional narrative and subjectivity, and the Western metaphysics that underlie them, and enacts new forms of narrative and subjectivity as means of positing possibilities for a new female subject and artist and new modes of representing them. While Molly Hite has similarly noted that "the critique of ideology" in *The Golden Notebook* goes "beyond narrowly Marxist principles to the more general set of presuppositions governing Western culture in the modern period, ultimately addressing the assumption that any world view can be adequate, that reality is the sort of thing that can be held together as a unified whole," she also asserts that novels by writers like Lessing are "recognizably distinct from the postmodernists."[4] In contrast, I argue that the effect of *The Golden Notebook*'s critique of Western metaphysics, and its use of various disruptive strategies, indicates a movement toward the postmodern that coincides with and even propels forward the novel's more subversive feminist aims.

Lessing's long novel is a compilation of various pieces or texts. A short five-chapter frame novella, entitled "Free Women," is written in conventional realist narrative form. However, fragments of four notebooks kept by the central character of "Free Women," Anna Wulf, intersperse the chapters of "Free Women." She uses each of the notebooks, distinguished by color, to record a different aspect of her life: the "Black Notebook" focuses on Anna the writer and on the memory of her early experiences in a communist cell in Africa; the "Red Notebook" records her intensely conflicted relationship with the British Communist Party; the "Yellow Notebook" fictionalizes Anna's own life, particularly her love affair with Michael, in the form of a novel entitled *The Shadow of the Third;* and the "Blue Notebook" is closer to a diary and tends to focus on states of mind. Eventually Anna ends each of the four notebooks and begins a new "Golden Notebook," which records her descent into madness with her new American lover Saul Green. The novel as a whole is also circular; it has no set beginning or ending. Near the end of the novel, Saul gives Anna the lines that begin the novella, "Free Women," and the novel, *The Golden Notebook*. Anna's various pieces of writing thus construct the novel: fragments of a novella and of five different notebooks, and the editorial notes that introduce and order the fragments.

Critics have hotly debated whether *The Golden Notebook* is a feminist novel. Many have argued that it is not, on the grounds that Lessing herself, in a rather bitter 1971 introduction to the novel, claims that *The Golden Notebook* is "not a trumpet for Women's Liberation" or merely a book "about the sex war."[5] Her comments, however, are not necessarily incompatible with a view of the novel as feminist, since a novel can be feminist in perspective and aims without centering thematically on specific movements such as Women's Liberation or the sex war. As a specific and engaged political stance, feminism can address or encompass virtually any topic or theme. Moreover, Lessing does not claim that her book is *not* about Women's Liberation or the sex war but rather argues that these are not the novel's primary themes. Indeed, the novel has such a large scope that it cannot be reduced to a specific theme.[6] Margaret Drabble calls the novel "prophetic," suggesting that Lessing took for granted things that had not yet been achieved for most women and was therefore not prepared for the novel's reception as a book championing Women's Liberation.[7] Lessing herself admits that "This book was written as if the attitudes that have been created by the Women's Liberation movements already existed."[8] Indeed, the novel includes but moves beyond specific issues and movements, as it attempts to depict human beings trying to cope with the violence, terror, and fragmentation of the postwar atomic age. As Linda

Kauffman argues, Lessing's novel "situat[es] women's struggle in relation to other emancipatory struggles around the globe."[9] However, the novel's specific focus on a female protagonist and the need for transforming the various institutions and thought systems that contain women in different ways than men highlights its feminist standpoint.[10] On a thematic level, for example, the novel focuses on Anna's precarious position on the margins of a culture that is physically in upheaval and yet clings to traditional values that rigidly circumscribe women. Her position is precarious precisely because she has rejected a traditional loveless marriage, preferring to live and raise her daughter on her own, and because she firmly believes that "there are whole areas of me made by the kind of experience women haven't had before."[11] However, if the novel is attempting to create a new female subject, it does not follow that the character Anna necessarily embodies that subject; rather, Anna is the site of the development of such a new subject. Anna does not have to be a feminist, nor does Lessing have to name herself a feminist, for the novel to contribute to feminism. Although Lessing chose not to identify herself with organized movements or to be a spokeswoman for her period, her novel nevertheless foreshadows many of the questions that subsequent literary feminists have claimed as central. Moreover, I argue that many of the novel's innovative structural and thematic strategies serve specifically feminist aims.

The Golden Notebook's positioning of Anna as a developing subject carefully delineates the ways in which subjectivity is linked to the historical, cultural, economic, political material situation and the psychic patterns it has engendered; and it does so using a combination of realist, modernist, and postmodern strategies. Although Anna attempts to reject the traditional roles that Western culture has assigned to women, she is unable to shed completely the various social conventions and values that have shaped her and that still surround her. The novel's extremely ironical treatment of Anna and her friend Molly as *free women* emphasizes Anna's collusion with and victimization by her culture at the same time as she attempts to break from it. While her rejection of a "traditional, rooted, conservative" perspective and refusal to be defined "in terms of relationships with men" (4–5) subvert the status quo, Anna admits that her "loyalties are always to men" (48) and that she still feels a "need to bolster men up" (484). Moreover, although she is in one sense a free woman, that very status as free woman constitutes a source of her victimization by married men, who view sexual relations with her as carrying no emotional attachments.[12] The novel in this way demonstrates that women cannot be free within existing social and ideological structures. As Kauffman notes, Lessing's novel "situates the subject as a product of power relations."[13] Given the context in which she lives, Anna cannot fully liberate herself even though she has achieved a certain degree of independence and is actively engaged in trying to situate herself as a new and free woman. However, Anna's growing awareness of her own collusion with the system she seeks to reject functions as a first step toward redefining herself.[14]

The novel complicates the issue of Anna's subjectivity by presenting Anna as more than just a character in a novel. The realist portrait of Anna that "Free Women" offers cracks as the narrative shifts from novella to editorial notes, to notebooks, and to various texts that make up the notebooks. Indeed, *The Golden Notebook* contains various versions of a character called Anna, as well as a writer and an editor also named Anna. This multiplicity of Annas on various levels calls into question not only conventional notions of character and narrative but also the humanist concept of the whole unified integrated self. There exists no essential Anna in *The Golden Notebook;* instead, the novel offers many versions of Anna on several narrative levels, so that the name *Anna* can at best refer to a composite of various roles, functions, and representations. Anna is the editor of her various pieces of writing that she organizes to form *The Golden Notebook;* Anna is the author of various private notebooks; Anna is the author of a traditionally written novella entitled "Free Women"; Anna is the subject-character of the notebooks; Anna is a character in "Free Women"; and Ella is a fictional representation of Anna in the "Yellow Notebook." None of these Annas, however, *is* Anna. Instead, these versions of Anna suggest or approximate what the human being or character named Anna might be like.[15]

The Golden Notebook pushes beyond not only realist but also modernist notions of the subject. Although modernism begins to question the traditional humanist subject, the modernist subject's alienation and internal fragmentation are a direct result of the multiplicity of available perspectives rather than of some schism in *Being* itself (which would be postmodern). Modernists still tend to view the subject as always working toward a re-centering and uphold the illusion of the subject as a coherent and unique entity, grounded in an external reality that underlies all perspectives. For example, although Virginia Woolf's *The Waves* reduces characters to named voices that tend to blur as they recount their alienation and fragmentation, the novel ultimately focuses on Bernard, who works toward a unity of consciousness. While Woolf's novel suggests that there is no center of identity and that the self is fluid, it presents selves that are complementary and combine to form a complete and whole self, epitomized by Bernard's plural and yet unified consciousness.

In contrast, Lessing's novel offers a subject who is literally a composite of various socially constructed roles or positions—not perspectives—that cannot be reconciled: social self, political self, sexual self, gendered self, parenting self, artistic self. The only thing that unifies Anna is her name. In this sense, Lessing is moving toward a postmodern notion of the subject as a dynamic set of culturally constructed positions. The novel engages the post-war nihilism that has created a rift in *Being* and has necessitated a reconceptualization of the subject as decentered and dispersed. Moreover, the postmodern challenge to the illusion of the subject as whole is compatible with feminist aims, in that it allows for the construction of alternative notions of the subject. The movement toward postmodern subjectivity enables *The Golden Notebook* to approach a delineation of a new female subject that is not grounded in any transcendental or essentialist notions of *Being* but that, instead, posits the subject as a constructed set of positions and functions within a specific configuration of material and cultural conditions.[16]

Although the novel focuses on its female protagonist and delineates a specifically female subject, it does not privilege women and, indeed, addresses men alongside women.[17] The novel depicts men and women as equally constructed and victimized by Western culture, a strategy that has generated some dissent among critics as to the feminism of the novel. Gayle Greene convincingly argues, however, that Lessing "demonstrates that men's behavior is, as surely as women's, a crippling adjustment to an intolerable world" and that no man "is untouched by his culture's image of masculinity." Although Greene's assertion that the novel "affirms that contemporary society is 'worse for' men than for women, leaving them damaged, divided, dehumanized" is debatable, to the extent that the novel depicts both women and men as victims of their culture, *The Golden Notebook* does depict women as "tougher" (663) than men and as more aware of their positions as victims.[18] The novel indicates that women are likely to have a clearer or more immediate view of the oppressing quality of their society than do men, since women are victims in a more overt and concrete sense: many women daily undergo physical and psychic violence at the hands of fathers, husbands, or lovers in a male-dominated culture; many women face concrete barriers to higher education, professional endeavors, and public office in a culture that asserts a division between a public and private realm and assigns women to the latter; many women perform menial tasks or jobs that Western culture has traditionally associated with women; and many women are constrained by their own reproductive potentials in a culture that relegates child care to women and views pregnancy as a disability. Indeed, male lovers, friends, and roommates psychically abuse Anna; the communist party relegates her to social work; and her position as a single mother gives her the constant responsibility for her daughter's care. While *The Golden Notebook* reveals the ways in which both men and women take up the various gendered roles that their culture provides for them, it also indicates that women are more aware of this role playing. Anna finally confronts and accepts her various roles and her fragmented self through her relationship with Saul, which is also a descent into madness. Saul, however, does not benefit from the experience in the same way, since, unlike Anna, he refuses to reemerge from the madness. In a dream, Anna realizes that "I was playing roles, one after another, against Saul, who was playing roles," and that "We played against each other every man-woman role imaginable" (603–04). Anna's recognition of these polarized roles highlights the means by which Western culture constructs and retains oppositions, like the one between men and women, which have concrete effects on human and power relations and on subject formation. By underscoring the constructed quality of gendered roles, the novel attempts to explain both the fragmentation inherent in human beings and the breakdown of relations between the two sexes in a decaying society in which chaos reigns and roles can no longer remain fixed.

Through its questioning of conventional notions of subjectivity, gender, and gender roles, Lessing's novel begins to challenge the binary logic that dominates Western thought and culture and positions women in inferior opposition to men. *The Golden Notebook* announces its impulse to disrupt established Western dichotomies in the novel's first section through the voice of Anna, the character of "Free Women": "Anna laughed. 'Men. Women. Bound. Free. Good. Bad. Yes. No. Capitalism. Socialism. Sex. Love ... '" (44). Not only does Anna laugh at the oppositions, but she imposes her own order on the list; she does not place in first position the traditionally dominant term; for example, she lists "bound" and "sex" on the side of "man" whereas "free" and "love" appear on the side of "woman." The novel neither reverses nor rearranges the oppositions in any rigid order, as evidenced by the ironical use of the term "free women." Anna and Molly are simultaneously free and not free: they are free to reject traditional familial arrangements but not free from Western ideologies of romantic love or from victimization by male lovers (see earlier discussion). By highlighting the instability of the notion of freedom, the novel inherently disrupts binary logic, which depends on fixed concepts. In demonstrating that women both are and are not free, the novel opens up the possibility that other concepts are similarly unstable and need not be associated exclusively with either women or men. As a result, the oppositions between man and woman, male and female, masculine and feminine break down. These dichotomies become meaningless as Anna slowly recognizes that neither creativity nor violence and destruction—traditionally positioned as binary opposites associated with men—are male principles: Anna dreams of "the malicious male-female dwarf figure, the principle of joy-in-destruction" (594). The indeterminate sexual nature of the dwarf in her dreams suggests to Anna that neither creativity nor destruction have innate ties to biological sex, which helps her overcome the historical association of authoring and maleness or masculinity.[19] The novel thus exposes the link between maleness and the creative and destructive principles as a cultural construction with no basis in biological difference.[20] Moreover, *The Golden Notebook* proceeds to challenge the entire system of binary oppositions initially mocked by the character Anna, as the novel moves toward the creation of a new female subject and toward aesthetic means of depicting that new subject.

Since Western culture has traditionally positioned woman on the object side of the classical dichotomy between subject and object, the first step toward creating a new female subject is to destabilize the opposition. Lessing's novel takes up this challenge by positioning Anna as both subject, or teller, and object, or character, of her story. There is a constant process of difference and deferral, as Anna shifts to occupy both and neither poles of this opposition. As editor, author, and character of *The Golden Notebook,* Anna's position within the dichotomy between subject and object is no longer stable. The same is true of the related opposition between self and other. The Annas who are the objects of the notebooks and the characters of the various fictional pieces are the *Other* of the author-self Anna, and all of these Annas are ultimately the *Other* of the editor-self Anna. Anna's ability to both represent and recognize her *Other* in its various guises suggests that the novel conceives of the *Other* in modernist rather than postmodern terms—the postmodern *Other* being precisely that which cannot be recognized or represented and yet which constitutes the self. Anna's recognition of her *Other* in the characters of her pieces of writing has much in common with Clarissa Dalloway's recognition of Septimus Smith as her *Other* in Virginia Woolf's modernist novel *Mrs. Dalloway.* Yet Lessing does tug a little at the modernist conception of the *Other* in her presentation of Anna's *Other* in the form of versions of Anna so that the *Other* is less vividly separate and more explicitly part of the subject herself than in the case of Woolf's Clarissa Dalloway.

The concept of the *Other* in *The Golden Notebook* is closer to the Lacanian *Other*, which seems to lie between the modernist and postmodernist *Other*. Jacques Lacan begins to disperse the subject by suggesting that it is composed of a dynamic interaction between a speaking subject, an alienated subject of identification or ego, identificatory objects, and an *Other* that is for Lacan knowable only inasmuch as it speaks through the unconscious—its language.[21] The Lacanian *Other* both constitutes and inhabits the human subject and is not directly perceivable. Anna's *Other,* discerned indefinitely in the fragments of her writing, similarly composes and is contained by the human being designated by the name Anna. The Lacanian *Other* is ultimately not postmodern, however, since it insists on a set structure to explain and tie together the dispersed elements that make up the human subject. Lessing's novel likewise challenges but retains the opposition between self and other. *The Golden Notebook* approaches a conception of the dispersed, decentered postmodern subject only when it investigates madness, toward the end of the book. Nevertheless, since the novel conceives of both the self and other as constitutive of and contained by the subject, it succeeds in breaking down the hierarchical arrangement by which women have traditionally been placed in the position of *Other*. Anna is not *The Other;* she is a subject in her own right and encompasses the positions of both self and other.

Throughout most of the novel, however, Anna the character and writer of notebooks tries to secure a humanist concept of the whole integrated self by compartmentalizing her life. Although she lives in a world in which roles and selves have become increasingly fragmented, Anna rejects "Alienation. Being split" and tries to hold on to a "humanism" that "stands for the whole person, the whole individual" (360). Paradoxically, her attempts at wholeness involve a division of herself into smaller wholes, as she works to keep her roles as writer, communist, friend, mother, and lover distinctly separate. In a diary entry of the "Blue Notebook," Anna admits that "The two personalities—Janet's mother, Michael's mistress, are happier separated. It is a strain having to be both at once" (336). The difficulty here is twofold: Anna feels unable to combine the roles of mother and lover not only because she seeks wholeness but also because Western culture has structured these two roles as incompatible, as antitheses. The centered humanist subject thus denies women multifaceted existence; women are either wives and mothers or they are whores and mistresses. In her writing Anna uses four separate notebooks to order the various aspects of her life, feeling that otherwise "it would be such a—scramble. Such a mess" (266). Indeed, Anna reveals herself to be very much a product of a Western culture that opposes and privileges order and reason against chaos. She has convinced herself that the division of her life into four notebooks will stave off the chaos of contemporary existence and enable her to retain a concept of wholeness; it is her way of staying "above all this—chaos" (407). She creates an artificial form of split personality to guard herself against real madness; but in the end she cannot sustain the inherent contradictions of this enforced division in the name of an illusion of wholeness. Not until Anna deliberately ends her four separate notebooks and begins to write in a single "Golden Notebook" does she finally accept the formlessness of life and of the individual.

In its exploration of subjectivity, *The Golden Notebook* challenges not only the oppositions between subject and object, self and other, but also the related dichotomy between the inner self and the outer world. When Anna recognizes that dividing herself into various roles is an evasion of and an attempt to ward off the chaos of the contemporary world, she is forced to acknowledge that there exists no neat dividing line between the chaos of the outer world and her own consciousness. Anna's question, "What anonymous whole am I part of?" (49), unsettles the conventional distinction between the inner self and the outer world, even if it is still based on a concept of wholeness. Moreover, through her relationship with Saul, Anna recognizes that there are no absolute divisions between individuals. Their relationship is a site of the novel's strongest challenge to the stable opposition between self and other; both Anna and Saul play out a series of roles until Anna can "no longer separate [her]self from Saul" (587). It is not that the two characters merge into one but rather that they are no longer sharply delineated one from the other.

Once she has accepted the world's chaos by willingly descending into madness and by writing in only one notebook, the "Golden Notebook," Anna not only recognizes that "a world of disorder lies behind" (633) the surface of things and people but also accepts that she occupies a multiplicity of irreconcilable positions or selves. Although Anna feels "threatened with total disintegration" as she sinks into chaos through dreams, her experience of seeing herself "sleeping, watching other personalities bend over to invade her" (614), as she becomes "an Algerian soldier" (600) and a Chinese "peasant woman" (601), frees her from her divided self. Her acceptance of fragmentation and chaos as multiplicity and formlessness, rather than as division, pushes *The Golden Notebook* beyond realism and modernism. By presenting fragmentation as a function of *Being* itself rather than as the result of a plethora of subjective interpretations, the novel has stepped decisively toward the postmodern: after all, Anna's dreams emphasize that she fills a variety of subject positions. Indeed, postmodern notions of identity posit sets of dynamic roles, in which human beings constantly take up and give up various sociocultural subject positions and thus have no singular unified stable subjecthood (see Chapter 1).

Many critics have argued, however, that in the "Golden Notebook" Anna becomes whole and integrated in the traditional sense.[22] For example, Mary Cohen argues that "The focus of the book is Anna's attempt to become a 'whole person'";[23] Roberta Rubenstein asserts that Anna ultimately "synthesizes" the "divisions in her consciousness"[24]; and Betsy Draine claims that Anna's resolve to write in a single notebook demonstrates that "Anna has at last synthesized a balanced self."[25] All of these arguments assume not only that the novel's aim is an integrated wholeness but also that the novel shares Anna's aims. In contrast, I argue that, although the character Anna, in most of the notebooks and in "Free Women," clings to a humanist concept of the self as whole and unified, *The Golden Notebook* challenges that very notion of the integrated self through its various versions of Anna and through the recognition by the Anna of "The Golden Notebook" that chaos is part of her existence and thus part of her identity. Anna does not synthesize her various selves but rather accepts multiplicity as a function of *Being* itself. While Anna achieves some kind of balance, it is a new kind of balance that defies conventional notions of wholeness, and the binary logic on which they depend, and instead embraces multiplicity.

But it is in its treatment of madness as a vortex of oppositions that Lessing's novel most decisively tests, explores, and dissolves humanist notions of the subject. The male-centered nature of the opposition between sanity and insanity is particularly evident in the traditional association of sanity with reason, order, and men and of insanity with emotions, chaos, and women. Challenging what is essentially a deeply male-centered Western opposition therefore becomes a potentially feminist as well as postmodern move. Anna, in fact, plays into the conventional set of hierarchical oppositions when she attempts to hold on to her reason as a means of staving off chaos and madness: "she set her brain on the alert, a small critical, dry machine. She could even feel that intelligence there, at work, defensive and efficient—a machine. And she thought: this intelligence, it's the only barrier between me and—but this time she did finish it, she knew how to end the sentence. Between me and cracking up. Yes"

(395). As the novel progresses, however, the dichotomies between sanity and insanity, reason and madness, slowly disintegrate to the point of meaninglessness.

The Golden Notebook demonstrates that chaos can no longer remain outside the individual in a world in which "destruction" is acknowledged "as a force" (589) and in which "war" and "the immanence of war" are "the truth for our time" (591). The novel depicts Anna's wilful descent into madness as a means of acknowledging and accepting chaos and formlessness, thereby highlighting the interconnectedness of identity and historical material conditions. Barbara Rigney suggests that, in *The Golden Notebook,* "To go mad in a positive sense is to give up all certainty" and "to lose the distinction between the real and the not-real, between the self and the not-self"; madness itself undermines the traditional oppositions between self and other, self and world, reality and fiction (I will discuss this last opposition later in the chapter). Yet Rigney's assertion that, in the novel's world, "Only through the recognition of one's own madness as a reflection of the world's madness can a higher sanity be achieved" is problematic, since it inherently assumes an opposition between self and world and between sanity and madness and posits sanity as the hierarchically superior and desirable term over madness.[26] But Lessing's novel questions the rigidity of these dichotomies and reveals that madness and sanity are not opposites but are merely culturally constructed labels for the two extremes of an unstable continuum: Anna recognizes that "the word sane meant nothing, as the word mad meant nothing," and that she "could see no reason why I should be mad or sane" (594). Moreover, the novel presents Anna's madness as a function of her identity rather than as a "reflection of the world's madness," as Rigney puts it.

The novel does not reverse the dichotomy and embrace madness, however, as Anna's emergence from her exploration of insanity to go on and write "Free Women" and *The Golden Notebook* makes clear. Anna does not achieve "a higher sanity" but rather reaches a point at which she accepts the continuous process of difference and deferral that destabilizes the rigid boundary between sanity and insanity. Anna understands that she can neither disown her own madness nor allow it to render her socially paralyzed: "it's not a question of fighting it [madness], or disowning it, or of right or wrong, but simply knowing it is there, always. It's a question of bowing to it, so to speak, with a kind of courtesy, as to an ancient enemy: All right, I know you are there but we have to preserve the forms, don't we?" (634). Although the experience of her own madness allows Anna to transgress traditionally imposed limits or boundaries, she cannot let herself sink into madness and still function within a social system that depends on set forms. In order to position herself as an active social agent, Anna must accept the chaos and madness intrinsic to contemporary existence and identity and yet not reinscribe hierarchical oppositions by privileging chaos and madness over order and sanity. Indeed, Anna surfaces from her experience of madness to write a novel that aims to represent the development of a new female subject, and thus has a specific political agenda, through a combination of subversive and established aesthetic strategies. The novel presents Anna's madness as both a symptom of and a cure for the fragmentation, formlessness, and violence of the contemporary world.[27] Lessing's novel neither glorifies nor dismisses madness; it explores it.

Within *The Golden Notebook,* madness takes the form of split personalities that both parallel and intersect with the fragmentation and chaos inherent in contemporary existence. Anna is disconcerted by Saul's inconsistent behavior, until she understands that he is struggling with madness and *is* in effect various persons: "What was strange was, that the man who had said No, defending his freedom, and the man who said, pleading, It doesn't mean anything, were two men. I couldn't connect them. I was silent, in the grip of apprehension again, and then a third man said, brotherly and affectionate: 'Go to sleep now'" (562). By presenting human beings as conglomerations of dispersed personalities, the novel reveals that the notion of a centered self is at best only an illusion. Saul's constant shifts from one self to another indicate that the human subject is in process and can never be fixed. Anna's own encounter with madness further emphasizes human beings' simultaneous occupation of various subject positions; she is "conscious of two other Annas, separate from the obedient child—Anna the snubbed woman in love, cold and miserable in some corner of myself, and a curious detached sardonic Anna, looking on and saying: 'Well, well!'" (562). Lessing seems to suggest that pathological split personalities are in effect only extreme versions of the schizoid contemporary subject.[28] Anna describes madness as "the place in themselves [people] where words, patterns, order, dissolve" and as something that "is there, always" (634). When Anna re-emerges from her wilful descent into madness, she retains a split self. Saul refers to two of Anna's selves when he gives her the first line of "Free Women" and of *The Golden Notebook:* "I'm going to give you the first sentence then. There are the two women you are, Anna. Write down: The two women were alone in the London flat" (639).

Not only does Anna's experience of madness serve as a means of disrupting and reconstructing notions of subjectivity, but it also exposes the coexistence of chaos and creative tension within the realm of madness. In a metafictional twist, Ella in Anna's "Yellow Notebook" envisions the story of Anna and Saul's experience inside madness: "A man and a woman—yes. Both at the end of their tether. Both cracking up because of a deliberate attempt to transcend their own limits. And out of the chaos, a new kind of strength." Although this notion of transcendence is problematic and even contradictory in a novel that calls into question culturally imposed limits, *The Golden Notebook* nevertheless asserts a positive and creative side to chaos and madness. Yet the novel does not slight the negative side of madness that is destructive of self and others and that informs Anna and Saul's bitter fighting. But if the negative side of madness leads Anna and Saul to fight, its positive side leads them to help each other find "a new kind of strength" (467) with which to write their respective books. Moreover, the reappropriation of madness within the novel, which coincides with the dismantling of hierarchical binary oppositions, supports Shoshana Felman's observation that "the issue of madness has been linked" to "the current upheaval in the status of knowledge."[29] By the end of the "Golden Notebook," Anna understands that her writer's block has been rooted in her inability to deal with the world's chaos and violence:

> "I can't write that short story or any other, because at that moment I sit down to write, someone comes into the room, looks over my shoulders, and stops me." [Anna]
>
> "Who? Do you know?" [Saul]
>
> "Of course I know. It could be a Chinese peasant. Or one of Castro's guerrilla fighters. Or an Algerian fighting in the F.L.N. Or Mr Mathlong. They stand here in the room and they say, why aren't you doing something about us, instead of wasting your time scribbling?" [Anna] (639)

Anna's particular political and aesthetic dilemma stems from a metaphysical crisis within Western culture. Its binary system of thought and the aesthetic forms it has produced invite Anna to think and write in ways that do not allow her to engage the chaos that surrounds and constructs her. Since Western rational thought privileges and opposes reason over madness and order over chaos, reason can engage with chaos only as a fixed adversary. In contrast, a non-binary, non-hierarchical notion of madness engages chaos more fully and productively in Lessing's novel.

Moreover, the novel's depiction of mad men as well as mad women undermines the traditional association of madness and women. The novel depicts the madness of both men and women as based in an inability to deal with their culturally imposed roles in a world that has become increasingly violent and chaotic. However, the sources of women's and men's madness differ in a culture that polarizes men and women and relegates them to different spheres of life. When Anna is out canvassing for votes, she is fascinated to find "lonely women going mad quietly by themselves, in spite of husband or children or rather because of them" (167). These women's madness serves as a symptom of a world in which "injustice and cruelty is [sic] at the root of life" (636), including the specific injustices and cruelties with which male-centered cultures oppress women. *The Golden Notebook* delineates the grim material situation of women and yet never divorces women's specific oppression from larger problems and structures. Greene is very much on target when she argues that Lessing is a "'feminist' in the broadest sense, in the sense defined by Adrienne Rich, as concerned with 'a profound transformation of world society and of human relationships.'"[30] Indeed, the novel reveals its feminist perspective by focusing on the problems of the entire structure of existing Western society and culture and their effects on women.

In conjunction with its challenge to the humanist subject and delineation of a new female subject, *The Golden Notebook* disrupts established aesthetic forms and moves toward a more dynamic novel form designed to better capture a chaotic world in which identity is no longer stable or centered. In much the same way as it presents the new subject as a multiplicity of selves in process, *The Golden Notebook* depicts the process of creating a new kind of novel—itself—made up of a multiplicity of forms and segments. The interrelated fragments exist on various narrative levels and resist synthesis into one piece; yet the fragments do not indicate divisions but rather combine to form a text-novel, which becomes in effect an intricate tissue of texts.[31] The novel physically enacts contemporary theory's notion that all texts are penetrated by and composed of traces of other texts, so that there is no originary or ultimate reality or meaning. This does not mean, however, that Lessing's novel lacks coherence or consistency: its fragments are specifically designed and ordered so that they enter into dialogue with each other and so that the gaps between them create a web of meaning.[32] Despite its formal disruptions, *The Golden Notebook* presents itself as a novel and as such retains some kind of form. However, through its emphasis on textuality and its often ironic juxtaposition of pieces, the novel criticizes and physically disrupts the conventions of realism and certain modernist modes even while it at times uses them. The result is a novel that is readable and yet subversive, a novel that presents recognizable characters and yet disrupts established aesthetic forms for depicting characters and notions of fixed identity, a novel that draws its readers into a conventional narrative and then explodes that narrative, a novel that is very structured and yet resists form, a novel that tells a story and yet challenges the very conventions by which stories have been told within Western culture. In order to tell-write, and thus communicate, a contemporary woman's story-history, the novel must hold on to narrative. At the same time, however, the novel disrupts the various narrative forms it co-opts by highlighting the ways in which they have been constructed within, and bear the marks of, a male-centered culture that privileges rational discourse and binary logic. But, although its disruptions are at times radical, the novel never severs ties to established conventions (especially realist ones) or to material conditions and therefore retains a wide reading audience, which in turn opens up the potential for social praxis through literature (see Chapter 1).[33]

Paradoxically, although *The Golden Notebook* overtly resists form, a great number of critics have devoted much energy to explaining the novel's structure. While critics have praised Lessing's novel for challenging traditional narrative form, many have insisted on describing the function of the novel's various parts, and the relations they have to each other, to such an extent that these critics are in fact imposing their own versions of a form onto the novel. The novel, undeniably, has a form, insomuch as all writing has form; but form in *The Golden Notebook* remains elusive, as it continually undermines itself through its overt circularity and metafictional structure.[34] Greene is right on target when she asserts that, in Lessing's novel, "form is accepted within full ironic recognition of the limits of form."[35] Since the various parts of the novel occupy different narrative levels and yet intersect, the novel defies a stable structure as well as critics' attempts at analysis and synthesis.

Some critics have worked themselves into corners attempting to provide definitive explanations of the relation between the novel's parts. A surprising number of critics, for example, have read "Free Women" as the novel Anna, the writer of the notebooks, ultimately writes after she overcomes her writer's block.[36] They base their interpretation on Saul's giving to Anna at the end of the "Golden Notebook" section the first line of the novel she is to write, a line that is the first line of "Free Women: 1." What these critics seem to ignore is that this line is also the first line of *The Golden Notebook,* which complicates the idea of authorship since it makes Anna the author of the whole novel as well as of its parts.[37] If Anna writes the entire novel, then she is also the editor, whose bracketed notations explain and comment on the various sections; and these editorial notations exist on a different narrative level from the other segments. Furthermore, Anna as author of *The Golden Notebook* makes for a complex relationship between Lessing and Anna. The novel does not collapse Lessing and Anna, since the two exist on different levels, and yet their voices within the novel are difficult to distinguish one from the other. Through elements such as this ambiguity of voice and superimposition of distinct narrative levels, the novel continually disrupts its own narrative structure and thereby resists a rigid form. Moreover, the indeterminacy of voice challenges the modernist belief in the expressive function of aesthetics through its distribution and dispersion of authorial control.

The Golden Notebook's multiple forms and fragments testify not only to a rejection of realism's mimetic aesthetics but also to simultaneous moves beyond modernism and toward feminism. The canonized version of modernist aesthetics is based on a categorical distinction between high art and mass culture, a dichotomy that

Andreas Huyssen convincingly argues "has been gendered as masculine/feminine from Flaubert" up to "French poststructuralism."[38] A challenge to the modernist novel thus also functions as a challenge to the rigid distinction between a masculinized high art and a feminized mass culture and, potentially, also as a feminist move: after all, feminism has everything to gain from a disassociation of women and low, or inferior, culture and from disruptions of the binary logic that facilitates Western culture's construction of women in inferior positions. Moreover, Lessing's novel implicitly suggests that the contemporary woman—and man, although the novel focuses on a woman—cannot be represented using aesthetic forms that do not account for the world's violence, fragmentation, and multiplicity or for the culturally imposed gender roles that fragment the individual and divide the sexes. Indeed, I argue that the novel refuses to separate aesthetics from the material situation and instead emphasizes the connections between all aesthetic forms and specific historical material conditions.

The novel within the novel, "Free Women," functions on one level as a parody of the conventional realist novel form by pointing out its limitations. "Free Women" is a third-person chronological narrative with a clear plot and story but with no in-depth analysis of the chaos that inhabits its characters' lives. The five chapters of "Free Women" make up less than a fourth of *The Golden Notebook,* and this space allotment alone demonstrates that traditional narrative has limitations. The division of "Free Women" into chapters interspersed by long notebook fragments further highlights the inability of the conventional novel to depict contemporary existence by itself.[39] It is noteworthy, however, that chapters of "Free Women" both begin and end *The Golden Notebook,* which indicates that the novel disrupts but does not altogether throw out traditional narrative. The novel must retain some degree of narrative structure to communicate the development of a contemporary woman's dynamic subjectivity to traditionally trained readers. Indeed, "Free Women" functions both as a parody of the conventional novel and as a basis or organizing principle for *The Golden Notebook.*

Although chapters of "Free Women" physically begin and end *The Golden Notebook,* the metafictional quality of the novel defies the very notions of beginning and ending. If Anna is the author-editor of *The Golden Notebook,* then the process of editing the various parts that make up the novel and choosing a sequence for the fragments is in effect the only tangible culmination. The existence of *The Golden Notebook* is an ending of sorts—but never actually an end—to the process of depicting a contemporary woman's story-history and creating a new novel form. That Anna as editor of the novel chooses to place "Free Women: 5" at the physical end of the book does not make this chapter the ending of the novel, since *The Golden Notebook* includes but goes far beyond the short conventional "Free Women." Moreover, "Free Women: 5" cannot be the ending of the novel as a whole, since it ends with Anna deciding to engage in marriage counseling for the working class and to give up writing, an ending that *The Golden Notebook* belies by its very existence as a product of Anna's writing-editing.[40] The penultimate section of the novel, the "Golden Notebook" fragment, is not the novel's ending either. The "Golden Notebook" segment ends with Saul providing Anna with the first line of both "Free Women" and *The Golden Notebook*, which gives the novel circularity and overtly defies any notion of a definitive ending or beginning.[41] Indeed, the degree to which the novel disrupts traditional narrative strategies extends far beyond high modernism's rejection of linear or chronological narrative. T.S. Eliot's modernist "The Love Song of J. Alfred Prufrock," for example, rejects chronology as it offers a series of atemporal images from modern life, but it nevertheless retains a distinct beginning and ending. Eliot's poem demonstrates a belief that art has an expressive function—expressing authorial intention and control over the chaos of the modern world—while Lessing's novel challenges that expressive function by presenting notions of beginning and ending as inherently indefinite.

The disruption of notions of beginning and ending associated with traditional narrative is simultaneously a feminist move in Lessing's novel. The implicit rejection of "Free Women: 5" as an ending is a rejection of both conventional narrative and the conventional roles imposed on women. "Free Women" ends with Molly's marriage and Anna's decision to engage in marriage counseling for the working class. By thrusting the novella's two female characters into conventional women's roles—wife, social worker, and expert on marriage—and giving the novella the ironic title "Free Women," *The Golden Notebook* mocks the pretense that women can be free within existing sociocultural structures. At the same time, Lessing's novel pushes beyond this cynical and ironic resolution by making Anna the author of "Free Women" and of *The Golden Notebook* and thereby providing alternative or multiple endings. The novel does not negate the ending of "Free Women," however, since it places it in final position; instead, it offers a multiplicity of endings and thus a greater number of possible roles for women: Anna as social worker-marriage counselor, Anna as author of "Free Women," and Anna as author-editor of *The Golden Notebook*. Similarly, the novel has no real beginning. "Free Women: 1" opens the book and yet does not begin the story or the writing process that the novel delineates, since Saul gives Anna its first line in the "Golden Notebook" section that is located almost at the end of the book. The "Black Notebook" fragment that is in second position is not a beginning either, since it jumps back and forth between the present and Anna's past. Through its disruption of the concepts of beginning and ending, the novel rejects the definitive limits of conventional narratives that have traditionally constrained women to particular roles and plots.

The Golden Notebook challenges not only conventional narrative form but also established notions of representation, particularly through Anna's incessant attempts to capture reality in her writing. The notebooks contain recollections, fictionalizations, and analyses of past as well as recent events in Anna's life; newspaper clippings dealing with war, atomic and hydrogen bombs, and violence in general; and various attempts to record the *truth* of events by writing in ever briefer and terser styles. As Anna struggles to depict and communicate her experiences through her four notebooks, she slowly recognizes that she has no direct unmediated access to reality or truth and therefore cannot represent raw experiences in her writing.[42] The novel in this way moves toward a postmodern notion of representation, which views raw experiences as always already mediated, and away from both realist and modernist fiction, which assume (albeit in different ways) a categorical distinction between reality and fiction as they seek to represent events and experiences. In *The Golden Notebook,* Anna's repeated unsuccessful attempts to capture reality signal the artificiality of the binary opposition between reality and fiction. Once Anna accepts that she cannot recuperate past experiences, she can move on to depict her existence in new ways that move beyond the established male-centered binary logic.[43] By undermining notions of objective reality and mimetic representation,

Lessing's novel creates a space for positing and constructing a plurality of dynamic realities and thus allows for women's traditionally effaced and undervalued stories-histories.

Anna learns that a coherent past exists only in retrospect, as a function of the way the mind imposes patterns onto past events: "It's only now, looking back, that I understand" (120), since it is only after "one has lived through something, [that] it falls into a pattern." On one level, then, the novel relativizes reality through its insistence that, since memories are subjective, the remembered past is inevitably "untrue" (227–28). But the novel more thoroughly undermines notions of reality by highlighting the mediated nature of all experiences and representations of experiences. Unable to separate her lived experiences from her memories of those experiences, Anna asks, "How do I know that what I 'remember' was what was important?" (137) or that what she emphasizes is "the correct emphasis?"; she eventually understands that "I was unable to distinguish between what I had invented and what I had known" (619). Moreover, Michael's declaration that "Anna, you make up stories about life and tell them to yourself, and you don't know what is true and what isn't" (331) and Anna's argument that "there's never any way of really knowing the truth about anything" (163) indicate a recognition of the instability of rigid distinctions between reality and fiction. However, the novel does not collapse reality and fiction; rather, it posits levels of fiction or reality. For example, Anna's overtly fictional "Yellow Notebook" remains distinct from her attempts to reconstruct her lived experiences in her other notebooks; the "Yellow Notebook" engages in a more overt and complete fiction-alization of Anna's experiences and yet is no less true or false than her diary entries.

In its disruption of notions of reality and representation, *The Golden Notebook* neither pretends to be a mirror of reality nor claims to be neutral in any sense. After experimenting with various styles of recording events, Anna recognizes that her "terse record of facts" is "as false as the account" that is full of "emotionalism" (468). This recognition not only emphasizes the inherent fictionality of all writing and the impossibility of mimetic representation but also reveals that the rationality traditionally associated with men is no guarantee of fact or truth and, in fact, serves only to create the illusion of fact or truth. Indeed, the novel depicts the writer Anna's growing recognition that writing or "Literature is analysis after the event" (228) and, as such, is always subjective and always already represented—in the sense that events cannot exist outside of layers of representation. The same is true of characters, who are never equal to the human beings they represent: "I, Anna, see Ella. Who is, of course, Anna. But that is the point, for she is not. The moment I, Anna, write: Ella rings up Julia to announce, etc., then Ella floats away from me and becomes someone else" (459). However, the recognition that all representations are mediated does not necessarily deny literature any political force. While *The Golden Notebook* highlights its own fictionality, it succeeds in communicating a contemporary woman's story-history without divorcing itself from material existence. Rather than presenting the reader with a supposedly neutral representation or copy of a real woman, Lessing's novel offers multiple versions or images of Anna as the only means of approximating such a woman living in the contemporary world.

The Golden Notebook's attempt to develop an aesthetics that does not deny or leave behind the historical and material situation is linked to its feminist impulses. Although the novel treats large topics—such as the role of aesthetics, mass political movements, war, atomic weapons, racism—it does not neglect the more personal issues that many contemporary women confront on a daily basis.[44] The novel presents Anna not only as a writer and a political activist but also as having to deal with her own female body, with the grocery shopping, with her young daughter, and with her lover. When Anna notes that her menstrual periods are starting on the day she has chosen to record objectively, she has a moment of doubt before proceeding as planned: "(I wondered if it would be better not to choose today to write down everything I felt; then decided to go ahead. It was not planned; I had forgotten about the period. I decided that the instinctive feeling of shame and modesty was dishonest: no emotion for a writer.)" (339). Her self-conscious choice to record her moment of doubt and then to include the physical details and feelings that dominate her day as a result of her period indicates that the novel rejects the traditional veiling of the female body and its functions. Menstrual cycles are part of women's physical existence and their presence within the novel is a political statement: it signifies the inclusion of women's specific perspectives and experiences within a new aesthetics that challenges the dichotomy between high art and mundane physical existence. Anna also describes how she is taken over by "the housewife's disease" peculiar to women: "I must-dress-Janet-get-her-breakfast-send-her-off-to-school-get-Michael's-break-fast-don't-forget-I'm-out-of-tea-etc.-etc." (333). The novel points to the political and aesthetic implications of these activities, which have traditionally been relegated to the domestic or private sphere and which fragment Anna.[45] Western culture's insistence on separating private and professional life—which is linked to the dichotomy between the sexes and to binary logic in general—forces Anna to keep separate her roles as writer and political activist from her roles as mother and lover. The novel emphasizes the interconnectedness of Anna's fragmentation into her various roles and the fragmentation of the world in which she lives and calls for a novel form that can encompass this fragmentation.[46]

Anna's dream of an art object that is "a mass of fragments, and pieces" (252) demonstrates her need for an aesthetics adapted to the fragmentation that is part of her life and of the world at large. Much of the novel focuses on Anna's search for this new novel form. Anna's assertion in "Free Women: 1" that "as far as I can see, every-thing's cracking up" (3) situates the world the novel is attempting to depict. Moreover, Anna quotes an artist saying that "the world is so chaotic art is irrelevant" (42), which sets up the challenge that underlies the novel's quest for a new and relevant aesthetic form. In the first fragment of the "Black Notebook," Anna suggests that "the function of the novel seems to be changing; it has become an outpost of journalism; we read novels for information" rather than for "philo-sophical statements about life," and that "the novel-report is a means" by which fragmented human beings grasp "for their own wholeness." This acknowledgment of the state of the novel opens the way for *The Golden Notebook's* search for a new novel form that would "create a new way of looking at life" (60–61) in all its fragmentation and chaos rather than serve as an escape from the world. The novel disrupts conventional representation with a stance that combines feminist and postmodern impulses and enables the novel to destabilize Western thought and aesthetics and to create a novel form that disrupts rigid dichotomies and allows for the chaos and fragmentation of the contemporary world. Through its challenge to the dichotomy between reality and fiction and its emphasis on the interrelation between the material situation, politics, and aesthetics,

The Golden Notebook challenges the conventional distinction between high art and daily life and redefines representation. The novel breeches the dividing line between public and private events and life, insisting for instance on the way in which Anna's life as a member of the Communist Party interweaves with other aspects of her life and identity, such as her relationship with Michael, her bodily functions, her caring for her daughter, her grocery shopping. Moreover, although Anna writes in her notebooks to record her life, the notebooks contribute to a new art form when they are inserted into the novel's structure.

The Golden Notebook disrupts not only established narrative and aesthetic forms but also language and writing itself. While the five chapters of "Free Women" demonstrate conventional language usage, the various fragments that make up the five notebooks offer a wide range of forms and styles. Most of these sections engage in untraditional uses of language, particularly grammatical fragmentation or disjunction. The lack of connectives, for example, resists the order, linearity, and continuity usually associated with narrative and yet results in a different kind of fluidity. At the same time, the novel engages questions of language thematically, particularly traditional conceptions of the stability of language. Anna's awareness that "words lose their meaning suddenly," and that there exists a "gap between what they are supposed to mean, and what in fact they say" (300), illustrates contemporary theory's recognition of language as an unstable system in which meaning is always sliding and shifting. Anna's experiments with writing ironical pastiches that others then read seriously convince her that a "thinning of language against the density of our experience" (302) accompanies the fragmentation and chaos of the contemporary world. If meaning is no longer stable, then irony becomes impossible, since irony depends on a stable basis of value and meaning. Anna at one point suggests not only that "words lose their meaning" but that they have nothing to do with the images they are supposed to be representing: "I keep *seeing,* before my eyes, pictures of what we are talking about— scenes of death, torture, cross-examination and so on; and the words we are using have nothing to do with what I am seeing" (352). By highlighting that words do not exist in any one-to-one relationship with a given meaning, the novel not only undermines the notion of language as stable but also highlights the difficulty of representing material conditions through the mediation of a language that Western culture has structured to uphold a particular status quo.

Lessing implicitly raises the contemporary theoretical notion that there is no permanent tie between signifier and signified since the pairing of the two terms is a convention rather than a fixed or natural relation. The novel suggests that, before she can create a new type of novel, Anna must not only accept that "words are faulty and by their very nature inaccurate" (653) but also accept the challenge of finding a way to use language regardless of its instability. Lessing is aware of the inherent instability of language as well as of the necessity of using language if she is to communicate to her readers and thereby engage in political praxis (see Chapter 1). As a piece of writing aimed at human beings, *The Golden Notebook* necessarily uses language even if it simultaneously calls language into question. By questioning the way in which language as an ordering mechanism has been employed by Western culture to ensure the hegemony of white bourgeois males, Lessing's novel challenges Western male-centered culture itself. For instance, the novel reveals the way in which the process of *naming* works to order the world's chaos in a culture that places value on order, form, structure, and reason. Anna comes to see naming as "a bit of rescue work, so to speak, rescuing the formless into form. Another bit of chaos rescued and 'named'" (470), and thus as a means of containment.[47] *The Golden Notebook* avoids naming Anna rigidly, by presenting multiple versions of Anna and her experiences and allowing a certain degree of chaos, formlessness, and fragmentation to infect the form of the novel.

Lessing moves away not only from a realist mimetic view of language but also from a high modernist view of language. Although modernists view language as in need of revitalization and experiment with language, they retain a belief in its expressive potential.[48] In contrast, postmodern theories and fiction demonstrate a more profound skepticism toward language and stress the gaps in signification that make it impossible for language to be truly expressive. Lessing's dependence on physical form to communicate Anna's search for identity and a new novel form in *The Golden Notebook* signals skepticism as to the expressive potential of language. The novel also literally fragments and de-orders language in its frequent omissions of connectives and neglect of correct grammatical structures, particularly in the notebook segments. The deliberate use of sentence fragments is one way in which the novel destabilizes conventional language usage and the notion of language as a rigid structure and opens up a space for a certain degree of formlessness. The beginning of the first fragment of the "Black Notebook" exemplifies this pulling towards formlessness within language:

> Every time I sit down to write, and let my mind go easy, the words, It is so dark, or something to do with darkness. Terror. The terror of this city. Fear of being alone. Only one thing stops me from jumping up and screaming or running to the telephone to ring somebody, it is to deliberately think myself back into that hot light ... white light light closed eyes, the red light hot on the eyeballs. The rough pulsing heat of a granite boulder. My palm flat on it, moving over the lichens. The grain of the lichens. Tiny, like minute animals' ears, a warm rough silk on my palm, dragging insistently at the pores of my skin. And hot. The smell of the sun on hot rock. Dry and hot, and the silk of dust on my cheek, smelling of sun, the sun. (56)

The novel does not unsettle language to the extent that communication is lost, however; rather, it calls into question conventional language usage, as well as notions of language as inherently expressive, through a manipulation of language. It opens up a space for new forms to communicate previously marginalized or unconstructed experiences and identities, such as new female subjectivities and new aesthetic modes that exist outside of binary structures. Indeed, for Anna, language itself serves as a barrier to the confrontation of chaos and formlessness. Anna recognizes the inability of language to depict madness, the world of chaos, formlessness, dissolution: "Words. Words. I play with words, hoping that some combination, even a chance combination will say what I want ... The fact is, the real experience can't be described. I think, bitterly, that a row of asterisks, like an old-fashioned novel, might be better" (633). Only after her exploration of madness and confrontation with chaos is Anna able to write again, for she now understands both the instability and power of language and is in a better position to both expose the limitations of language and strategically manipulate language to fulfill her own aims.

The novel's exploration of language also leads to a parallel exploration of interpretation. In the absence of stable meaning, interpretation constantly shifts and slides. If interpretation is unstable, then a space opens up for new interpretations or reinterpretations.[49] Lessing thus foreshadows the work of feminist scholars since the 1970s, which has exposed conventionally fixed interpretations as inherently male-centered and championed reinterpretations from feminist perspectives. Within Lessing's novel, the various equally flawed versions of Anna's past in Africa demonstrate the inherent instability and biases of interpretation. Although Anna's novel about her African experience, *Frontiers of War*, does not itself figure in *The Golden Notebook*, Anna notes in the "Black Notebook" that it was based on a "lying nostalgia" and did not capture "the truth" (63). Anna then tries to recount her African days in a more "objective" style, only to find that what she has written is once more "full of nostalgia" (153). Moreover, she refuses to sell movie rights for her book, on the basis that the directors and film companies are not interpreting it correctly. Later in the novel, Anna dreams that she is watching a film version of *Frontiers of War* and "began to feel uneasy" when she "understood that the director's choice of shots or of timing was changing the 'story.'" But when she complains to the director, he asserts that he "only filmed what was there," prompting Anna to accept that what she "'remembered' was probably untrue" (524–25). The novel also implicitly questions the director's interpretation, which is dependent on his own male-centered view and on film technology. The director's and the camera's eyes affect the story too; it is never already present. In the "Golden Notebook" segment, Anna has a dream in which an invisible projectionist shows her film clips of her life, and again Anna protests that none of the depictions are accurate. However, when Anna sees that the film credits include *"Directed by Anna Wulf,"* she understands that her naming or interpretation of events in her life have been biased and filled "with untruth" (619). At the same time as it calls into question the possibility of a correct or truthful interpretation, *The Golden Notebook* also challenges the role of author as expressive unity, by depicting a new mode of authorship that is not fixed and absolute and that belies intentionality: Anna does not know she is the author of the film's interpretation until she sees her name in the credits. The novel's offering of multiple versions of events and characters suggests that the only means of representing events or characters is through a plurality of interpretations, none of which are privileged over the others since they are only temporary approximations covering gaps in signification that cannot be filled definitively.

The Golden Notebook thus pushes beyond both realist and modernist modes in its attempts to delineate an aesthetics that is not divorced from physical existence and yet is aware of the constructed nature of any reality. The novel questions and disrupts the established status of fiction, of the author, and of conventional expressive representation. Lessing does not forgo representation, however, but rather lays the foundations for a new mode of representation that undermines binary logic and its inherent limitations and that no longer excludes the historical and material situation, with all its violence, fragmentation, and multiplicity. The experimental form of the novel, with its various indeterminate fragments, its overlapping narrative levels, and its lack of closure, physically invalidates sharp distinctions between reality and fiction, as well as between high art and mass culture. It is not accidental, for example, that more pages are given over to Anna's informal, unstructured notebooks than to her conventional novella, "Free Women." Since women writers have traditionally been marginalized from the realm of serious literature, challenging the distinction between high art and mass culture also undermines the opposition between white, bourgeois men and the rest of the human beings on earth. The novel's unconventional narrative engages in attempts to communicate a woman's story-history and to offer women a multiplicity of roles, identities, aesthetics, and endings, particularly ones that move beyond male-centered constructions.

The Golden Notebook seeks to create not only a new novel form but also a new, specifically female subject. Indeed, the novel's relentless questioning of received knowledge and challenges to the very structure of existing society are inextricable from the attempt to delineate a new female subject. The novel takes on a political and critical stance that focuses on the social construction of gendered beings and aims to expose the ways in which Western culture works to retain its white, bourgeois, male dominance. Although *The Golden Notebook* falls short of offering a blueprint for a restructured society, it does work toward a vision of a new subject independent of traditional binary oppositions and of imposed gender traits. The novel's Anna is not this new subject; but, by presenting multiple versions of Anna, the novel rejects illusions of the subject as unified or centered and pushes toward a postmodern notion of the subject as decentered and dispersed, and always "in a process of becoming other."[50] This move toward a new (postmodern) subject is simultaneously a feminist strategy, since it challenges the binary logic that organizes the world according to an opposition between the sexes and thus creates a space for creating new non-binary conceptual modes.

4. WORLDS IN CONFRONTATION: MARGE PIERCY'S *WOMAN ON THE EDGE OF TIME*

Marge Piercy's *Woman on the Edge of Time* (1976), published in the United States fourteen years after Lessing's *The Golden Notebook,* was written in the aftermath of the cultural changes of the 1960s and in the midst of a rapidly growing feminist movement. Given their different temporal and cultural contexts, it is not surprising that the two novels differ a great deal; yet, like *The Golden Notebook,* Piercy's novel contains various disruptive strategies, usually associated with postmodernism, that coincide with and even propel forward its feminist aims. More overtly feminist than Lessing's novel, *Woman on the Edge of Time* moves from challenging existing social structures to proposing a potential new system that does away with the oppressions built into present American society. Like Lessing's novel, *Woman on the Edge of Time* calls into question the whole system of hierarchical binary oppositions at the basis of Western thought and values; but, unlike Lessing, Piercy presents a vision of an alternative world that evolves from such a massive challenge to existing metaphysics. By delineating a potential feminist utopia and contrasting it to the present world, Piercy's novel both critiques the present and focuses on the reconstruction that deconstruction enables. Although the novel does not highlight deconstructive processes, it nevertheless substantiates the need for dismantling Western thought and societal structures in order to achieve the utopia it champions.

Stylistically, *Woman on the Edge of Time* is much more traditional than Lessing's novel. Indeed, Piercy's novel falls close to social realism, assuming a mimetic aesthetics to depict the material conditions of the various worlds it presents. However, disruptive strategies intrude within and unsettle the realist text, as the novel attempts to present both the present world and a potential future world free of human oppression. *Woman on the Edge of Time* retains a strong link to the material situation through its overt use of realist conventions, especially in the graphic descriptions of the means by which American culture physically and psychically oppresses its protagonist, Connie (Consuelo) Ramos. However, the novel also co-opts postmodern strategies to engage in deconstructive and, more importantly, reconstructive processes. While realist aesthetics serve to communicate to its readers (trained in realist modes) Connie's situation in the present world, the novel implicitly demonstrates the limits of realist aesthetics by having to break from realist conventions to create a space for constructing a feminist utopia. Created within and bound by binary logic and its notion of fixed subjectivity, realist aesthetics reproduces and reinforces hierarchical oppositions and cannot alone move beyond established social and thought structures.[1] To construct a specifically feminist utopia devoid of oppression and inequality, the novel must challenge Western metaphysics with its male-centered system of hierarchical oppositions that ground women's material subjugation. Piercy's novel adopts and transforms certain postmodern strategies in order to disrupt the status quo and open up a space for the new in specifically feminist terms: it engages in narrative superimpositions of temporally discrete worlds, creates ontologically indeterminate alternate worlds, and emphasizes what lies in the margins of the text, in between the worlds it presents. Although the novel never completely severs its ties to realism, this very conventionality gives its postmodern impulses explosive potential.

The novel's opening scene emphasizes the physical and psychic oppression of women in an overtly male-centered culture. Set in New York City during the early 1970s, the scene depicts Connie's attempt to protect her niece Dolly from Geraldo—Dolly's lover and pimp—by hitting him over the head with a bottle. Subsequently, Geraldo has Connie institutionalized, based on her past psychiatric record. Although the novel begins with Connie's second institutionalization and follows her through various psychiatric hospitals, it details events of her past life and of her first institutionalization through flashbacks sprinkled throughout the narrative. Connie's story is that of a poor Chicana whose first husband was killed by the police in a street demonstration, whose second husband physically abused her until she ran away, whose lover died of hepatitis while taking part in a medical experiment in prison, and whose daughter,

Angelina, was taken from her and put up for adoption on the grounds of child abuse. Moreover, Connie's violent behavior toward her child served as the grounds for her first institutionalization. The novel focuses on her life as a mental patient, particularly when she is chosen as a guinea pig for an experiment in which electrodes are implanted in patients' brains, with the aim of controlling anti-social behavior. While this realist plot records Connie's victimization by a society that labels her as *mad* for failing to conform to the roles expected of her, that of passive, successful wife and mother, a parallel plot depicts a possible future world, that of Mattapoisett in 2137, in which all persons and roles have equal status and authority. Luciente, the novel's protagonist from the future, links up with Connie through a process of psychic time-traveling. Although Luciente first appears in Connie's world, most of the time-traveling sequences involve Connie visiting the future world and learning about its different social, cultural, and thought structures that support an egalitarian society. Realist conventions break down, however, as the narrative alternates between the two plots more and more frequently, so that the two worlds become less and less distinct within the context of Connie's consciousness. Moreover, the very telling of Connie's story-history from her perspective disrupts society's labelling of her as mad or sick and gives equal reality status to the two worlds she experiences.

Piercy's novel, which critics have consistently read as a feminist utopian or science fiction novel, has generated little critical debate. Critics generally describe utopian fiction as a subset of the science fiction genre that concerns itself specifically with "the institutions and interactions of persons" and aims to "reconstruct human culture."[2] The boundary between utopian and non-utopian science fiction is so nebulous, however, that many critics have adopted the umbrella term "speculative fiction"—which includes "utopias, science fiction, fantasy, and sword and sorcery."[3] Furthermore, critics have demonstrated that feminist speculative fiction differs from the generic or traditional variety. The feminist versions are both "critiques of patriarchy"[4] and "framework[s] for exploring the consequences of full development of women's potential"[5]: typically, these feminist works begin "by showing how women are profoundly alienated and limited by patriarchal society; they then go on to acquaint the reader with an alternative society in which women could feel at home and manifest their potential."[6] Feminist versions of futuristic societies "seek solutions primarily within the public, political sphere"[7] and represent technology "as subordinate to the development of a society in which power is shared"[8]: these societies are "better in explicitly feminist terms and for explicitly feminist reasons."[9] Although *Woman on the Edge of Time* fits well within the broadly defined category of feminist speculative fiction, and is consequently often discussed as such, its complex construction using both realist and more subversive strategies deserves a more sustained exploration than simple reduction to an example of a predefined genre.

I argue that an incisive analysis reveals *Woman on the Edge of Time* to be a novel that co-opts and transforms postmodern adaptations of speculative fiction to further its feminist aims. In *Postmodernist Fiction,* Brian McHale suggests that "science fiction" is "postmodernism's noncanonized or 'low art' double, its sister-genre," in the sense that they are both "literature of cognitive estrangement" that place "worlds into confrontation." He further argues that postmodern fiction has tended "to adapt science fiction's motifs of temporal displacement" and that "in constructing future worlds, postmodernist writing tends to focus on social and institutional innovations rather than on the strictly technological innovations that are stereotypically associated with science fiction."[10] McHale's general conception of postmodern fiction's adaptation of certain science fiction motifs is extremely close to descriptions of feminist speculative literature, although he does not note the similarity. Indeed, discussions of postmodern fiction to date (including McHale's) tend to neglect the issue of feminism, as well as fiction written by women (see Chapter 1). In contrast, Marleen Barr does posit a relationship between postmodern fiction and feminist speculative fiction in her claim that "feminist fabulators deserve a prominent place in postmodern fiction." However, Barr bases her claim on the metafictional quality of much feminist speculative fiction, while I argue that what makes such feminist speculative fiction as Piercy's postmodern is its more radical strategy of placing worlds in confrontation.[11] The structure of *Woman on the Edge of Time* in fact depends on the conjoining of temporally discrete worlds, which leads to theoretical and aesthetic consequences that enact a more subversive feminist agenda. The transgression of traditional temporal boundaries allows Piercy to posit a plurality of worlds and realities and to destabilize the conventional dichotomies between reality and fiction and between presence and absence, so that the novel implicitly calls into question binary logic in general and "deconstruct[s] notions of historical inevitability, indeed of authority *per se*."[12] Piercy's superimposition of temporally disconnected worlds or realities has two consequences, both of which propel forward the novel's feminist aims: it highlights a thorough challenge to Western thought and values, and it opens up a space for the creation of a restructured world devoid of human oppression. Within this space, the novel creates a feminist utopia, "a society in the process of becoming" and thus always open to possibilities of constructive change.[13]

Before exploring the novel's construction of a feminist utopia, I will address its feminism. Indeed, its feminism is as complex as its form. Although discussions of *Woman on the Edge of Time* center almost exclusively on its feminist aspects, critics tend to overlook the type of feminism implicit in the text. I argue that the novel exhibits a tension between a liberal feminist and a more subversive feminist agenda that parallels its formal conjoining of realist and postmodern strategies. Written during the surging Women's Liberation Movement in the United States, the novel internalizes certain elements of a conventional bourgeois version of feminism (liberal feminism) at the same time as it pushes beyond them. The novel's adherence to leftist politics and to a more subversive feminism surface in the communistic aspects of Mattapoisett's social structure and in the choice of a non-romanticized working-class heroine. As an aging, man-less, poor, Chicana, Connie is an unconventional heroine for feminist fiction, even though as a madwoman she has many literary precursors—most notably Bertha in Charlotte Bronte's *Jane Eyre*. Connie's positions of marginality function to "subvert the patriarchal assumption of the hero as solitary, individualistic, isolated, contentious, and victorious."[14] However, the presence of certain liberal feminist notions in the consciousness of its working-class heroine indicates that the novel has not reconciled its leftist socioeconomic politics with its liberal feminist streak. The novel at times reads like an animated liberal feminist tract as it preaches for legislated equality between the sexes, insisting on an absolute juncture between biological and culturally imposed characteristics. One way in which Piercy's novel seeks to negate the relation between biology and women's oppression is to sever reproduction from the female body in its vision of the future world. The conservatism inherent in this stance lies in its view that imposing new laws will change social relations and result in equality. In contrast, other strands of the novel offer a more radical view, which insists that equality cannot be effected without a total change in thought and social structures. Nevertheless, the novel's at times very conventional feminism, and the didactic manner in which the narrative gives it a voice, serve a particular function and in no way negate the experimental aspects of the novel or its more subversive feminist impulses. Using the vocabulary and thought structure of liberalism in its presentation of feminism allows the novel to communicate more directly to readers steeped in the liberal tradition. At the same time, the novel disrupts its own (and subsequently readers') comfortable recognizable liberal feminism with more subversive feminist impulses that challenge and move beyond the status quo. However, the novel does not overtly conjoin its feminist politics with postmodern aesthetic strategies until it enacts Connie's psychic travel to Mattapoisett, a feminist utopia.

Nevertheless, although the novel's depiction of early 1970s America appears conservative in its dependence on social realism and liberal emphasis on legal inequalities, challenges to Western metaphysics nevertheless inform most of the scenes. *Woman on the Edge of Time* goes beyond pointing out inequalities in its incisive analysis of a society in which those in power—white, bourgeois males—remain in control through their victimization of those they regard as marginal to society, as *Other* within the limits of the classic opposition in which the self defines itself in opposition to an other. The novel's protagonist, Connie, is significantly a fourfold *Other:* she is female, Chicana, poor, and aging. In a society that has designated women to the roles of sex-object, wife, mother, and domestic servant, Connie is a failure. In its first pages, the novel presents her as man-less and child-less, and subsequent flashbacks describe how society systematically deprives her of two husbands, a lover, and a daughter. In each case Connie remains helpless, the object of powerful social forces that control the shape and direction of her life and ultimately leave her alone, poor, no longer young, and thus no longer a worthy sex-object. Not surprisingly, Connie has come to view herself as "second-class goods," as an object of little value.[15] The novel's delineation of Connie's treatment at the hand of a society that oppresses her in a variety of ways exposes and inherently challenges the workings of power relations structured within a male-centered binary logic that privileges men, white Europeans/Americans, the rich, the young and healthy. At the same time, the novel emphasizes the tangible material effects of these power relations on women's daily lives.

Since society defines her as *Other* and objectifies her, Connie is unable to escape the role of victim and the cycle of victimizations in which she is caught. Although the novel investigates sex, race, class, and age as factors determining Connie's fate, it emphasizes the role of sexual difference. It is not by chance that the main character is female or that the novel uses rape as the prevalent metaphor to describe society's violent manipulation of those it considers marginal and therefore threatening. Connie is not only sexually raped and abused by her second husband, and as a result instilled with fear—"He ... forced me" (145)—but she is raped in other physical and psychological ways. She feels the unnecessary hysterectomy performed on her as a violation, a rape that leaves her—as it previously left her mother—"no longer a woman. An empty shell" (45). The repetition of the hysterectomy image suggests that this is a raw point for Piercy and that she uses the image to capture the texture of women's hidden injuries. The novel further extends the notion of rape when Connie is due to have an electrode implanted in her skull as part of an experiment aimed at controlling behavior: the doctors "would rape her body, her brain, her self" (279). The novel indicates that an extreme manifestation of Western rational thought entails the control and even extermination of all that is considered irrational and that has traditionally been associated with women: "Suddenly she thought that these men believed feeling itself a disease, something to be cut out like a rotten appendix. Cold, calculating, ambitious, believing themselves rational and superior, they chased the crouching female animal through the brain with a scalpel. From an early age she had been told that what she felt was unreal and didn't matter. Now they were about to place in her something that would rule her feelings like a thermostat" (282). *Woman on the Edge of Time* uses the image of rape to expose the various means by which Western culture robs human beings, particularly, though not exclusively, women, against their will of some portion of themselves—be it physical and/or psychological.[16] By presenting Connie as a victim of various forms of rape, a word and a notion that carries a considerable charge, the novel engages in a penetrating exposition and scorching indictment of the violent and destructive measures that Western culture has enacted to ensure its hegemony.

The novel further exposes and criticizes Western culture's construction of categories to control and contain human beings through its analysis of gender and sexuality. Connie's fellow inmate Sybil makes it graphically clear that Western culture is to blame for constructing woman as a sexual object, as "a dumb hole people push things in or rub against" (85). Moreover, society imposes the roles of mother and domestic servant onto women by creating the housewife as the ideal for women: "an appliance on legs" batting "to and fro with two or three or four children, running the vacuum cleaner while the TV blared out game shows" (254). The novel's explicit and satiric depictions, which reduce the notion of woman to a "hole" and to an "appliance," serve to undermine conventional social roles by exposing the hidden agenda that produces them. This agenda includes subjugating women to ensure the continued hegemony of a deeply male-centered culture. Connie's culture controls her not only through an inescapable socialization process but also through specific institutions anchored in the dominant ideology and governed by those in power. She attempts but fails to escape the family, an institution that she recognizes as a powerful agent of oppression: "I'm not going to lie down and be buried in the rut of family, family, family! I'm so sick of that word, Mama! Nothing in life but having babies and cooking and keeping the house." Connie rejects her mother as a role model—"I won't grow up like you Mama! To suffer and serve. Never to live my own life! I won't!" (46)—and yet she is unable to escape the roles designated to women within her world's social structures. For instance, Connie has no choice but to quit college when she becomes pregnant and her white lover deserts her, which demonstrates how Western culture uses women's reproductive capabilities to limit and control them. Although she subsequently finds two husbands and a lover to support her economically and psychologically for short periods of time, she is ultimately left alone to eke out a living.

As bearers of children, women are expected to take charge of all mothering functions. As an uneducated single parent, however, Connie is unable to live up to her assigned role of *Mother*. After her lover Claud's death, Connie falls into a deep depression in which she "mourned him in a haggard frenzy of alcohol and downers, diving for oblivion and hoping for death" (61), until the day she strikes her daughter in frustration after Angelina kicks a hole in her shoes: "she screamed, and hit her. Hit too hard. Knocked her across the room into the door. Angie's arm struck the heavy metal bolt of the police lock, and her wrist broke. The act was past in a moment. The consequence would go on as long as she breathed" (62). The authorities not only take the child away from Connie, on the grounds of child abuse, but also institutionalize her for being a "socially disorganized individual" with "a tendency to act out problems with violent expression and hostile and extrapunitive tendencies" (377–78). In short, Connie is locked up in a mental institution for being a *bad mother,* for not living up to the romanticized ideal of motherhood—an ideal that has no link to the material situations of many women.[17] The novel implicitly exposes motherhood as an artificial role and ideal that is not only imposed onto all women who bear children but also depends on a stable nuclear family and a stable income. When Angelina kicks a hole in her shoes, Connie is overcome by the cycle of poverty and state dependence in which she is caught: "Those were the only shoes Angie had, and where in hell was Connie going to get her another pair? Angie couldn't go out without shoes. There rose before Connie the long maze of conversations with her caseworker, of explanations, of pleas and forms in triplicate and quadruplicate, and trips down to the welfare office to wait all day first in the cold and then inside in line, forever and ever for a lousy cheap pair of shoes to replace the lousy cheap pair Angie had just destroyed" (62). Piercy's novel emphasizes that, without a stable means of income or a husband-lover to support her, Connie's situation lacks essential elements on which the prevailing conception of motherhood depends; yet society expects Connie to live up to this ideal regardless of her material conditions. In this way, the novel emphasizes the artificial nature of Western ideals and norms and their incompatibility with the material situation that most human beings face. The seemingly conventional depiction of Connie's oppression thus includes a more subversive challenge to the prevailing male-centered relations of power and the binary logic that grounds them.

The psychiatric institution takes control of Connie's life once society has deemed that she is no longer successfully fulfilling her designated roles. The first time she is institutionalized, Connie accepts her society's verdict and internalizes the notion that she is mentally sick and in need of help: "she had judged herself sick, she had rolled in self-pity and self-hatred" and "She had wanted to cooperate, to grow well" (60). Connie becomes more suspicious, however, when Geraldo commits her again on the sole basis of her past record of violence and institutionalization. Men clearly occupy the positions of power in Connie's world, as evidenced by Geraldo's convincing the doctors that Connie was the aggressor in their confrontation: "Man to man, pimp and doctor discussed her condition" (19).[18] This scene particularly emphasizes the predominance of sexism over and above other forms of oppressions in Connie's case, since Chicano and white men join forces to subjugate her. No one in the hospital will believe or even listen to Connie's story. As a mental patient and a woman, she has become an object, a non-being: "She was a body checked into the morgue; meat registered for the scales," and nobody "paid attention to what she tried to say" (19–20). Connie's one act of violence against her child has unending reverberations, in that society secures its control of Connie through the negative label of madness.

Connie's victimization by the male-controlled psychiatric institution does not stop with its labelling and institutionalizing her, since she is chosen as a guinea pig for a brain control experiment. The doctors see their new technology as a positive innovation: "We can monitor and induce reactions through the microminiaturized radio under the skull. We believe through this procedure we can control Alice's [a patient] violent attacks and maintain her in a balanced mental state" (204). The patients, on the other hand, view the research strategy as an oppressive and dehumanizing means of "Control. To turn us into machines so we obey them" (200). Piercy's novel indicates that control of the mind through technological innovations is a potential means by which those in power can work to better secure their position of authority. Nonconformist actions, like Connie's striking out at her daughter and later at Dolly's pimp, are a threat to those who are in positions of power. Although incarceration and institutionalization are methods of controlling undesirable elements, the very necessity for these severe restraints points to weaknesses in the dominant ideology. Indeed, *Woman on the Edge of Time*'s blend of liberal and more subversive feminist agendas demonstrates the tangible negative impact of social forces on the multiply marginalized Connie, so as to not only expose current American society's oppression of human beings on the basis of sex, race, class, and age but also link that oppression to the perpetuation of a bourgeois, male-centered culture's hegemony.

———

However, the novel's more subversive feminism lies in its construction of a possible new and restructured future society through a (postmodern) narrative superimposition of present and future worlds. I am thus arguing that a link exists between the novel's more subversive feminism and its co-opting of postmodern strategies. By contrasting depictions of New York in the early 1970s and Mattapoisett in 2137, Piercy's novel demonstrates that differences in social and cultural structures are inextricably tied to differences in systems of thought. The future world illustrates the potential that exists once Western thought is thoroughly deconstructed and reconstructed.[19] In the space or gap between the novel's two contrasting worlds, a major metaphysical shift takes place. *Woman on the Edge of Time* depends on the processes occurring in the margins of the written novel itself, in ways similar to that of Woolf's *Between the Acts* (see Chapter 2). What lies *in between* the social, cultural, and thought structures of the present and those of the future is critical to one of the novel's primary feminist aims: to depict how a potential future world free of human oppression might come about.

By presenting a feminist utopian culture based on a non-hierarchical and non-binary system of thought, *Woman on the Edge of Time* indicates that the major problems of the present world result from elements within Western metaphysics and that a thorough questioning of the existing system of thought is a necessary first step toward the development of a world that would be better in feminist terms. Not surprisingly, Connie's first reactions to many elements of the future society she visits are negative, since her point of view is directed and limited by Western thought. She is shocked, for example, that the inhabitants of the future world do not live *with* their families and, initially, fails to understand the explanation Luciente gives her, since contemporary Western societies place emphasis on the family as a closed nuclear unit: Luciente explains that "we live *among* our family" but "we each have our own space" (72). Although the basis on which Mattapoisett's society organizes itself is foreign to Connie's mode of thought, she slowly recognizes that massive changes in thought and social structures are necessary to arrive at a better world free of the oppression under which she has suffered. Connie's eventual wish that her daughter could grow up in Mattapoisett, so that she would "never be broken as I was" and would "walk in strength like a man and never sell her body" (141), indicates that she has accepted and embraced this new and different world. The character Connie functions as a locus for bringing together the two different modes of thought and social structures and contrasting their effects on human life.

Although the depiction of Mattapoisett indicates that a thorough disruption of hierarchical binary oppositions takes place in between the present and future worlds, the process of deconstruction remains outside the written novel. However, the narrative highlights this (absent/invisible) process through its contrasting of the two worlds. In the first meeting between Connie and Luciente, for instance, Connie thinks that Luciente is a homosexual man, a judgment that she bases on her equation of men and authority and on her observation of a mixture of masculine and feminine gender traits in Luciente: "he was girlish" and "He moved with grace but also with authority" (40–41). Connie is dumbfounded when she recognizes that Luciente is female and that using conventional gender stereotypes to determine sex fails in Luciente's case: "Luciente spoke, she moved with that air of brisk unselfconscious authority Connie associated with men. Luciente sat down, taking up more space than women ever did. She squatted, she sprawled, she strolled, never thinking about how her body was displayed" (67). Luciente incarnates the destabilization of the traditional hierarchical oppositions between man and woman, masculine and feminine, male and female: "Luciente's face and voice and body now seemed female if not at all feminine; too confident, too unselfconscious, too aggressive and sure and graceful in the wrong kind of totally coordinated way to be a woman: yet a woman" (99). Although biologically female, Luciente possesses a combination of traits that Western culture has divided up and labeled as either feminine or masculine. The division is strategic in that all characteristics linked to power and authority are designated as masculine, and therefore reinforce male-dominated relations of power. Indeed, Piercy's novel disrupts this artificial binary logic, by exposing established notions of womanhood as constructions imposed upon females to ensure male authority and dominance: Luciente is female and yet possesses authority and confidence. However, the novel does not present inhabitants of the future world as androgynous beings, as some critics have suggested.[20] The novel depicts no fusion between the sexes in the future; instead, gender traits and biological sex are disassociated from each other. Luciente is a product of a society that encourages all persons to the outward show of emotion—"Touching and caressing, hugging and fingering" (76) and "weeping openly" (74)—and at the same time allows each individual to carry an equal amount of authority and self-respect. The utopia no longer associates emotions exclusively with females and authority with males. In Mattapoisett, individuals of both sexes can potentially possess any trait or characteristic, which helps to make possible a society devoid of hierarchies. Male, masculine, man no longer exist in hierarchical opposition to female, feminine, woman; binary logic no longer structures relations between the sexes.

Mattapoisett's language promotes and reflects this absence of hierarchy and opposition by being de-gendered. The noun "person" replaces all the traditional personal pronouns and "per" replaces the possessive pronouns. These changes in language call attention to the inherent biases of language used in the 1970s world, biases that serve to uphold various cultural or social structures. Moreover, Mattapoisett's new system of language points to the instability of language and its potential as a vehicle of sociocultural change.[21] The novel's approach to the issue of language pushes toward the post-modern notion of language as an unstable system in which meaning is forever sliding and slipping and of language as constitutive of subjectivity and social structures. Furthermore, the world of Mattapoisett dilutes the power of language to name and contain things, by allowing each person only one arbitrary and changeable proper name. The Western patriarchal convention of imposing the father's name on mother and children, which is also a means of structuring social and familial ties, has been eradicated. Individuals are free to change their name as often as they like once they go through their initiation rite of self-discovery, a "naming" that signals the "end-of mothering" (114).[22] Since names are no longer imposed or static, they cannot be used to structure social ties or fix individuals. This change in naming patterns is one of the ways in which Mattapoisett ensures equality between individuals.

Although the novel's construction of a utopia that depends on a thorough destabilization of Western metaphysics is the site of a conjoining of subversive feminist and postmodern impulses, traces of liberal feminism and of social realism remain. As I briefly mentioned earlier, Piercy insists on introducing a physical change in the workings of reproduction to help account for the restructured family and the resulting equality between the sexes in Mattapoisett. Rather than base change solely on the disappearance of the hierarchical opposition between women and men, Piercy seeks in a typically liberal feminist move to legislate equality through the removal of biological reproduction as a means of oppression. In the future world, babies are conceived and developed in a "brooder" where "genetic material is stored" and "the embryos grow" (101), so that reproduction is totally disconnected from the female body. Reproduction and sexuality are divorced from each other, allowing for more open sexual relations—even children are allowed to experiment with sex. In vitro conception also makes possible the use of a wide gene pool that ensures diversity and nullifies racism: "we [the future society] broke the bond between genes and culture, broke it forever. We want there to be no chance of racism again." Brooder reproduction replaces the concept of blood ties or "genetic bond" (104) between persons with community ties. While the novel's focus on in vitro reproduction suggests that the resulting lack of blood ties enables the mothering function to be disassociated from women's work, the novel's more subversive impulses indicate that it is possible to do away with the Western notion of motherhood by simply disrupting the metaphysical equation of mother and female and the opposition between father and mother.

In fact, the persistence of the term *mothering* in the future world attests to the conventional streak in the novel's otherwise more subversive feminism. After all, if pronouns have been de-gendered, then why not replace the ideologically loaded term *mother* with a new, gender-neutral term? In Mattapoisett, each infant is assigned three co-mothers, male and female, who care for the child until the initiation period at about twelve years of age. Hormonal technology even allows both sexes to breast-feed the babies, a notion that horrifies and angers Connie: "Yes, how dare any man share that pleasure. These women thought they had won, but they had abandoned to men the last refuge of women. What was special about being a woman here? They had given it all up, they had let men steal from them the last remnants of ancient power, those sealed in blood and in milk" (134). Connie feels that men do not have the "natural right" (135) to breast-feed and mother the babies. This emotional rejection of men as mothers is grounded in an essentialism, grounded in Western binarism, that the novel rejects since it ignores the egalitarian potential of such major changes in family structure. Nevertheless, through Luciente's voice, the novel falls into a conventional liberal feminism as she preaches that legislated changes in reproduction and mothering are a necessary step toward equality of all human beings. Moreover, the didacticism of these sections recalls social realism.

However, Luciente's discussions also make the more radical claim that these changes result from a massive destabilization of Western binary thought aimed at ridding society of oppression: "It was part of women's long revolution. When we were breaking all the old hierarchies. Finally there was that one thing we had to give up too, the only power we ever had, in return for no more power for anyone. The original production: the power to give birth. Cause as long as we were biologically enchained, we'd never be equal. And males never would be humanized to be loving and tender. So we all became mothers. Every child has three. To break the nuclear bonding" (105). The novel borrows this analysis of the role of reproduction in the oppression of women from Shulamith Firestone's ground-breaking but solidly liberal feminist *The Dialectic of Sex* (1970). Firestone argues that ending "The tyranny of the biological family" and the oppression of women requires "the seizure of control of reproduction" by women; she calls for the introduction of "artificial reproduction," so that "children would be born to both sexes equally, or independently of either."[23] *Woman on the Edge of Time* illustrates this liberal feminist solution by depicting a society in which in vitro reproduction is the norm and in which the notion of motherhood has been de-gendered (even if the term remains) and severed from blood ties. What is more radical, however, is that the word and concept *mother* has no opposite in the future world: the term *father* no longer exists.

Without the figure of the father, the patriarchal and nuclear family dissolves and authority is dispersed. On one level, then, artificial reproduction functions to reinforce the more general challenge to hierarchical oppositions that takes place in the margins of the novel. The new term *co-mother* denotes the space in which a process of infinite difference and deferral is unfolding as a result of the novel's disruption of the conventional opposition between father and mother.

By undermining the rigid dichotomy between man and woman and between father and mother, the novel wrenches the male from his traditional position of authority and dominance. A space for equality opens up once binarism no longer grounds social and thought structures. All human beings are on equal footing in Mattapoisett, performing productive and equally valued tasks within the non-hierarchical community, regardless of sex, race, or age. Class is not an issue, since the socioeconomic structure is one of small communal living with no ownership of private property. Connie is disappointed upon her first visit to find a world devoid of the "skyscrapers" and "spaceports" (68) that science fiction predicted; instead, she faces a future that has gone "Forward, into the past" (70). Small villages that emphasize the community rather than the individual have replaced cities. Although she later learns how the future society uses various technological advances, these changes aim to improve the quality of life and of the earth rather than to produce wealth or luxuries. Manufacturing and mining are automated, for example, because "Who wants to go deep into the earth and crawl through tunnels breathing rock dust and never seeing the sun? Who wants to sit in a factory sewing the same four or five comforter patterns?" (130). The greatest changes, however, concern social structures: Luciente refers to Mattapoisett as a "more evolved society" (125). Its social fabric is based on "social faith" (183) and is organized so that all persons share property, wealth, work, responsibilities, children, friends, and lovers. Mattapoisett's social structure has dissolved specific positions of authority and aims for complete equality between its citizens. All persons share authority equally, and there exists no ultimate or final authority. Even the government is a totally democratic one, in which all citizens have a voice and the power of veto. Although rotating representatives chosen by lot sit in at town and council meetings, "if it's a major proj—such as research on prolonging life would be—then everybody decides" (277), since it would affect each individual.

Without a locus of authority, the future society cannot and does not impose roles upon individuals. Each citizen is free to choose a variety of occupations and roles with no emphasis on priorities. Luciente is a plant geneticist, a "sender" to connect with Connie's world, a co-mother, a lover, a drummer; and all of these roles have value. The future subject is a composite of distinct non-gendered and non-hierarchical roles that has broken with the humanist concept of the privileged whole centered subject grounded in an opposition between subject and object. Moreover, the subject is always in process, as their taking up and giving up of names imply. In a society where all human beings are on equal footing, there are no subject and object or self and other positions per se; rather, persons occupy both and neither positions in an infinite play of difference and deferral. The communal aspect of life in Mattapoisett also works to undermine the conventional dichotomy between self and world. Luciente's claim that in Mattapoisett individuals live *"among"* rather than "with" their families suggests that there is no stringent demarcation between self and world or self and others (72). These classic hierarchical oppositions have undergone deconstruction in the margins of the novel, in between the present and future worlds; and Mattapoisett serves as evidence of the reconstructive possibilities that such a deconstructive process opens up.

Woman on the Edge of Time utilizes the depictions of two different societies both to reveal the problems within existing society and their ties to Western binarism and to delineate a potential future society, in which a non-binary thought system and non-hierarchical social structures have been erected. But, to reinforce its position, the novel dedicates one chapter to a depiction of another alternate future that is clearly a dystopia in feminist terms.[24] This other future world coexists temporally with Mattapoisett, so that the two possibilities for the future compete with each other. The emphasis in this alternate version of the future is on technological advances that increasingly benefit those in power rather than on quality of life for all persons. Ecology has no place in this plastic world of surfaces and appearances, in which buildings need no windows since the "air's too thick" (291) even to see through. No deconstruction of Western social structures has occurred; rather, culture has taken these structures to their extremes so that the rich are richer and more powerful, the poor are poorer and less powerful, and men have more authority and control over women than ever. The "Rockemellons, the Morganfords, the Duke-Ponts" (297), the same men who control Connie's 1970s world, have now acquired the technology to achieve immortality. The poor, or "duds," are "diseased" and are little more than "walking organ banks," who "live like animals out where it [the air] isn't conditioned" (291). Descendents of present multinational corporations, "multis own everybody" (300); the multis control and contain human beings by transforming them physically to better fulfill their assigned roles.

This future society has totally reduced women to objects for sex or for reproduction, exaggerating and reinforcing the traditional designation of women as either prostitutes or mothers. The woman Connie meets in this strange other future, Gildina, is a mid-level being, whose life is spent locked up in a windowless room. Her only visitor is the man who has contracted her out for sex: "Contract sex. It means you agree to put out for so long for so much" (289). Gildina's life consists of sampling the various drugs available in her "automated pill dispenser," watching pornographic videos on her "Sense-all" (292), and providing sex for her contractor. Physically, Gildina "seemed a cartoon of femininity, with a tiny waist, enormous sharp breasts that stuck out like the brassieres Connie herself had worn in the fifties—but the woman was not wearing a brassiere. Her stomach was flat but her hips and buttocks were oversized and audaciously curved. She looked as if she could hardly walk for the extravagance of her breasts and buttocks, her thighs that collided as she shuffled a few steps" (288). Piercy's novel demonstrates the destructive potential of Western notions of womanhood by depicting a society that takes such notions to their logical extremes. This future world so completely objectifies women as commodities that they can be made to order; women's bodies are artificially reconstructed to meet a male-centered society's absurd standards of femininity and feminine sexual appeal. While men have retained their positions of authority, they have also been reduced to automatons: their physical power has been increased artificially through genetic engineering, and their brains have been implanted with "superneurotransmitters." A central authority monitors and controls all persons through hidden microphones and, if need be, through "the electrical impulses in your brain" (298). The novel utilizes the sharp contrast between this negative version of the future and the positive depiction of Mattapoisett to support its claim that equality between human beings and a higher quality of life cannot be achieved without a major restructuring of existing thought and society.

But the introduction of this second possible version of the future serves another important function besides reinforcing the novel's feminist themes: it further disrupts the conventional oppositions between presence and absence and between reality and fiction. Piercy's novel does not merely present and contrast a good and a bad future society but, rather, underscores the multiplicity of possible futures, of which Mattapoisett is only one. Luciente makes it quite clear that her world exists only in potential and, as such, is not inevitable: "Those of your time who fought hard for change, often they had myths that a revolution was inevitable. But nothing is! All things interlock. We are only one possible future" and "Yours is a crux-time. Alternate universes co-exist. Probabilities clash and possibilities wink out forever" (177). By introducing indeterminacy into its narrative, the novel challenges Western culture's very concept of *Being*. Furthermore, the indeterminate nature of the future worlds affects notions of the past: Luciente argues that "the past is a disputed area" and that her world will prevail only "if history is not reversed" (267).[25] Although it presents a feminist utopia, the novel does not fall into a naively optimistic determinism. The feminist utopia of Mattapoisett is only one possibility, depending on the direction in which human beings move, as the negative future world makes clear. The novel implicitly calls for engaged political action directed toward the kind of society that Mattapoisett illustrates, and thus toward massive deconstructive and reconstructive processes.

If Luciente's and Gildina's worlds exist in the sense that Connie can visit and describe them and yet are only possible future worlds, then these futures simultaneously exist and do not exist, are present and yet absent. The novel's presentation of alternate future worlds challenges the Western concept of *Being* that is grounded in the opposition between presence and absence. Moreover, the destabilization of the status of *Being* of the future worlds also inherently calls into question the ontological status of the present world. Since the novel dedicates as much space to the depiction of Luciente's world as to Connie's world, and since Connie is alternately present in each world as a subjective observer, both of these worlds possess the same ontological status. The contemporary world is just as absent when Connie is visiting the future world as the future world is absent when Connie is in the contemporary world. To complicate matters, Connie is both or neither present and absent in both worlds when she visits the future. Connie's time-travelling is psychic, so that her body remains in the contemporary world in an unconscious state. It is her mind that reaches out to and connects with Luciente and vice-versa: Luciente explains that "As in dreams. You experience *through* me" but "you are not really here" (78–79). Likewise, when Luciente visits the world of the 1970s, she is "not here" but rather is "in contact" (53) with the 1970s world through Connie. Luciente is corporally visible and present to Connie—even leaving her chair warm after disappearing—and yet Luciente is also absent in a biological or physical sense. The same is true of Connie when she visits the future; for example, Connie can eat in the future, but the food does not actually nourish or sustain her. Piercy's novel gives equal ontological status to all worlds and persons based on sensory material experience: Connie and Luciente experience each other and each other's worlds and, on that basis, the novel grants both characters and worlds equal ontological status. Through its overt disruption of the conventional distinction between presence and absence, the novel is able to posit temporally disjointed worlds simultaneously and to depict their intersection through characters who possess strong psychic capabilities. Consequently, the novel provides a sharp contrast between radically disparate worlds that highlights the need for an engaged activist feminist politics.

Woman on the Edge of Time not only challenges the dichotomy between presence and absence through its superimposition of discrete worlds but also undermines the notion that there is one *Reality* or world. Instead, the novel insists on the plural nature of realities or worlds by severing the sharp distinction between reality and fiction. If Luciente's and Gildina's worlds are only potential future worlds, then what reality status can they have? Although it is arguable that the future worlds are figments of Connie's and/or Piercy's imagination, the novel in fact repudiates such readings by calling into question the opposition between reality and fiction and thereby problematizing these very notions. Indeed, since the novel presents all the various worlds from Connie's perspective, the depiction of 1970s American society is no less fictional and no more real than the presentation of the future worlds. Similarly, the views of the past held by the inhabitants of Mattapoisett often appear inaccurate, confused, and exaggerated as they tend to fuse together various discrete historical moments. Since the real and the fictional cannot be untangled, however, these terms lose their distinct meanings, as Luciente's blending of temporally disjointed historical figures and events demonstrates: "the feast of July nineteenth, date of Seneca Equal Rights Convention, beginning women's movement. Myself, I play Harriet Tubman. I say a great speech—Ain't I a woman?—that I give just before I lead the slaves to revolt and sack the Pentagon, a large machine producing radiation on the Potomac—a military industrial machine?" (173). By destabilizing notions of the past, present, and future as stable determinate entities, the novel exposes the neat distinction between reality and fiction as untenable. The novel does not collapse reality and fiction but rather demonstrates how they interact in a continuing process of difference and deferral that breaks down all notions of hierarchy and of binary opposition. Since the novel contains supporting evidence for both interpretations of Luciente and her world as real and as fictional, the status of the future world remains indeterminate. Ultimately the very categories *reality* and *fiction* are meaningless to the workings of the novel, for Luciente's world remains in either case a feminist utopia that contrasts sharply with the depiction of New York in the 1970s and that serves to validate the need for a restructuring of existing thought and society.[26]

The novel's destabilization of the dichotomy between reality and fiction is also at work in its treatment of perspective. The last chapter is a facsimile of "Excerpts from the Official History of Consuelo Camacho Ramos" (377), as reported by the various psychiatric institutions in which she is placed. These excerpts present society's version of Connie's life. The official records reduce Connie and her life to five pages of cold, detached, seemingly factual observations or, rather, judgments; in these pages, Connie is a case rather than a human being. Since 376 pages written from Connie's perspective precede this final chapter, however, a wealth of information—even if biased—about Connie, her life, and her society exists with which to compare and judge the clinical evaluation of Connie.[27]

Indeed, the content of the reports strongly reinforces the novel's insistence on the oppressive control wielded by those in power through various social institutions. Since the novel has presented Connie as a victim of an oppressive society, and since its final chapter is written from the perspective and inherent bias of those in power, the last chapter stands as already obviously fictional or false. The novel as a whole belies the clinical reports that distort Connie's life and reactions with biased assumptions and interpretations and that cloak arbitrary judgments with factual language. Under the intimidating and seemingly objective heading "MENTAL STATUS," for example, one section of the report describes Connie in purely subjective terms, with a list of details that are irrelevant to the stated topic: "MENTAL STATUS: This patient is disheveled and appears to be older than her stated age. She readily admits needing help. She is cooperative but confused and occasionally suspicious. Has not demonstrated assaultive behavior on the ward" (378). None of these points substantiate her status as mad and violent; rather they focus on her external physical appearance and deny any violence or lack of control. The novel presents the official version of Connie's life as no more true or real than Connie's version of her own life, so that the dichotomies between reality and fiction and between truth and falseness lose relevance.

Through its rejection of a true or real version of Connie's life, the novel also challenges the opposition between sanity and insanity that Connie's world uses to judge and control her. The overt unreliability of the official reports casts doubts on the institutional labeling of Connie as *mad* and confirms the novel's presentation of Connie as perfectly well aware of what is going on around her. From Connie's perspective, it is the doctors who are *mad* as they pursue technological means of controlling human beings; and the novel clearly sides with her point of view. Like Lessing's *The Golden Notebook,* Piercy's novel destabilizes the opposition between sanity and insanity. *Woman on the Edge of Time* presents sanity and insanity as artificial labels that vary from one culture to another and are not fixed. In the 1970s world, certain forms of madness are associated with behavior that threatens Western sociocultural norms: Connie's striking of a man, even if he is her niece's violent pimp; Skip's homosexuality and self-destructive impulses; Sybil's belief that she is a witch and can heal with herbs.[28] In contrast, Luciente's future world accepts madness as a potentially positive or renewing experience that has no association with illness or with shame: "We do not use these words ["Sick. Mad."] to mean the same thing." Madhouses in Mattapoisett are places to which people voluntarily retreat: "Our madhouses are places where people retreat when they want to go down into themselves—to collapse, carry on, see visions, hear voices of prophecy, bang on the walls, relive infancy—getting in touch with the buried self and the inner mind" (65–66). Madness is not a negative term in the future world. The notion of madness as a place of self-examination and of retreat from the world is also taken up by Lessing in *The Golden Notebook* and even more so in *The Four-Gated City* (1969).

The two very different notions of madness that Connie's and Luciente's worlds exhibit emphasize that the conventional Western view of sanity and madness as distinct and opposed concepts is culturally constructed and that any clear demarcation between the two terms is necessarily unstable. From the perspective of Mattapoisett's inhabitants, Connie is not mad: Luciente tells Connie, "in truth you don't seem mad to me"; "you seem too coherent" (65). That Connie is considered mad by the standards of her society and sane by those of Luciente's society reinforces the notion that these terms are far from stable, since their meanings can undergo shifts to the extent that they overlap. This is not to say that the novel collapses these terms or reverses the opposition. Rather, Piercy's novel points out that the negative label *madness* set in opposition to the positive *sanity* is an artificial relation used to ensure the hegemony of existing society. The novel's disruption of the opposition between sanity and madness serves as a strategic means of opening up a space for creating a new restructured society not grounded in such binary oppositions that result in human oppression.

Indeed, Connie seems to grow more sane from the reader's perspective as the novel progresses, not because she submits to treatment and is cured but rather because she becomes more aware of her situation and begins to act in her own behalf. The novel moves from a depiction of Connie as a subdued helpless victim to a depiction of Connie as a rebel against the society that oppresses her and so many others. As Connie asserts near the end of the novel, "For me this is war. I got to fight it the only way I see. To stop them" (366). The novel's penultimate chapter, the last chapter written from Connie's perspective, ends with her "act of war" (376): she lethally poisons four doctors and achieves her immediate aim of

bringing the electrode brain implant experiment to a halt. She justifies her actions by arguing that, since power equals violence in the
existing world, violence is the only means of challenging and affect-
ing those in power: "I murdered them dead. Because *they* are the
violence-prone. Theirs is the money and the power, theirs the poisons that slow the mind and dull the heart. Theirs are the powers of
life and death. I killed them. Because it is war" (375). Connie's act of
violence is in effect a violent narrative ending, since it cuts off
Connie's story and is not an end to the novel in any physical sense:
Connie's life apparently continues for a good many years, and the
novel does not close for another chapter. Moreover, the clinical
summary only briefly refers to Connie's act as an "incident" and
leaves unclear the effects of her act. All that is clear from the end of
the novel is that Connie remains institutionalized for years: "There
were one hundred thirteen more pages. They all followed Connie
back to Rockover" State Psychiatric Hospital (381).

The novel's use of Connie's violent act as an ending to her own
story-history has in fact elicited controversy among feminist critics.
Rachel Blau DuPlessis argues that the ending is problematic in that
there is no "evidence that others see and understand her message,
so that there are political consequences for her act."[29] On the surface, this argument is valid, but it seems to neglect the fact that this
is a literary text and that it does have an audience. The readers of
Woman on the Edge of Time do "understand" the message behind
Connie's act of war, since the book as a whole has prepared them for
it. Rather than judge Connie's act within the traditional moral categories of good or evil, the novel explains the act through its critical
depiction of Connie's society and through its positing of alternate
potential future worlds. The novel presents Connie's act as the only
means she has of fighting for the version of the future exemplified
by Luciente's world, a world that has been restructured to fulfill
feminist aims. Connie's act, then, does have political consequences,
but on the level of the novel's readership rather than within the
story itself. The ending serves not to advocate violence but rather to
reinforce the novel's insistence that an equitable and violence-free
society will not come into existence until a major questioning and
restructuring of Western thought and society has taken place. The
ending thus functions as a call for action aimed at the readers.[30]
Indeed, the abrupt shift from Connie's perspective to the excerpts
from official psychiatric records serves as a politically motivated dis-

ruption that re-emphasizes the oppressive nature of existing societal structures and encourages readers to criticize and even condemn the institutional version of Connie's story, which violently silences and objectifies her.

Narrative disruptions in fact structure the novel, which at first glance appears to uphold traditional narrative conventions. Although conventional narrative does not have to present a story chronologically, it still conceives of time as a linear and absolute dimension; two distinct moments in time cannot occupy the same space in the traditional model. Much of *Woman on the Edge of Time* recounts Connie's story using a standard linear narrative form. The story moves forward chronologically and occasionally jumps backwards in time, using flashbacks to fill in relevant gaps in Connie's personal history. However, the shifts between the present and the future disrupt the narrative by superimposing moments in time and destabilizing its temporal grounding. Connie's 1970s world coexists spatially with Luciente's 2137 world within the narrative, so that time becomes a flexible, non-linear dimension.[31] As the novel progresses, the shifts between the two temporally discrete worlds become more and more frequent, so that the present and future begin to intertwine. Furthermore, since Connie appears to exist in both time periods, temporal distinctions become irrelevant. The narrative's use of these temporal disruptions, typical of postmodern fiction, to structure the novel serves both to challenge traditional conceptions of time and narrative and to achieve a more vivid contrast, from a feminist perspective, between the worlds it presents.

Through its simultaneous use and disruption of conventional narrative, Piercy's novel exemplifies the new type of art it attributes to the world of Mattapoisett. In Luciente's world, "art *is* production" (267)—it has a use value—and its interest in "Boundaries dissolving" (265) indicates a political dimension. For instance, the "holi" (hologram) Jackrabbit shows Connie presents power as "energy" rather than as "power over people" (265) and, as such, both deconstructs established conceptions of power and reconstructs a new notion of power that is not dependent on oppressive relations of power. In a similar vein, *Woman on the Edge of Time* produces a critical reading of contemporary society from a feminist perspective and posits choices for the future. Its feminist utopia rests on a thorough deconstruction of traditional humanist concepts and of the boundaries erected to create the hierarchical binary oppositions that structure Western thought and society. Although this deconstructive process takes place in the margins of the novel, in between the depictions of the present and the future worlds, the novel highlights its necessity as a precondition to constructing a new non-hierarchical social order. Moreover, Piercy's novel presents itself as functional, as having a use value in its overt call for engaged political action, which assumes "the power of the word to move an audience to action."[32]

Through its transgression of established temporal boundaries, its creation of ontologically indeterminate alternative worlds, its emphasis on what lies in the margins of the text, and its general destabilization of Western binary logic, *Woman on the Edge of Time* acknowledges the need for deconstructing established paradigms while focusing on the subsequent reconstructive processes through its delineation of a blueprint for a feminist utopia. Indeed, disruptive postmodern strategies propel forward the novel's more subversive feminist aims.[33] The novel achieves a sharper contrast and a more incisive feminist critique by superimposing temporally disjointed worlds and allowing its protagonist, Connie, to experience both present and future worlds and to choose to fight for one particular future. At the same time, however, the novel's social realism, which surfaces in its many detailed descriptions of daily existence, keeps the narrative focused on the oppressive conditions that structure Connie's life and identity in the present world and on the material changes that potential disruptions of male-centered relations of power enable in Mattapoisett. Likewise, the novel's at times liberal feminist streak functions to anchor the narrative in the concrete inequalities within Western institutions that daily enact physical and psychic violence upon human beings. I thus argue that, while the novel's liberal feminism and social realism function to highlight how material conditions affect human relations and existence on a concrete level, its more subversive feminism co-opts postmodern strategies to expose the link between Western metaphysics and oppressive relations of power and to propose a potential feminist utopia constructed in the space cleared by a thorough deconstruction of Western thought and societal structures.

5. THE GAP BETWEEN OFFICIAL HISTORY AND WOMEN'S HISTORIES: MARGARET ATWOOD'S *THE HANDMAID'S TALE*

Although Margaret Atwood's *The Handmaid's Tale* (1985) fits into the category of "speculative fiction," it differs sharply from Piercy's *Woman on the Edge of Time,* in that Atwood chooses to depict a feminist dystopia rather than a utopia as a means of criticizing from a feminist perspective the conservative and even reactionary American politics and culture endemic to the 1980s.[1] Moreover, the proximity of Atwood's dystopia, set in the 1990s, eliminates any sense of temporal displacement and effectively prevents the "suspension of disbelief" that most works of speculative fiction require. This effect of the temporal setting may account for the large number of reviewers who questioned the "plausibility" of the world that the novel depicts—an unusual criticism to level at a work of speculative fiction.[2] Charges of implausibility stem from a refusal by some critics to acknowledge not only the possibility of such an abrupt change of regime but also the potency of reactionary elements present within American culture in the early 1980s.[3] The novel in many ways warns its contemporary readers of the potential backlashes to which late twentieth-century Western cultures are susceptible, given that reforms have occurred primarily through the legal system (and thus are always open to reconsideration) and have had little effect on Western male-centered modes of thought. More specifically, Atwood's novel engages in social critique by demonstrating the ways in which sweeping changes in modes of thought have not accompanied or resulted from women's recently won civil rights, making legal reversals not only possible but even probable given the conservative climate of the United States in the 1980s. By creating a lack of distance between the two societies that "The Handmaid's Tale" section presents, the novel disrupts the conventional demarcation between reality and fiction, between

1980s America and 1990s Gilead, thereby forcing readers to recognize seeds of the dystopian Gilead in 1980s American culture. Moreover, the novel's final framing chapter depicts a post-Gileadean society in the year 2195 that has such close affinities to 1980s America as to again disrupt temporal boundaries as well any clear distinction between reality and fiction, strategies that critics attribute to postmodern fiction. In contrast to Piercy's *Woman on the Edge of Time,* Atwood's novel superimposes temporally discrete worlds by emphasizing their underlying similarities rather than through characters' psychic time travel. However, like Piercy's novel, *The Handmaid's Tale*'s narrative disruptions function to further its social critique by highlighting the sexism that underlies established Western modes of thought and by demonstrating the impossibility of radical change in feminist terms without concurrent metaphysical shifts.

Although Atwood's narrative is conventional in form, combining social realism and stream-of-consciousness, the framing chapter undermines the very groundings of these forms through its thorough assault on Western metaphysics and the binary logic on which it depends. The novel begins with a lengthy first-person narrative set in the 1990s, followed by a short final chapter labeled "Historical Notes on 'The Handmaid's Tale.'" Set about two hundred years after the first section, at an "International Historical Association Convention," the "Historical Notes" section takes as its subject the longer piece that precedes it, so that *The Handmaid's Tale* is overtly self-reflexive, metafictional.[4] As in the case of *Woman on the Edge of Time's* final chapter, Atwood's last segment is a commentary on the narrative that makes up the majority of the novel, from the point of view of a male-centered culture that is grounded in the very Western metaphysics that the novel calls into question. The "Historical Notes" section is more complicated than Piercy's last chapter, however, in that it draws the reader into complicity with its surface liberal stance. Indeed, many critics have asserted that the world it presents is a positive one. Although the world of 2195 is clearly more open and less dystopian than the world of Gilead, the novel indicates that the seeds of Gilead's culture are present in this future world just as they are in 1980s America. More specifically, the novel's last chapter sharply delineates the means by which Western cultures have ensured their dominance through an erasure of women's voices and stories-histories. Although the "Historical Notes" section offers the most sustained challenge to the status quo, and is therefore crucial to the novel's feminist agenda, the narrator's tale that makes up most of the novel also engages in disruptions that in many ways prepare the reader for the novel's final metafictional twist and critique of Western metaphysics.[5] "The Handmaid's Tale" section addresses the problem of defining a female subject in a world in which set roles are imposed on women and in which social structures are inherently inequitable. The self-conscious first-person narrator, Offred, yearns for, but cannot grasp, a stable identity. The narrative demonstrates not only that centered fixed identity is a fiction but also that subjectivity is inextricably linked to relations of power that assert themselves in all aspects of existence and that cannot be reduced to neat divisions of victimizer and victim: victimizers are often also victims, and victims are often complicit in the systems that ensure their status as victims. Indeed, the novel subtly indicates the instability of all relations of power and thus the possibilities for transformation inherent in all systems. The novel explores in particular the relationship between subjectivity and power within the realms of sexuality, desire, and language. Moreover, like the novel as a whole, Offred herself addresses the problems of representation as she attempts to tell her story-history and recognizes that no representation can escape fictionalization. Both of the novel's sections ultimately challenge Western transcendent notions of reality, truth, and history as male-centered concepts that inevitably lead to inequitable material conditions. The novel is not solely deconstructive, however, since its challenges to Western metaphysics open the way for a multiplicity of histories and realities that are neither male-centered nor fixed. Indeed, as I will argue, Atwood's novel manages to offer traces of Offred's story-history and her material existence, even though all the texts that make up the physical novel are ultimately male-centered.

———————

"The Handmaid's Tale" section depicts the Republic of Gilead in the late twentieth century, shortly after a coup permits a group similar to the Moral Majority to assume power and to impose its preferred social and cultural system onto what had been the United

States. The new rulers replace the American Constitution with a rigid adherence to patriarchal principles found in the Bible, particularly in Genesis, and deprive women of personal wealth, education, and civil rights. Although on the surface Gilead appears foreign, the novel highlights the ways in which its social structure and material conditions merely *exaggerate* the situation within 1980s America.[6] Atwood's novel criticizes existing conditions in Western cultures by way of Gilead's horrifying regime. For instance, Gilead values women primarily for their childbearing potential not only because of Biblical precedent but also as a means of countering the decrease in childbirth brought on by various disastrous wars, diseases, and ecological problems. Male-centered Western culture here responds to disasters of its own making with reactionary male-centered responses. Although Offred compares her negative life as a handmaid to her more positive life before the inception of Gilead, the novel (and even Offred at times) clearly rejects such an oversimplified dichotomy. Instead, the narrative forces the reader to recognize and criticize the similarities at the bases of both cultures. While the novel does not collapse the two societies, it nevertheless disallows any easy association of Gilead with fiction in contradistinction to the *real* world. As an exaggeration of existing relations of power, Gilead has truth value at the same time as it exists as a fiction. Indeed, to a certain degree, Gilead contains 1980s American culture. Atwood's narrative strategy disrupts conventional boundaries as a way of exploring the means by which male-centered cultures ensure their own hegemony.

As a military theocracy, Gilead features an extremely hierarchical social structure, with men in power over women and with set classes of men and women controlling other classes of men and women respectively. However, the novel insists that the change in social structure is one of degree but certainly not of kind. Indeed, Gilead's extreme categorization of its human population highlights the oppressive potential of establishing fixed boundaries according to a binary logic that necessarily engages in constructing hierarchical oppositions and in effacing that which does not fit neatly within the boundaries. In Gilead, the Commanders occupy the top positions of power and oversee the three military divisions, made up of men distinguished by the color of their uniforms: the Eyes, the secret police force, wear black with a gold eye; the Angels of the

Apocalypse, the state's military force, wear plain black; and the Guardians of the Faith, a local force "used for routine policing and other menial functions" (27), wear green. A certain degree of mobility exists within these three divisions, so that Guardians are usually young men who then move up to the position of Angel and, even sometimes, of Eye. The system rewards men who adhere to its principles.[7] However, these categories apply only to Anglo-Saxon men; men and women of other races or ethnicities are banished to the colonies (where they die) or simply killed. As with its differentiation of classes of men, Gilead marks the categories that distinguish women by the specific color of their clothing (full-length gowns): Wives, women married to the members of Gilead's ruling class, wear blue; Handmaids, unmarried fertile women appointed to ruling class homes for the purpose of procreation, wear red; Aunts, older unmarried and infertile staunch reactionary women who train the handmaids in military fashion for their functions, wear brown; Marthas, lower-class unmarried and infertile women designated as servants, wear green; Econowives, lower-class married women who have to perform the functions of wives, handmaids, and servants, wear striped blue, red, and green; and Unwomen, infertile and/or uncooperating women, such as feminists and lesbians, are banished to the colonies, where they clean up toxic waste until they die. Unlike men, however, women can aspire to no mobility, except down to the category of Unwoman and thus death. Otherwise, they remain in fixed positions and have few options except cooperation.[8] Gilead's overt positioning of women as inferior to men, regardless of class, parallels the less overt ways in which 1980s American society sets glass ceilings that women only rarely smash, while men of no greater accomplishments still dominate positions of power. In addition, however much Gilead's fixed categories of women appear harsh and rigid, the novel subtly indicates that they are only exaggerated versions of the classes of women that exist in contemporary American society. The only new official class of women in Gilead is that of the Handmaids; however, the developing arena of surrogate motherhood, and the battles between women it has engendered, indicates that even this supposedly *new* class of women parallels an existing subsection of contemporary American society.

　　Not only does the sphere of men dominate over that of women, but women have little real power within their own realm.[9] Gilead divides men and women into separate and unequal spheres, a function of the hierarchical nature of binary logic. Although Gilead has a women's culture, it is one that men in positions of power have structured for the purposes of inducing an increase in the birth rate and of limiting women to the domestic arena. Moreover, the system ensures that women will not unite to secure changes, by pitting the categories of women against each other. Wives are "defeated women," since they have been "unable" (62) to bear children in a culture that views reproduction as the primary function of women. They are understandably jealous and resentful of the handmaids assigned to their households, whom they view as "Little whores, all of them" (147). The handmaids in turn envy the wives their husbands and children, since a handmaid is shipped out of a household after she gives birth. The Marthas, as servants, envy both the wives and handmaids for their privileged positions. Although the Gileadean households are technically women's spheres, the narrator reflects that it is not the kind of women's culture that her mother fought for as a feminist activist: "Mother, I think. Wherever you may be. Can you hear me? You wanted a women's culture. Well, now there is one. It isn't what you meant, but it exists" (164). The novel indicates that a women's culture that is imposed by and subordinated to a primary culture controlled by men and that is structured by a rigid class system, embodied in the distinct colors of the women's gowns, is not compatible with feminism. Gilead's rigid categorization of women exposes (by exaggerating) the present divisions among women that work against unified action to combat oppression at the hands of a deeply male-centered culture.

Gilead maintains control of its women not only by creating divisions among them but also by ensuring their collusion in the system, and Atwood's novel intimates that control through collusion has roots in 1980s America. Indeed, the narrator's reluctance to fight against the new regime when signs of its increasing power first become apparent enables Atwood to criticize the 1980s as an age of "moral cowardice," as Barbara Hill Rigney puts it,[10] and of a dangerous proclivity toward self-interest: "I [the narrator] didn't go to any of the marches. Luke [her husband] said it would be futile and I had to think about them, my family, him and her," since "Nobody wanted to be reported for disloyalty" (233). Both cultures ensure cooperation from its victims by making them believe that they are in control, that they participate in victimization, that they are victimizers. Binary logic not only structures the hierarchical opposition between victimizer and victim but also assures that victims will collude with the system if they are allowed to occupy the position of victimizer, even if only temporarily and in highly orchestrated settings. The narrator divulges examples of her collusion with the Gileadean regime, of which she is ashamed: "I don't want to be telling this story" (351). She describes how the handmaids are made to participate in "Salvagings" (hangings) and in "Particicutions" (group killings of supposed rapists): "I've leaned forward to touch the rope in front of me, in time with the others, both hands on it, the rope hairy, sticky with tar in the hot sun, then placed my hand on my heart to show my unity with the Salvagers and my consent, and my complicity in the death of this woman" (355). Although she has to participate to ensure her own survival, Offred is aware of the treacherous role she willingly plays. Her shame increases as she admits how she allows herself to be manipulated into an active participant in what is essentially ritual murder: "A sigh goes up from us; despite myself I feel my hands clench ... It's true, there is a bloodlust; I want to tear, gouge, rend. We jostle forward, out heads turn from side to side, our nostrils flare, sniffing death, we look at one another, seeing the hatred" (358). Atwood's novel demonstrates how systems ensure collusion from their victims, in Gilead's case by allowing the handmaids to participate in and therefore share in the responsibility of the regime's killing of undesirables.[11]

The narrative's depiction of the transition from contemporary 1980s American culture, in which women have gained a good number of civil rights and a degree of independence, to Gileadean culture, in which they are again denied those rights, demonstrates the impact of social and economic organization and its legislation on individual freedom as well as the fragility of legal changes unaccompanied by more radical metaphysical changes. Atwood's novel indicates that, if male-centered rational thought and binary logic remain intact, changes that appear to satisfy feminist aims are likely to be more cosmetic and/or temporary than truly subversive. "The Handmaid's Tale" opens with the narrator, a young woman renamed Offred by the Gileadean regime, describing her life as a handmaid in the Commander's household and ends with the escape that enables her to tell her story. Flashbacks serve to describe the shift in government as it affects the narrator, a married college-educated working mother now turned handmaid. Offred's memories of her past life as an independent American woman and of the changes that bring Gilead into being demonstrate the novel's feminist perspective and, more specifically, illustrate both how thought systems structure oppression and how economic structures effect oppression. Gilead relegates women solely to the function of reproduction through laws that strip women of their money, material possessions, and jobs, things which the novel implicitly suggests are vital to women's freedom from oppression. The narrator recalls how paper money evolved to credit cards and then to a central "Compubank" system. Keeping all monetary exchange within a computer network makes it easy for the new regime to freeze all women's assets once it passes a new law against women holding property. The narrator recognizes that the non-liquid economy enables the Gileadean regime to take control "in the way they did, all at once, without anyone knowing beforehand. If there had still been portable money, it would have been more difficult" (224): "Any account with an F on it instead of an M. All they needed to do is push a few buttons. We're cut off" (231). Moreover, the new laws forbid women to hold jobs, and millions of women are instantly let go, so that an era in which "women having jobs" is "considered the normal thing" (224) comes to an end. Simultaneously deprived of their monetary wealth and their positions in the work force, women are instantly reduced to an inferior standing of dependency. Atwood thus demonstrates the connection between the status of women and their participation in the exchange economy. Without the ability to earn and possess money, women lack economic independence and power, since they are forced to depend on men for physical survival. The narrator recalls that even in her relationship with her husband, Luke, before they are separated, "something had shifted, some balance": "We are not each other's anymore. Instead, I am his" (236) and "Already he's starting to patronize me" (332). Clearly, the seeds of change are present in 1980s culture, enabling the new regime to establish its dominance. The ease with which Luke assumes dominance and ownership indicates the male-centered modes of thought which still undergird late twentieth-century Western cultures, even if legal reforms veil their sexism. In short, the Gileadean regime does not have to restructure established thought systems—these are already male-centered—but merely has to enact legal changes. Indeed, the novel indicts Western modes of thought themselves and not just particular social systems.

Moreover, *The Handmaid's Tale* disallows any simplistic denouncement of Gilead by highlighting its dependence on rational thought and binary logic and thus its connection to present Western cultures. For instance, Gilead co-opts a rationalistic rhetoric to support its oppressive treatment of women when it emphasizes the advantages of the new society for women. The novel in this way reveals the relativity of any notion of freedom, which necessarily exists within a specific sociohistorical context. The aunts show the handmaids violent pornographic films and ask them to "Consider the alternatives": "You see what things used to be like? That was what they thought of women, then" (152). Gilead subtly redefines the notion of freedom for women, turning it on its head. Although the narrator remembers the control she had over what she chose to do in her past life, she also recalls that "Women were not protected" from rape and violence: "I remember the rules, rules that were never spelled out but that every woman knew: Don't open your door to a stranger, even if he says he is the police. Make him slide his ID under the door. Don't stop on the road to help a motorist pretending to be in trouble. Keep the locks on and keep going. If anyone whistles, don't turn to look. Don't go into a laundromat, by yourself, at night." In contrast, women can walk alone in Gilead, and "no man shouts obscenities at us, speaks to us, touches us. No one whistles." At the same time, women are not free to do as they like: "There is more than one kind of freedom, said Aunt Lydia. Freedom to and freedom from. In the days of anarchy, it was freedom to. Now you are being given freedom from. Don't underrate it" (32–33). The novel not only rejects freedom as a fixed transcendent entity or essence but politicizes notions of freedom by questioning *who* is benefitting from any given version of freedom. Although the narrator's recollection of the potential for rape and violence in her life under the American system demonstrates that Atwood is well aware of the problems and fears facing women at present, the novel's depiction of the Gileadean version of freedom for women as oppressive suggests that Atwood does not view protection legislated through terror—violators are condemned to death—and through the reverence of women as agents of reproduction or wombs as freedom in feminist terms. The novel implicitly suggests that freedom for women requires a change in thought patterns, and not merely stricter laws, and that a feminist version of freedom cannot be an either/or choice between "freedom to" and "freedom from." The narrator at one point accuses the aunts, and by implication the regime as a whole, of being "in love with either/or" (10) and thereby participates in a challenge to the binary logic on which Western thought and culture is based and by which Gilead justifies its new norms.

Although *The Handmaid's Tale*'s critique of Western culture and metaphysics is feminist in impulse, the novel nevertheless criticizes forms of feminism that border on fanaticism. Lorna Sage suggests that Atwood earmarks "the tendency in present-day feminism towards a kind of separatist purity" that "threatens to combine with the language of conservatism" and issues a warning as to the possible consequences of these exclusionist and dogmatic trends.[12] The narrator recollects being taken by her mother to burn "bad rubbish," pornographic magazines, over a bonfire in the park: the book-burners' "faces were happy, ecstatic almost" (51). By paralleling this feminist anti-pornography activity with Gilead's anti-pornography stance, the novel highlights the dangers inherent in all forms of censorship, since they ultimately work against freedom.[13] The novel rejects both a separatist women's culture and one imposed and constructed by a male-centered culture; instead, the novel points toward an as yet undelineated new culture devoid of debilitating hierarchies for both women and men. Gilead not only outlaws all pornographic materials and masturbation but also strictly regulates sexual intercourse itself, allowing it only for the purposes of procreation between married individuals or with an assigned handmaid. Homosexuality, known as "Gender Treachery" (57), and all non-designated sexual contacts are punishable by death. The narrator suggests that this obsession to purify sex of any associations with desire has devastating consequences and is inhumane: "They [young men] have no outlets now except themselves, and that's a sacrilege. There are no more magazines, no more films, no more substitutes" (30). Gilead's severe anti-pornography and anti-sex laws serve as a warning that censorship always has the potential of becoming a form of oppression, particularly if taken to extremes. By demonstrating that both pornography and censorship of pornography can be oppressive depending on context, the novel seeks to move beyond the binary system that poses them as opposites.

Moreover, Atwood's novel rejects the notion that biology or reproduction is in itself a source of women's oppression; instead, *The Handmaid's Tale* demonstrates how specific cultures utilize reproduction as a means of oppressing women. Having inherited a world in which the birth rate has declined dangerously, Gilead promotes a worship of fertility and reproduction, using biblical principles phrased by men to ground its policies. Gilead objectifies the fertile handmaids as "two-legged wombs, that's all: sacred vessels, ambulatory chalices" (176);[14] all other women perform tasks related to reproduction, such as training handmaids and running the households that sustain the handmaids' precious bodies. The new regime labels abortions "atrocities," and doctors who performed them prior to Gilead's inception are punished by death: "their crimes are retroactive" (44). In the same spirit, Gilead condemns the use of birth control as "Scorning God's gifts" and refers to women who previously used birth control as "Jezebels" and "sluts" (144). That biology determines women's but not men's lives indicates that biology is a source of oppression only if manipulated as such. According to Gileadean law, for example, "There is no such thing as a sterile man anymore, not officially. There are only women who are fruitful and women who are barren, that's the law" (79). The novel demonstrates how Gilead manipulates legal and thought structures to uphold its hegemony. As a male-dominated regime, Gilead cannot admit that men have any biological deficiencies; instead, the regime blames women for all failures at reproduction. As Offred explains, "It's only women who can't, who remain stubbornly closed, damaged, defective" (264). In Gilead, a woman's reproductive capacity determines her success as a woman; if she bears children, then she is deemed fertile—a real woman. In contrast, the Gileadean male's ability to impregnate remains unquestioned; since he does not physically bear the child, any lack is easily hidden and unacknowledged. The new regime successfully manipulates perception and even *Being* itself. If Gilead asserts that men are never sterile, then men effectively become non-sterile in the world's eyes, regardless of biological realities.

As it sketches Gilead's established system of thought and laws, the narrator's tale criticizes and deconstructs the male-centered Western metaphysics that produces them. However, the tale also points toward reconstructive possibilities in its delineation of the varied ways in which daily life departs from the rigidity of official structures. Offred's story both challenges Gilead's official history and constructs new histories by filling in the gaps that separate official existence from daily life as individuals experience it. The novel's focus on that which exists in the margins or gaps of the official Gileadean regime enables it to demonstrate that possibilities for change always exist, since there are gaps in all systems. The novel highlights all that binary logic hides or veils, all that lies in between the two rigidly demarcated sides of any given dichotomy. Official considerations strategically leave out the realm of the *in between* precisely because it threatens the system of binary oppositions which grounds Western thought. Atwood's novel enacts the double agenda at work in the postmodern recognition and analysis of the gaps that inherently exist in Western systems: challenging those systems and opening up possibilities for change—strategies that have feminist potential. The narrator's old college friend Moira exemplifies that which official history marginalizes and, yet, is revolutionary in nature. Moira, a lesbian feminist activist, escapes twice from the Red Center, the handmaid training facility: the first time she is recaptured and tortured, but the second time she remains at large for months. She becomes the handmaids' "fantasy." Her escape gives them hope, by exhibiting that the regime's "power had a flaw to it": "Moira had power, she'd been set loose, she'd set herself loose" (172). Eventually Offred meets her again at the hotel-turned-whorehouse to which the Commander takes her. As one of the "incorrigibles" (323)—most of whom are former professional women—Moira does not fit within Gilead's social structure and is banished to its margins, in a brothel that does not officially exist, among women who do not officially exist: "Certainly I [the narrator] am not dismayed by these women, not shocked by them. I recognize them as truants. The official creed denies them, denies their very existence, yet here they are. That is at least something" (306). For the narrator, the very existence of the age-old traditional house of prostitution testifies to cracks in the regime and offers the hope that it may not be as monolithic as it appears.

The narrator's tale abounds with references to things that exist in the gaps of official Gileadean life. She receives various hints, later substantiated by Moira, that a resistance group using the password "Mayday" (261) and an "Underground Femaleroad" (320) exist. When Offred finds out that "There is an *us* then, there's a *we*," she feels a sense of "hope" and of "opening" (218). Her tale ends with her arrest and removal in an Eyes van, but she is told by her lover Nick—the Commander's chauffeur—that these Eyes are part of Mayday, and her only hope is to trust him: "I snatch at it, this offer. It's all I'm left with" (377). The existence of her taped story is evidence that she is able to escape, at least long enough to record her tale. Black market trading is another solid institution that thrives unofficially and in which even high-ranking officials like the Commander take part. Although Gileadean strictures prohibit the handmaids from engaging in sex except once a month with their assigned Commander, the Commander's wife attempts to get Offred pregnant through Nick and Offred's gynecologist offers his services, suggesting that even the tightly controlled realm of sexual inter-course has gaps. Suicide, especially within the ranks of handmaids, is another occurrence that does not officially exist but that everyone seems to be aware of and concerned about: the narrator's predecessor as well as her walking partner both commit suicide. The narrator's description of her room emphasizes that "They've removed anything you could tie a rope to" and that the window "only opens partly" (9). The regime wants to prevent suicide as an act of courage and defiance, as a form of power. For example, Offred's walking partner commits suicide to prevent the authorities from learning about the resistance movement in which she is involved. What occurs in the gaps of official culture is subversive in the sense that it threatens the control, authority, and power of the official culture by revealing that it is not monolithic.

The novel's analysis of the complexities of relations of power also serves both deconstructive and reconstructive functions. By demonstrating that traditional views on relations of power as static fixed systems are oversimplified and deceptive, *The Handmaid's Tale* creates a space for changes in relations of power and the social and thought structures that both create and are created by those

relations. Moreover, the narrator's tale indicates that subjectivity is
in part a function of relations of power. Atwood's novel focuses its
exploration of relations of power and subjectivity particularly on the
realms of sexuality and language. The narrator experiences Gilead
in its early years of transition, in which late twentieth-century
American notions of sexuality are still widespread. As Nancy
Hartsock convincingly argues, since "sexuality" is "culturally and
historically defined and constructed," any shift requires time.[15] If
Gilead resorts to regulating sexuality with strict laws limiting
sexual intercourse to procreation, then the version of sexuality it
seeks to suppress must be a powerful and feared entity.[16] In other
words, Gileadean repression of existing sexuality signals the potential dangers it presents to the system. Indeed, Western cultures
have always censored desires and attempted to erase and/or rewrite
sexuality, realms that threaten the preeminence of the rational discourses that uphold those cultures. Western societies have tended to
link desire and sexuality with negative terms within its system of
hierarchical oppositions: irrationality, animalism, barbarism, evil,
women. What make desire and sexuality dangerous, however, is
that they are deeply implicated in power relations, which indicates
that rationality and binary logic in general do not dominate to the
extent that Western metaphysics assumes and asserts.

Gileadean culture attempts to suppress all that is tied to sexuality—sensuality, desire, love—by bringing sexual intercourse into
the public arena and making any kind of private social or sexual
intercourse illegal. Sexuality becomes an impersonal and public act
of duty devoid of "passion or love or romance" or of "sexual desire"
for either party. The regime enacts the ultimate objectification of
women, as it transforms sexual intercourse into an act that a man
performs on an inert body-womb: "What he is fucking is the lower
part of my body." Offred describes the monthly fertilization
"Ceremony," which brings together Commander, wife, and handmaid, as a perversion of sexuality:

> Above me, towards the head of the bed, Serena Joy [the
> wife] is arranged, outspread. Her legs are apart, I lie between
> them, my head on her stomach, her pubic bone under the base
> of my skull, her thighs on either side of me. She too is fully
> clothed.

My arms are raised; she holds my hands, each of mine in each of hers. This is supposed to signify that we are one flesh, one being. What it really means is that she is in control, of the process and thus of the product. If any. The rings of her left hand cut into my fingers. It may or may not be revenge.

My red skirt is hitched up to my waist, though no higher. Below it the Commander is fucking. (121–22)

As Barbara Hill Rigney suggests, this obscene performance is both "pornographic and asexual."[17] The Ceremony is a staged travesty of sexual intercourse at the same time as it attempts to negate the erotic aspects of "fucking." The term *pornographic* is an apt one since the official encounter positions women as both objects and victims: objects, since they are forced to be passive, and victims, since the only control they are given is illusory. Both wife and handmaid have the option either to participate in the Ceremony as prescribed or be sent to the contaminated colonies as Unwomen. Although the authorities distort the notion of choice by limiting women's choices to subjugation or death, they still manage to obtain the women's collusion within the system: Offred admits that "There wasn't a lot of choice but there was some, and this is what I chose" (121). Yet the narrator also stresses that the perverse and false picture of unity evoked by the two women lying on the bed in unwilling submission is a crime against both of them: "Which of us is it worse for, her or me?" (123). The situation denies both women any release for their desires, any means of expressing their sexuality. Although the Commander does not enjoy the Ceremony either, he at least has the more active role and is ultimately in control of the situation: the Ceremony ends with his ejaculation.

Atwood's novel undermines Gilead's (and Western Cultures' in general) official erasure and condemnation of sexuality by highlighting both the presence and potential power of sexuality. Offred's narrative is filled with sexual allusions, demonstrating both her need and desire for the sexual contact she is denied and the state's inability to eradicate desire and sensuality from the everyday world at large. The narrator returns again and again to descriptions of the household's garden in sexual and erotic terms: "The tulips are red, a darker crimson towards the stem, as if they have been cut and are beginning to heal there" (16). The sensuality of the language is heightened by the play on words between "tulips" and "two lips," and the sexual connotation is made more explicit by later references to flowers as "the genital organs of plants" (105), as "swelling genitalia," as the "fruiting body" (195). Out in the garden on a Spring day, the narrator is overcome with the "liquid ripeness" that surrounds her: "The summer dress rustles against the flesh of my thighs," and "the air suffuses with desire. Even the bricks of the house are softening, becoming tactile; if I leaned against them they'd be warm and yielding" (195–96). She longs to indulge the sensuality she is forced to repress: "I hunger to touch something, other than cloth or wood" (14). The sight of "stains on the mattress" in her room leaves her yearning for "love or something like it, desire at least, at least touch" (68). When she stumbles onto the Commander's chauffeur in the sitting room at night—both are there illegally—desire flames between them: "I want to reach up, taste his skin, he makes me hungry. His fingers move, feeling my arm under the nightgown sleeve, as if his hand won't listen to reason. It's so good, to be touched by someone, to be felt so greedily, to feel so greedy" (127–28). Offred subsequently indulges in an illicit affair with Nick, whom she sneaks up to see at night. Through these passages filled with desire and eroticism, Atwood indicates that social norms and laws cannot totally eradicate sexual desire and sensuality—although in time they can rechannel them—which is precisely what makes them potentially dangerous to a regime that wants to be all powerful and to control human beings completely.

The novel explicitly links desire with that which is secretive, illicit, or against accepted social norms. Desire functions in the novel as one of the gaps that exist between official history and personal daily life. Even the Commander indulges in activities that are against the law to fulfill his own desires, such as his secret relationships with his handmaids and his occasional visits to a brothel. Although Offred is afraid the first time the Commander calls her into his office, she quickly recognizes that his wanting her gives her a degree of power: "To want is to have a weakness. It's this weakness, whatever it is, that entices me. It's like a small crack in a wall, before now impenetrable" (176). Offred's arrangement with the Commander becomes a conspiracy in which she holds power, if only by knowing that illegal meetings are taking place. The Commander's attentions reinforce her earlier feeling that she holds a certain degree of power merely by being a young attractive woman in a world that does not allow any form of intercourse between the sexes: "I enjoy the power; power of a dog bone, passive but there." Her sense that she can still move men with her sex appeal empowers her; for instance, she explains that swinging her "hips a little" in front of the sexually repressed guards is "like thumbing your nose from behind a fence" (30). The episodes with the Commander and the guards empower her precisely because she affects men through sexual desire; she flaunts the survival of that which the official regime supposedly effaces. Indeed, the power that desire and sex appeal affords her indicates why male-centered cultures like Gilead (but also like most Western cultures) feel threatened by realms associated with sexuality: they disrupt male-centered and -dominated relations of power.

Although the narrator treasures the "luxury" of the "freedom, an eyeblink of it" (180), that she enjoys in the Commander's office where she is allowed to read, write, and speak, she is unable to give him the intimacy he seeks precisely because she is not a totally passive victim and does retain a degree of control or power: "What he wants is intimacy, but I can't give him that." As a member of the ruling class, the Commander participates in the restructuring of society and is therefore above Offred's pity. She refuses to buy into his justifications for the repressive social changes. He argues, for example, that in the 1980s there was nothing left for men anymore: "the sex was too easy. Anyone could just buy it. There was nothing to work for, nothing to fight for. We have the stats from that time. You know what they were complaining about the most? Inability to feel. Men were turning off on sex, even. They were turning off on marriage" (273). He also asserts that the changes are in the interest of women as well as men: "We've given them [women] more than we've taken away, said the Commander. Think of the trouble they had before. Don't you remember the singles' bars, the indignity of high school blind dates? The meat market. Don't you remember the terrible gap between the ones who could get a man easily and the ones who couldn't? Some of them were desperate, they starved themselves thin or pumped their breasts full of silicone, had their noses cut off. Think of the human misery" (283–84). Although the Commander's justifications have some validity and indicate that Atwood severely criticizes the existing condition of women's lives, the narrator and the novel reject the Commander's answer to the problems he lists as just another form of oppression. When he effectively tells Offred that "his wife didn't understand him," she feels that it is the "same old thing" and is just "too banal to be true" (203): "The fact is that I'm his mistress. Men at the top have always had mistresses, why should things be any different now? The arrangements aren't quite the same, granted … But underneath it's the same. More or less … It's my job to provide what is otherwise lacking" (210). As I have indicated, although the novel presents Gilead as a regime in which the surface social structure has changed from that of the present day, it becomes clear that things have not changed very much in actuality: both 1980s America and Gilead are male-centered cultures, and both contain ruptures.

Relations between the sexes have remained remarkably intact: men still dominate and yet women's desirability disrupts male power. Only the objects of desire have changed somewhat as a result of Gilead's stricter laws against all intercourse between the sexes, which have transformed many previously non-sexual activities into ones that possess sexual overtones. For instance, the Commander's wish to play "Scrabble" with Offred surprises her, since she has been expecting him to want "Something unspeakable, down on all fours perhaps, perversions, whips, mutilations" (198); but she soon understands that the notion of playing Scrabble has changed. It is no longer a game for "old women, old men, in the summers or in retirement villas." Now that reading and writing are against the law for women, "it's something different. Now it's forbidden, for us. Now it's dangerous. Now it's indecent. Now it's something he can't do with his Wife. Now it's desirable" (179).[18] Although different activities become desirable, the motives remain the same; men still yearn for what they are not allowed, and men still objectify women with the gaze. When the Commander allows her to read, he "sits and watches" her so that his "watching" her "illicit reading" becomes "a curiously sexual act" (239), a new type of voyeurism. However, she herself feels the awakening of power and sensuality when he allows her to write, thereby allowing her to engage in the illicit, in the satisfaction of desires: "The pen between my fingers is sensuous, alive almost, I can feel its power" (241).[19] Although Gilead structures itself rigidly, it cannot eradicate desire and the power that engaging in the forbidden engenders.

Atwood's novel also links desire and the power it engenders to subjectivity. On one level, the Commander's desire for intimacy demonstrates that he himself wants to be recognized as a subject. The paradox is that only another subject can recognize him in those terms, so that Offred is both the object of his desire and the subject who can substantiate his subjecthood. He wants her to be a subject, but *his* subject. Since she is in the position of denying him the intimacy he desires, Offred holds a degree of power over the Commander at the same time as he constructs her as a subject.[20] The novel disrupts the classical opposition between subject and object by depicting Offred as occupying both and neither position simultaneously. Furthermore, her relationship with the Commander undermines the designated limits of her role as a handmaid restricted to breeding purposes: the "functions" of wife and handmaid "were no longer as separate as they should have been in theory" (208). The blurring of the demarcation line between wife and handmaid signals Offred's indeterminate position within the household, which unmasks the fixed categories that name women as oppressive constructions intended to objectify women and ensure male dominance. Since the oppression of women has traditionally included sexual oppression and repression, whether it be in the form of rape and violence, as in the America of the narrator's earlier life, or of the obscene Gileadean fertilization Ceremony, an assertion of sexuality signifies an assertion of subjecthood. Although Offred claims that the power she feels is passive, it is a conscious and active passivity rather than the passivity of the unknowing and powerless victim; as such, it threatens the conventional polarization of activity and passivity, subject and object. By disrupting established boundaries and highlighting indeterminacy, Offred in effect subverts not only the Gileadean system but also Western metaphysics in general, which is grounded in binary logic and set boundaries. Moreover, Offred's indeterminate position as subject and object, as mistress and handmaid, indicates not only that she occupies a multiplicity of officially incompatible positions but also that her identity is fluid, in process, rather than fixed and stable.

The narrator's giving to Nick the intimacy she refuses the Commander is another sign that she occupies the position of subject as well as that of object. It is telling that she and Nick "make love" (346); her choice of words suggests that she is an active participant in the sexual intercourse, in contrast to her inert role when "the Commander fucks" (121) her. She also stresses that she engages in an illicit sexual relationship with Nick for her own pleasure rather than for purposes of procreation; she defies Gileadean law and culture by asserting her own subjecthood: "I did not do it for him, but for myself entirely" (344). The hint that she may be pregnant with Nick's child further flaunts her independent existence as a subject: "I put his [Nick's] hand on my belly. It's happened, I say. I feel it has. A couple of weeks and I'll be certain" (348). The possibility of her pregnancy suggests that she can be both an active sexual partner and a potential childbearer, challenging Gilead's attempt to suppress sexuality and desire in the name of healthy mothers. She even tells Nick, but not her audience, her name from her earlier life: "I tell him my real name, and feel that therefore I am known" (347). The new regime names the handmaids according to the Commander to which they are assigned, so that their names indicate their positions as objects owned by men and have nothing to do with the person that fills that position. The narrator's name *Offred* marks her as the possession of a Commander named Fred, *Of-fred;* and all handmaids attached to Fred's household in the past or the future bear the name Offred. This naming process objectifies the handmaids. The narrator treasures her old name precisely because it helps her retain a sense of her own being as subject: "My name isn't Offred, I have another name, which nobody uses now because it's forbidden. I tell myself it doesn't matter, your name is like your telephone number, useful only to others; but what I tell myself is wrong, it does matter. I keep the knowledge of this name like something hidden, some treasure I'll come back to dig up, one day. I think of this name as buried. This name has an aura around it, like an amulet, some charm that's survived from an unimaginably distant past" (108). While the narrator holds on to her "real name" (347) as a conventional means of securing her own identity, she nevertheless recognize the arbitrary but strategic nature of all names when she compares her old name to a telephone number. In fact, what she values most about her old name is that it is illicit and unknown to those around her.

Moreover, the novel's failure to disclose that name indicates its criticism of forms of naming as means of fixing and oppressing human beings.[21] The novel underscores the oppressive potential inherent in naming, which derives from its process of delimiting and circumscribing its object: Gilead constructs the handmaids as objects by giving them names that define their positions as possessions. Likewise, the narrator creates her own version of herself as subject by holding on to her old and now illegal name. However, the narrator and Atwood have very different strategies. By deliberately leaving the narrator's pre-Gilead name out of the novel, Atwood challenges the traditional equation of fixed identity with subjecthood and presents a more fluid version of the subject. The novel's suspicion of naming and consequent refusal to name the narrator pushes toward a view of language as unstable, as both potentially oppressive and liberating. In much the same way that Gileadean culture names the narrator as a means of positioning her to ensure male dominance, Atwood's novel strategically does not name the narrator so as not to fix her in any set role. This possibility of manipulating language to support feminist politics demonstrates that language can be a powerful emancipatory tool.

The Republic of Gilead's tight control and even suppression of language in general is a testimony to language's potential power and threat. Gileadean laws restrict women's direct access to written language, which enables the regime to more easily relegate women to object positions, since using and manipulating language is inextricably tied to being a subject and to having power in Western culture. After all, Western cultures historically have privileged the written word and until relatively recently restricted its use to the ranks of those in positions of power, that is to white European/American men with money and/or rank. In Gilead, the Bible itself is "kept locked up" (112), and only the Commander is allowed to (mis)read it or to (mis)read passages from it to the women in the household. Consequently, men have sole control of how the *Word* is translated into law and into the system of thought that regulates society. Although Moral Majority thought is based on a literal reading of the Bible, *The Handmaid's Tale* indicates that, since reading or interpretation always contains a degree of subjectivity or bias and since language itself is far from stable, any supposed *literal* reading is in actuality a version that works to the advantage of those in power. Since women are forbidden to read or write, they lack the means to challenge the Gileadean regime's interpretation of the Bible and of history; moreover, they lack the tools to document their lives. Atwood's novel examines the political implications of the notion that a gap necessarily exists between a text and any reading of it, demonstrating an awareness of the inevitable gap that exists between signifier and signified as well as of language as unstable and therefore open to subversion. Gileadean culture covers over this gap at the same time as it fully exploits it. Indeed, the regime selectively pulls quotations from the Bible and distorts them to suit its own purposes: for instance, the regime attributes the slogan "From each according to her ability; to each according to his needs" to "St. Paul" (151) rather than to Marx and strategically replaces a masculine pronoun with a feminine one; and it adds "Blessed are the silent" (115) to the beatitudes of the Sermon on the Mount.[22] The narrator's skepticism is apparent, however, in her comments on these biblical passages quoted to her: "It was from the Bible, or so they said" (154), and "I knew they made that up, I knew it was wrong" (115). Offred retains the memory of another reading or version of these biblical verses. Although she holds on to the traditional dichotomy between a right and a wrong reading, between fact and fiction, the novel challenges that opposition through its offering of multiple official versions of the biblical verses. If more than one official version exists, then there exists no one real or true version, and binary logic breaks down.

To further cover over the gap between signifier and signified and eliminate at least a degree of the indeterminacy inherent in language, the Gileadean regime replaces verbal signs with visual ones whenever possible. Shops exhibit pictorial illustrations of the products they sell, and the color of clothing or uniform distinguish the various classes of men and women.[23] For example, the narrator's bright red gown and white headdress visually signal her status as a handmaid; the color of her attire "stands for" something (13). Red, "the color of blood," defines the handmaids' association with menstrual and birthing blood, and the white wings, which "keep us from seeing, but also from being seen" (11), define them as chaste and guarded possessions. The handmaid's clothing signals her function and position; she has no other identity.[24] But the narrative's play with words highlights the associative powers of language that Gilead unsuccessfully attempts to suppress. For instance, the narrative underscores the irony inherent in the handmaid's resemblance to an inverted nun—"A Sister, dipped in blood" (11)—in the sense that she is supposed to be chaste in all but procreation. The handmaid becomes a parody or reversal of Hester Prynne and the scarlet "A" stigmatizing her as adulteress in Nathaniel Hawthorne's *The Scarlet Letter;* Gilead has legitimized and institutionalized the scarlet-clad handmaid. These examples demonstrate not only the extent to which signs can be and are manipulated to reinforce oppressive systems but also the great malleability of language. If language is malleable, then it can have both oppressive and emancipatory potential. Indeed, Offred co-opts language to eventually tell her story. However, her story remains oral: she records her story onto tapes. By recording her experiences without resorting to written language, she challenges Gilead's locating of authority in the written word.[25]

Moreover, Offred is a very self-conscious narrator, who questions language and the possibility of telling a story accurately even as she attempts to tell her own story. Although she is aware of the impermanence of oral tales, she rejects the notion that writing is more *real* or *true* than speech, since language and subjectivity render mimesis impossible. As a narrator, she demonstrates a postmodern sensibility in her rejection of the dichotomy between reality and fiction, in her emphasis on the gaps in language, and in her investigation of the constructed quality of language. She is aware that there is no one static reality and that what is designated as reality is in fact only the official "version of reality" (261), which changes with any given regime.[26] She even asserts that her *truth* is neither stable nor fixed. When she describes three different versions of what could have happened to her husband Luke after they were separated, she emphasizes that all three variants are true in the sense that she believes them all to be possible: "The things I believe can't all be true, though one of them must be. But I believe in all of them, all three versions of Luke, at one and the same time. This contradictory way of believing seems to me, right now the only way I can believe anything" (135). The novel offers truth or reality as a function of available information and, therefore, as inherently provisional. Through its use of a self-conscious narrator, the novel presents reality as "no longer a world of eternal verities but a series of constructions, artifices, impermanent structures."[27] Knowledge rests on assumptions or provisional truths that are continually shifting and changing. But, although the novel disrupts the opposition between reality and fiction, it neither equates nor reverses the terms. The narrator's claim that she must tell her story precisely because it "includes the truth" (344) indicates that Atwood is trying to distinguish between reality and fiction at the same time as she rejects them as opposites. Although the narrator emphasizes that her story is merely a reconstruction of events and is, as such, a fiction, the novel differentiates between a textual version of the material historical situation and the constructed fiction of novels. The narrator's story is fictionalized but is not entirely arbitrary, since it follows a given set of lived events; she even wishes that "this story were different. I wish it were more civilized" (343). Hence, Atwood's *The Handmaid's Tale* exists on a different level than the narrator's oral tale: Atwood's novel is a creative piece of fiction; the narrator's story is a reconstruction of her experiences in Gilead as a handmaid. Both are fictional in the sense that life and novels can exist only "within 'textual' boundaries," or frames, and that "neither historical experience nor literary fictions are unmediated or unprocessed or non-linguistic."[28] Atwood demonstrates that novels and history are inevitably constructions or fictions, since everything is always already represented; yet they exist on different fictional levels, since they are framed differently. This distinction is important from a feminist perspective, because recuperating women's often oral stories-histories demands a new mode of thought and approach and yet cannot relegate physical existence and oppression to the realm of fiction. Although unstable and fictionalized, these stories nevertheless work to represent their narrators' material situations and experiences.

While Atwood's narrator is intent on representing her lived experiences as a handmaid in Gilead, she manifests a shrewd (postmodern) awareness of the inherent gaps in signification and the impossibility of filling those gaps to retrieve any true order of things or events. She acknowledges the inability of her story to mirror or replicate the events and feelings she attempts to describe: "It's impossible to say a thing exactly the way is was, because what you say can never be exact, you always have to leave something out, there are too many parts, sides, crosscurrents, nuances; too many gestures, which could mean this or that, too many shapes which can never be fully described, too many flavors, in the air or on the tongue, half-colors, too many." Her disbelief in the possibility of mimesis undergirds her repeated warning that her story is merely a reconstruction: "All of it is a reconstruction" (173–74). When the narrator describes her first visit to the Commander's office, she notes that "He was so sad" and then immediately counters that statement with "That is a reconstruction, too" (181), demonstrating her recognition of the gap that exists between events and their recollections. An intensified manifestation of the narrator's skepticism over the possibility of representation occurs in her multiple attempts to recount her first secret visit to Nick's room. She breaks off her first description by denying its validity—"I made that up. It didn't happen that way" (338)—and then starts describing the scene all over again. Her second version of the events is also marred by falsehood, but now she understands and accepts that any attempt to tell this story will always be only an approximation at best: "It didn't happen that way either. I'm not sure how it happened; not exactly. All I can hope for is a reconstruction" (340). Moreover, the narrator argues not only that the story she retrospectively recounts into the microphone of a tape recorder is a reconstruction but also that her thoughts and memories while she is a handmaid are already reconstructions: "It's a reconstruction now, in my head, as I lie flat on my single bed rehearsing what I should or shouldn't have said, what I should or shouldn't have done, how I should have played it … When I get out of here, if I'm ever able to set this down, in any form, even in the form of one voice to another, it will be a reconstruction then too, at yet another remove" (173).[29] The novel's recognition that versions of events are necessarily mediated, and that fiction will contaminate any version of reality, demonstrates a postmodern impulse. But disrupting the conventional binary opposition between reality and fiction also has feminist implications, in that it allows women's oral stories to function as histories. Although these stories necessarily involve fictionalization, they also maintain close ties to the material situation, as in the case of Offred's tale.

Atwood's novel also links language and subjectivity, through its insistence that the narrator exists only in the telling of her story through the medium of language. The novel indicates that her narration is a politically engaged move that counters the passivity and collusion she exhibits during the shift in government as well as prior to Gilead's inception, when she ignored "newspaper stories" reporting violence perpetrated against women and chose to live "in the blank white spaces at the edges of print," "in the gaps between the stories" (74). As a handmaid in Gilead, and therefore an object denied subjecthood or active engagement with life, she feels she is "a blank, here, between parentheses, between other people" (295). Only by co-opting language and inserting herself within a story, her own story-history, does she become an active subject in her own right.[30] She even compares an active purposeful life to a plot in a story: "But people will do anything rather than admit that their lives have no meaning. No use, that is. No plot" (279). Moreover, to assert herself as a subject, the narrator needs not only to tell her story but to tell it to someone. She specifically addresses her audience as *you* and thereby wills it into existence: "I must be telling it to someone. You don't tell a story only to yourself. There's always someone else" (52–53). Throughout her narration she speaks directly to a *you* that she creates out of a need to have her story-history known to others. She must believe in a potential listener if her narration is to have any point or meaning: "By telling you anything at all I'm at least believing in you, I believe you're there, I believe you into being. Because I'm telling you this story I will your existence. I tell, therefore you are" (344). Her belief that her own lived experiences must be passed on as a history necessitates her creation of an audience. By using the word *you,* Offred is able to create or construct an addressee through the medium of language, which in turn helps her construct her own subjectivity. While this process of subject formation occurs within the realm of language, it never severs its ties to material conditions; the story she must tell is about her physical experiences under the Gileadean regime. She must tell her story to alert immediate and future audiences to the potential for dehumanization that marks Western modes of thought with their male-centered binary logic.

While it presents language as a dynamic system, *The Handmaid's Tale* nevertheless exposes the ways in which language can stagnate and become drained of meaning if it is circumscribed too narrowly. Indeed, the narrator at one point asserts, "I don't listen. I've heard this speech, or one like it, often enough before: the same platitudes, the same slogans, the same phrases" (353). Offred's failure to listen to the speech indicates that, once meaning becomes static and empty, language loses its power to construct both subjects and objects. However, the narrator's choice to tell her story indicates her recognition of the liberatory potential and power of language. After all, the very instability of language makes it a tool that opposing political forces can co-opt. Offred's story exists as evidence that human beings can tap language as a powerful force to use against repressive systems. She literally tells herself into existence, into subjecthood. Offred refuses to give up access to language and eventually uses it, even as she questions it, to tell her story and thereby subvert Gilead's system that denies women that power. She seizes upon language, the very tool utilized by Gilead to objectify her, to assert herself as a female subject actively engaged in reconstructing her Gileadean experiences. However, the subject she creates is a new version of the subject that is not set in opposition to an object and is neither static nor unitary. The process of recounting her experiences in Gilead becomes simultaneously a process of constructing her own subjectivity. The novel leaves the reader with a subject in process, a subject that is a function of the process of story-history telling. Furthermore, by providing the reader only the narrator's Gileadean name, the novel undermines not only traditional notions of subjectivity but also of authorship as the expression of a specific individual with a documented identity. The novel's last section, which frames "The Handmaid's Tale," more fully demonstrates the effects of this lack of signature or concrete attribution of authorship.

As I intimate in the introduction to this chapter, the "Historical Notes" segment is crucial to the novel as a whole, allowing *The Handmaid's Tale* simultaneously to engage in a more thorough disruption of a host of traditional Western concepts and to strengthen its feminist stance. Atwood's novel offers this final chapter as a facsimile of "a partial transcript of the proceedings of the Twelfth Symposium on Gileadean Studies, held as part of the International Historical Association Convention" in 2195 (379). Although it is set in the distant future, the symposium replicates and parodies the present world of the 1980s, so that the present is, in effect, also included in the novel as text. The symposium's keynote speaker,

Professor Pieixoto, reveals through his discussion of "The Handmaid's Tale" that his culture is just as biased as the one of the 1980s: it is male-centered and rests on a system of hierarchical binary oppositions that privileges concepts such as truth, reality, author, subject, history, and writing.[31] His speech manipulates and finally effaces the female subject as well as women's histories. Atwood uses this thinly disguised version of the future to demonstrate how male-centered academic institutions have always appropriated women's experiences and co-opted women's voices for their own ends.[32] The effects of this final chapter are not purely deconstructive, however, in that the narrator's physically absent oral tale and signature remain as traces—both and neither present and absent—within the novel's pages, pointing to possibilities of recuperating women's voices, stories-histories.

The title of Pieixoto's talk, "Problems of Authentication in Reference to *The Handmaid's Tale*" (380), highlights his culture's dependence on metaphysical notions of truth, reality, and origin as absolutes. The professor is overtly uncomfortable with the object of his talk, precisely because the narrator's oral tale is not a well-defined object and contains indeterminacies. His reference to it as a "soi-disant manuscript" and his "hesitat[ion] to use the word *document*" (381) demonstrate Pieixoto's suspicion of a text discovered in the form of a recorded oral tale. But the scholars have appropriated the tale by transcribing and editing the tapes, ordering the narrative segments, and affixing titles to the various sections and to the work as a whole. Although the speaker admits that the "arrangements are based on some guesswork" (383), the reconstructed version of the story carries authority since (male) scholars have written and arranged it.[33] They have transformed the narrator's oral story into a tangible object of study. The translation of thirty unnumbered cassette tapes into a written tale consisting of fifteen titled sections and forty-six chapters serves as evidence of the scholars' manipulation of the oral story. Indeed, they have reshaped and restructured the narrative and have named the segments and the whole in an effort to transform it and thereby legitimize it as a serious and credible manuscript: "Strictly speaking, it was not a manuscript at all when first discovered and bore no title. The superscription 'The Handmaid's Tale' was appended to it by Professor Wade, partly in homage to the great Geoffrey Chaucer" (381). By naming the story "in homage" to Chaucer, the scholars are reshaping it so that it will fit within the tradition of texts accepted by the male-centered academic institution.[34] In other words, to validate the unconventional text, they must make it fit within an accepted tradition.

Further to establish the work's legitimacy, the speaker spends a great deal of energy attempting to name the narrator. His obsession with attributing an author to the story exhibits a belief in and reliance on the concept of origin and the equation of fixed identity and being: "If we [the scholars involved in the project] could establish an identity for the narrator, we felt, we might be well on the way to an explanation of how this document—let me call it that for the sake of brevity—came into being" (384). The scholars' intensive research to uncover the narrator's "original name" (387) exposes their association of story with authorial intention. They are threatened by the narrator's failure to name herself and thus to offer a guarantee of meaning grounded in her existence as originator of the story. As Catherine Belsey explains, conventional notions of literature assume that it "reflects the *reality* of experience as it is perceived by one (especially gifted) individual."[35] Although the narrator herself hangs on to her name and to traditional notions of identity, the novel's refusal to name her both indicates its criticism of conventional notions of identity and origin and demonstrates how vital these notions are to Western thought and culture. Indeed, the scholars' attempt to name the narrator is also an attempt to objectify her. They want her as the object of their research and not as the subject of her story, and so they work to co-opt her story and make it their own. The scholars want to tell her story and, to a certain extent, they succeed in doing so by being the authors of the story's written structure.[36]

Professor Pieixoto's talk devalues the oral story by questioning its importance or relevance as a historical document. He blames the narrator for not providing enough historical details on the Gileadean era and spending too much time on *her* story: "many gaps remain. Some of them could have been filled by our anonymous author, had she had a different turn of mind. She could have told us much about the working of the Gileadean empire, had she had the instincts of a reporter or a spy. What would we not give, now, for even twenty pages or so of print-out from Waterford's [a high-ranking Commander] private computer!" (393). Pieixoto clearly wishes to transform the narrator's tale into a different story, one that conforms to the conventions of written male-centered history and focuses on an objective retrospective of another time or world and its official structures. From his point of view, the narrator's story is marred by subjectivity, since it centers on quality of life, on how the state structures affect individuals—particularly women.[37] Moreover, by accusing the narrator of not providing enough information about Gilead's official history, the speaker trivializes the nightmarish experiences of women in Gilead as well as the entire realm of the personal and of daily life. Indeed, Pieixoto's speech emphasizes his own adherence to the traditional Western notion of history as objective and factual and set in binary opposition to that which is subjective and fictional. Furthermore, his wish for computer printouts from the Gileadean period highlights his assumption that a fixed or true history exists and that it is to be found duly recorded in written form. His mourning over the scarcity of "surviving records" in Gilead, which he attributes to the regime's "habit of wiping its own computers and destroying print-outs after various purges and internal upheavals" (385), exhibits his equation of authentic history with written official documents.

Through Pieixoto's speech, the novel overtly criticizes the traditional Western tendency to view history as a fixed entity and to view officially recorded history as *the* valid and authentic representation of past events. In the telling of her story, the narrator herself falls prey to the notion that oral records are not as authentic as written ones: "I can't remember exactly, because I had no way of writing it down" (317). The novel demonstrates, however, that all versions of history, oral or written, are necessarily fictionalizations in the sense that they are always reconstructions rather than mimetic representations. The narrator admits that her story is a reconstruction, but the novel stresses that the scholars' readings of her story and of the Gileadean period are also only reconstructions. Atwood's novel does not reject written official history altogether but rather relativizes it by demonstrating that no version of history can reflect events mimetically, even if those in power assert that their version is the true one. For instance, although Pieixoto acknowledges that his version of Gilead and his attempts to name characters in the narrator's story are based on "guesswork," he immediately assumes that his suppositions are true: "This is our guesswork.

Supposing it to be correct ... " (393). By demonstrating that Pieixoto's notion of history is no more authentic than the narrator's own personal history, Atwood's novel exposes all histories as strategic reconstructions of events from specific perspectives.

Moreover, the speaker manifests an overt masculinist bias in his discussion. His opening joke points out the wordplay between "tale" and "tail" in the title given to the document by Professor Wade and thereby indicates that the audience he speaks to is receptive to sexist humor: "those of you who know Professor Wade informally, as I do, will understand when I say that I am sure all puns were intentional, particularly that having to do with the archaic vulgar signification of the word *tail;* that being, to some extent, the bone, as it were, of contention, in that phase of Gileadean society of which our saga treats." This joke, which opens the seminar, effectively downplays Gilead's harsh sexual politics and its victimization of women; the joke reduces the handmaids' lives as breeders to a bawdy pun.[38] Referring to the narrator's story as a "saga" further trivializes the handmaid's plight. He makes an even more overt sexist wordplay when he refers to the "Underground Femaleroad" as the "Underground Frailroad" (381). Indeed, Pieixoto's discussion demonstrates not only his sexism but his total lack of interest in the handmaids or in the story at hand.[39] Since he is unable to trace the identity of the narrator, he spends the greatest part of his talk attempting to determine the identity of the Commander in whose household the narrator resided. Although he has little information to go on and has himself decried the lack of records, he posits two possible known high-ranking officials as the *origin* of the narrator's Commander: "Frederick R. Waterford and B. Frederick Judd" (388). Again, the speaker exhibits a need to name the story's characters in order to authenticate the narrative as historically correct; yet, all he can offer is his own reconstruction based on the slim clue provided by the name *Fred,* as derived from the narrator's Gileadean name— Offred.[40] He does not even entertain the possibility that the narrator could have fictionalized the name in her endeavor to remain anonymous, although he is quick to accuse her of "malicious invention" in naming the Commander's wife "Serena Joy" (394). This double standard is in itself a sign of ingrained sexism.

Further evidence of Pieixoto's sexism surfaces in his enthusiastic discussions of Gilead's regime and the two Commanders he researches, with which he is clearly impressed. His assertions that Gilead's "genius was synthesis" (389) and that Waterford was "in his prime, a man of considerable ingenuity" (391) expose the speaker's affinities with Gilead's male-centered regime and its male architects. However, the most telling evidence of Pieixoto's masculinist bias is his injunction to the effect that Gilead must be studied objectively and that the task of scholars "is not to censure but to understand": "we must be cautious about passing moral judgment upon the Gileadeans. Surely we have learned by now that such judgments are of necessity culture-specific" (383). By refusing to pass judgment, the speaker depoliticizes the Gileadean epoch and makes it into an object that is disconnected from his own world. He thus circumvents vital issues "under the guise of scholarly objectivity."[41] Pieixoto further normalizes Gilead by calling attention to the existence of "historical precedents" (390) for many of its practices, which has the effect of downplaying the specific horrors perpetrated by the Gileadean regime and watering down its guilt. While still acknowledging historical precedent, Atwood's novel *does* pass judgment on the Gileadean regime, the academic institution to which Pieixoto belongs, and contemporary American society by inherently comparing and contrasting these three worlds and highlighting their shared dependence on male-centered modes of thought which translate into sexist oppressive social systems.

The recognition that Pieixoto and his fellow academics have manipulated and appropriated "The Handmaid's Tale" is unsettling for the reader. The novel's presentation of the ways in which the scholars have subsumed the narrator's voice and arranged the structure of the story to fit their preconceived notions of narrative throws into question "The Handmaid's Tale" portion of the novel. Pieixoto's reference to "the difficulties posed by accent, obscure referents, and archaisms" (383) further suggests that significant alterations may have been made to the oral story during the process of transcription. Emphasis and tone are also lost in the written version. The result is that the narrator's oral tale, its written version, and Pieixoto's discussion of it challenge and undermine each other's stability and authority. Atwood's introduction of a frame for "The Handmaid's Tale" narrative in the novel's last pages relativizes reality by destabilizing all of the worlds presented: 1980s American society, the Gileadean period, and the distant future.[42]

Without one true reality, the rigid opposition between reality and fiction breaks down, and indeterminacy creeps into the novel. A gap opens up between the narrator's oral story and the scholars' reading and writing of her story. Within this gap lies the novel's most subversive feminist thrust.

Indeed, I am arguing that Atwood's novel accentuates its feminist agenda by emphasizing the gap that exists between women's lived material existence or histories and official history. The narrator's oral tale is central to the novel and yet is not tangibly present in its written pages. The novel places the oral story under erasure; it is both present and absent and as a result disrupts the Western metaphysical opposition between these two terms. The academic institution's version of the narrator's story demonstrates not only that history does not exist as such but also that Western history is inherently male-centered. Official history has traditionally been the history of "the winners" and of "the male sex,"[43] "written by and about males,"[44] and as such tends to either marginalize or co-opt women's versions of history. By deliberately not naming the narrator, Atwood's novel allows the narrator to stand as a female subject with her own story in the gap between the novel's two sections; without a name, the scholars are unable to completely objectify her or to totally co-opt her story. The narrator exists as both a subject telling her own story and as the object of both her own story and the scholars' version of her story; her indeterminate position simultaneously internalizes and problematizes the traditional Western dichotomy between subject and object. Not only do the novel's disruptive gestures undermine binary logic, but they serve the novel's feminist aims by disrupting the conventional notion of history as an objective unitary entity and the whole Western tradition of reading and writing history. Moreover, these deconstructive strategies open up a space for creating and reclaiming multiple histories. The scholars' preservation of the narrator's emphasis on her story as a reconstruction in their written version of "The Handmaid's Tale," presumably because it reinforces their view of oral history as inaccurate, in fact criticizes the scholars' own belief in and dependence on a monolithic conception of history. The narrator's awareness of the inevitable fictionalization inherent in all attempts to record history allows her to tell her story outside the margins of mainstream history and thus to problematize history itself.[45] Atwood has created a character who can tell her story precisely because she has evaded some of the restraints of Western conceptual boundaries and binary thinking, even if readers can find only traces of her story in the physical novel itself.

As a self-conscious text that highlights its existence as a physical object with distinct sections or texts and with overt gaps or absences, Atwood's novel enacts the ways in which stories and histories are always reconstructed and calls into question notions of authorial control. Atwood writes "The Handmaid's Tale" as a document written by male scholars based on an oral story recorded onto tapes by an anonymous narrator. This superimposition of authorial voices challenges the notion of author as expressive unity by fragmenting and dispersing the authorial position to the point of indeterminacy. Authorship in the novel is neither fixed nor absolute. With a nebulous authorial position, authorial intent becomes indeterminate, and uncertainty menaces interpretation.[46] However, the novel's assertion of itself as a text allows it to highlight gaps that cannot be filled and yet are powerfully present as absences. As a text made up of various texts, some of which exist in written form and some of which exist within the gaps between written texts or as traces within written texts, Atwood's novel depicts how male-centered cultures marginalize and efface women's stories-histories by privileging fixed metaphysical conceptions of history, writing, truth, reality, and origin and the binary logic on which these concepts depend. Indeed, Western cultures have consistently positioned men in positions of power and privileged written official documents as the most authentic sources or forms of representation for material events: the result has been an erasure of women's stories-histories.

By framing "The Handmaid's Tale" with a reading, and writing, of the tale by a scholar who lives in 2195 and yet whose culture is similar to that of the present, Atwood's novel is able both to criticize existing Western thought as male-centered and to issue a warning against sweeping changes that do not challenge the metaphysics that undergirds all of Western culture and therefore do not ultimately change sociocultural structures. Although the scholars discuss the Gileadean period as an oddity of the past, they still retain its inherent sexism. In fact, sexism and social inequities inform all of the historical periods discussed in the novel; and, although Gilead's inequities are the most overt and drastic, they are only exaggerations of those existing in the present and in the more distant future.[47] Indeed, the novel exhibits an uneasiness toward the cyclical pattern that results in cultures in the 1980s and the 2190s that are based on the same seemingly liberal and yet clearly male-centered system of thought. The novel verbalizes its cautionary gesture through words spoken by the narrator's mother, a feminist activist banished to the colonies by the Gileadean regime, and recalled by the narrator as she tells her story: "History will absolve me ... You young people don't appreciate things, she'd say. You don't know what we had to go through, just to get you where you are. Look at him slicing up the carrots. Don't you know how many women's lives, how many women's *bodies,* the tanks had to roll over just to get that far?" (156). Although the novel presents the narrator's mother as a fanatical feminist and thus as a threat to the possibility of restructuring society to ensure equality for all persons, her words foreshadow both the Gileadean regime and the circular movement of history that can cancel changes, even those acquired at great costs— recent U.S. Supreme Court decisions limiting hard-won abortion rights are cases in point.[48]

Atwood's novel does not ultimately offer a blueprint for a better society in feminist terms, but it nevertheless issues warnings against reactionary and fanatical trends both in culture at large and within feminism itself.[49] Unlike George Orwell, who upholds humanist concepts and values in his dystopian novel *1984,* Atwood creates a dystopia as a means of criticizing transcendental Western concepts such as freedom and truth and of highlighting the political potential of the indeterminacy and relativity that Orwell condemns. If concepts are relative, then oppressive conceptualizations can be deconstructed and created anew. For instance, the novel demonstrates that feminists need not choose between "freedom to" and "freedom from"; they can reconceptualize freedom in non-binary terms as a means of evading the oppressive potential inherent in oppositional thought. As I have argued, *The Handmaid's Tale* engages both deconstructive and reconstructive (postmodern) strategies in order to criticize the inherent biases in Western culture's notion and reading of history as a mono-lithic objective entity, while simultaneously inserting a woman's oral story-history within the margins or cracks of the texts written by men; as a result, these subversive strategies relativize history and open up a space for women's traditionally marginalized stories-histories. Moreover, Atwood's novel formulates a more fluid female subject by disrupting the conventional opposition between subject and object and by resisting naming processes that circumscribe human beings. The anonymous narrator's legitimacy as teller of her own story exists independently of her identity, which strategically remains outside of the book's written pages and clearly shifts. While readers glimpse only traces of the narrator's oral tale and material existence, these traces nonetheless point to the possibilities that open up as a result of challenges to the status quo. By disrupting conventional notions of history, reality, truth, Atwood's novel points the way to the creation of multiple histories, realities, truths. In feminist terms, this constructive impulse allows not only for the acknowledgement and representation of women's material existence but also for changes in women's material situations.

6. FANTASY AND CARNIVALIZATION
IN ANGELA CARTER'S *NIGHTS AT THE CIRCUS*

With extravagant playfulness, Angela Carter's *Nights at the Circus* (1984) weaves together elements of the carnivalesque and fantastic with those of harsh material realism as vehicles for feminist aims. Carter's novel is the literary heir of Virginia Woolf's *Orlando* and Djuna Barnes' *Nightwood,* both of which engage the fantastic and the carnivalesque, and indeed is more literary or fully artificial than the novels of Lessing, Piercy, and Atwood. Set in 1899, *Nights at the Circus* purports to usher in the twentieth-century. Carter's depiction of the past is strikingly familiar, however, which suggests that the present is effectively her target and that 1899 and the 1980s are not worlds apart. The novel is set not only in the past but also in places that are out of the ordinary—a whorehouse, a museum for women monsters, a circus, St. Petersburg, and Siberia—which enables Carter to engage in flights of imagination that do not directly contradict the immediate context of the contemporary reader.

The feminism of *Nights at the Circus* is complex in that it brings together more than one strand of feminism, an engaged Marxist feminism and a subversive utopian feminism.[1] Lizzie and her adopted daughter Fevvers serve, respectively, as mouthpieces for each of these two feminisms, although there is an overlap as the two characters influence each other. The novel's omniscient narrative voice strives to conjoin these two strands of feminism, in order to posit a feminism that would be liberating while retaining a sociohistorical grounding: a feminism that would free human beings from the hierarchical relations in which Western culture, with its binary logic, has entrapped them, without becoming disengaged from the material situation. In order to analyze the status both of women and of existing relationships between women and men within Western culture and, more radically, to propose possible avenues for change, Carter pits a Marxist feminist realism against postmodern forms of tall tales or autobiographies, inverted norms, carnivalization, and fantasy. Disruptive strategies usually associated with postmodernism pervade *Nights at the Circus* to a greater extent than any of the other novels I have discussed so far; but, like the others, it uses postmodern aesthetic strategies specifically to strengthen and further its feminist aims.[2] Even as she appropriates extraordinary and fantastic elements, Carter retains certain conventions of realism and a firm connection to the historical material situation as means of securing her novel's feminist political edge and ensuring that her novel remains accessible to most readers.[3]

To accomplish its aims, the novel engages and attempts to resolve the tensions that have characterized the uneasy relationship between Marxist feminism and postmodernism. Marxist feminism has generally rejected postmodernism on the grounds that its tendencies toward abstractions give way to a disconnection from the material world and from history, that it rejects metanarratives (such as Marxism and gender theory), and that it dissolves the subject. In contrast, Marxist feminists emphasize the material world in which women are daily oppressed as women and situate their analyses of women's oppression within specific political, cultural, historical, economic, ideological contexts. As Toril Moi explains, "patriarchy itself persists in oppressing women *as women*," so that "as feminists we need to *situate* our deconstructive gestures in specific political contexts."[4] Materialist feminism takes as its point of departure "the oppression of women" and asserts "the social origins" of that oppression, employing both micro- and macro-analyses. Furthermore, as "a social movement," a "revolutionary movement" actively seeking to change the world, Marxist feminism requires active agents/subjects.[5] However, as I argue in Chapter 1, postmodernism is a slippery area of contention that cannot be reduced to any oversimplified characterization. Indeed, the work of critics such as Fredric Jameson, Andreas Huyssen, Linda Hutcheon, Nancy Fraser, and Linda Nicholson demonstrates that postmodernism is not inherently antithetical to feminism and Marxism, that it is very much tied to the material world, that it actively engages history, that it does not necessarily invalidate all metanarratives, and that it seeks to reconstruct and reconceptualize, rather than negate, the subject. Similarly, Carter's novel aesthetically engages and conjoins Marxist feminism and certain postmodern aesthetic strategies in an effort to construct an engaged feminism with liberatory potential.

Carter's novel highlights its own textuality with its three labeled parts and its presentation of a metafictional narrative in which the sheer number of embedded narratives undermines notions of authorship and single-leveled reality. As with the other three novels I discuss in this study, one of the central preoccupations of *Nights at the Circus* is its challenge to the traditional Western opposition between reality and fiction. However, Carter's novel uses different strategies than the other novels to disrupt that dichotomy: the construction of carnival spheres, the relativizing of time, and the creation of fantastic images. The novel's rejection of any neat demarcation between reality and fiction functions as the pivotal strategy for undermining the Western conception of the subject and of traditional gender categories and for offering forms of liberating power. This liberating power carries with it possibilities for change in the realms of subjecthood and the relations between the sexes and also anticipates potential new forms for feminist fiction.

Nights at the Circus is divided into three parts labeled in terms of geographical location: "London," "Petersburg," and "Siberia." The movement toward increasingly foreign and remote places parallels a movement away from any stable grounds of reality and toward the ever more fantastic. The narrative is fragmented by various embedded stories, told by and about women, that further destabilize conventional notions of reality, truth, and authorship. Although the omniscient narrator purports to concentrate on the central male character's point of view, the narrative's perspective continuously shifts as it is appropriated by women characters telling their stories-histories in long monologues that often include vivid dialogue exchanges.

The novel's focus and central character is Fevvers, a huge female *"aerialiste"* with wings, whose fame rests on her indeterminate identity and origins: her slogan reads, "Is she fact or is she fiction?"[6] Lizzie, a staunch Marxist feminist, is Fevvers' adopted mother and companion, who took her in as a foundling. The "London" segment of the novel consists of an interview of Fevvers, in Lizzie's presence, by a young American journalist, Jack Walser. Walser's initial purpose is to expose Fevvers as "a hoax," as one of the "Great Humbugs of the World" (11). Although Walser is the interviewer, Fevvers and Lizzie control the session by telling Fevvers' life story and challenging his disbelief and skepticism. Walser's curiosity is only awakened by the women's "performance" (90) during the interview, and he decides to join the circus in order to follow up on this story. The second part, "Petersburg," focuses on Walser's transformation into a clown as he becomes subsumed within the magical circus world and recognizes that he has fallen in love with Fevvers. This segment relies more heavily on authorial narration, although it also includes segments of dialogue as well as embedded stories of the abused female circus performers befriended by Fevvers. By the novel's last section, "Siberia," the fantastic has taken over. The train carrying the circus crashes and the various characters wander around Siberia in various groups, meeting extraordinary people and situations. Walser and Fevvers are separated, and the novel ends when they are reunited. In this segment, the narrative shifts among Fevvers's and Walser's stream of consciousness, dialogue, embedded stories, and authorial narration.

Feminist and postmodern elements are so enmeshed in *Nights at the Circus* that any discussion of either necessarily overlaps with the other. It is, nevertheless, useful to begin with the more overt feminist currents. From its first page, Carter's novel begins to undermine conventional notions of gender construction and sexual hierarchy.[7] Fevvers asserts authority over her own story-history and evades attempts by Walser to fix an identity upon her. As in *The Handmaid's Tale,* a male writer is intent upon naming and thus objectifying a female character; but, in *Nights at the Circus,* his quest begins rather than ends the novel, which announces from the start the subversion of his attempts to appropriate Fevvers. Carter in this way begins to call into question accepted notions of identity and the binary logic on which they depend, as she attempts to create a new female subject that seeks to satisfy feminist aims.

Fevvers defies Walser's attempt to prove her a fake not by refusing to answer his questions but by taking command of her own self-definition as she tells him her story and thereby assumes a position of authority. As Teresa de Lauretis asserts, "strategies of writing *and* reading are forms of cultural resistance," and this argument surely can be extended to oral storytelling.[8] By having Fevvers read her own life and write, or rather tell, her own story-history as she chooses, the novel challenges the traditional appropriation of women's lives and histories endemic of Western male-centered culture. Furthermore, Fevvers deliberately flirts with the boundary between truth and non-truth. Her story is both an autobiography and a tall tale and, as such, destabilizes both male definitions of women and notions of identity, truth, and reality.

The novel opens with Fevvers' assertion that she "never docked via what you might call the *normal channels,* sir, oh, dear me, no; but, just like Helen of Troy, was *hatched*"; and the narrative specifies that she accompanies her statement with direct eye contact "as if to dare him: 'Believe it or not!'" The reference to the mythical Helen, engendered by Zeus in the form of a swan and Leda, ironically links Fevvers' self-definition to the history of Western culture by raising her to mythic or at least fantastic proportions. The narrative normalizes the comparison, however, by playfully debasing it to the level of ordinary family resemblances: "Evidently this Helen took after her putative father, the swan, around the shoulder parts" (7). Moreover, according to Ricarda Schmidt, Fevvers' claim that she was hatched suggests that she "fantasizes a beginning for herself outside the Oedipal triangle" associated with the nuclear family and subject formation.[9] To more thoroughly mystify her biological origins, Fevvers further asserts that she was a foundling. As a half-woman, half-swan orphan, Fevvers challenges prevailing notions of identity that are grounded in verifiable origins and binary logic.

By allowing her origins to remain a mystery and encouraging speculation about them, Fevvers maintains her status as "Heroine of the hour" (8). Her fame depends precisely on her being suspect, whether or not her wings are real. Although Walser is skeptical of Fevvers' claim that she is a "genuine bird-woman," he "contemplate[s] the unimaginable" while watching her perform on the trapeze and recognizes the "paradox" that, "in a secular age, an authentic miracle" would have to "purport to be a hoax, in order to gain credit in the world" (17). Walser's reflection highlights the precarious nature of the opposition between reality and fiction by suggesting that the concepts are intertwined. Fevvers' indeterminate identity and her insistence on preserving its mystery threaten the dichotomy between reality and fiction.

"At six feet two in her stockings" (12), Fevvers disrupts the conventions of female characters. She asserts her authority by simply taking up space: "Fevvers yawned with prodigious energy, opening up a crimson maw the size of that of a basking shark, taking in enough air to lift a Montgolfier, and then she stretched herself suddenly and hugely, extending every muscle as a cat does, until it seemed she intended to fill up all the mirror, all the room with her bulk." Walser is threatened by her appropriation of space and attempts to escape the room so that "he might recover his sense of proportion" (52), which is clearly male-defined. The novel's simultaneous insistence on Fevvers' bodily presence and on her self-construction frustrates the traditional Western dichotomy between soul-self and body, in which the body—and in turn the material world—is relegated to irrelevance and inferiority.[10] Fevvers significantly fills the mirror before she fills the room, highlighting the postmodern notion that nothing exists outside of representation or a specific context; yet she nevertheless fills the room as well, fulfilling the feminist insistence that representation retain a firm link to the material situation.[11]

Fevvers's "raucous" voice and her "grand, vulgar" (12–13) gestures indicate that she is comfortable with herself and has chosen her own codes of behavior. She takes up a traditionally masculine role by asserting herself as the author of her own actions and words. Having internalized conventional categories, Walser describes Fevvers as having a "strong, firm, masculine grip" (89) when she shakes his hand. The narrative also stresses her femininity, however, by describing her dressing room as "a mistresspiece of exquisitely feminine squalor" (9), using deliberately feminized language. Moreover, the depiction of one of her feminine flirtatious gestures, when "she batted her eyelashes at Walser in the mirror" (40), again presents Fevvers via the mediation of a mirror. Fevvers is altogether an ambivalent figure who threatens traditional binary categories: she possesses masculine strength and authority as well as feminine charms and wiles.[12] The interview reduces Walser, rather than Fevvers, to a passive state: "It was as if Walser had become a prisoner of her voice" (43). Carter's novel challenges the traditional association of female with femininity and male with masculinity through the depiction of characters who confound accepted gender norms and polarity. As Sally Robinson suggests, "For Carter, gender is a relation of power, whereby the weak become 'feminine' and the strong become 'masculine.' And, because relations of power change, this construction is always open to deconstruction."[13] Indeed, the novel does deconstruct the hierarchical opposition between masculine and feminine by presenting Fevvers as co-opting both masculine *and* feminine characteristics to establish her power over Walser. Fevvers and Lizzie assume control of the narrative in the novel's "London" section, unfolding Fevvers's life story-history through long dynamic monologues, interrupted by dialogues between the two women. The customary association of authorship and activeness with the male is here reversed: Fevvers and Lizzie are the active speakers-writers and Walser is the passive spectator-reader. Fevvers is able to "challenge and attack" (54) Walser's attempt to fix her identity, and thus objectify her, by constructing her own self and story-history. Fevvers exhibits herself as object for an audience's gaze; yet, as the author of herself as object, she is also a subject who has control over how much she will allow herself to be consumed by her viewers: "Look at me! With a grand, proud ironic grace, she exhibited herself before the eyes of the audience as if she were a marvellous present too good to be played with. Look, not touch" (15).[14] Fevvers begins her working career by posing as a *"tableau vivant,"* actively constructing herself as an object to be seen but not touched: as a child she is "Cupid" (23), and as she matures she becomes "Winged Victory" (25) and then "Angel of Death" (70). Although Fevvers objectifies herself, she remains a subject by constructing her own objectified image. By destabilizing and yet retaining the conventional opposition between subject and object, the novel moves toward non-hierarchical and non-binary notions of subjectivity while simultaneously engaging and highlighting issues of power relations. Although feminists such as Nancy Hartsock have criticized postmodernism for "getting rid of subjectivity or notions of the subject," *Nights at the Circus* illustrates ways in which postmodern notions of subjectivity can be tapped for feminist purposes without disintegrating subjectivity to the point where it no longer exists. Carter's novel never loses touch with the material oppression of women even while it attempts to offer new forms of subjectivity that are not based in the binary thought system that has helped to oppress women in Western culture. The novel does precisely what Hartsock claims is necessary for feminism to move forward: "we need to engage in the historical, political, and theoretical process of constituting ourselves as subjects as well as objects of history," and "we need not only to critique the dominant culture but also to create alternatives."[15]

Carter's novel differentiates among those who are performing the objectification of women and for what purposes. Fevvers's existence as both subject and object challenges the type of objectification by which "male-subjectivity creates its Other precisely to designate itself as its superior, its creator-spectator-owner-judge."[16] Fevvers vehemently rejects her own objectification by men: "I did *not* await the kiss of a magic prince, sir! With my two eyes, I nightly saw how such a kiss would seal me up in my *appearance* for ever!" (39). The threat of being forced into the position of static object to be viewed and dominated is all too tangible for Fevvers, who is again and again faced with attempts to fix the ambivalent figure she presents to the world.

The novel contains two separate instances in which men literally attempt to objectify Fevvers. In each case, the men seek to dominate her by depriving her of control over her own life. Their attempts to transform her into a corpse in one instance and into a toy in the other support the notion that "you can only objectify the living by taking away its life; by killing it either in fact or fantasy."[17] In the first episode, a wealthy gentleman purchases Fevvers from the museum of women monsters and attempts to kill her with a blade. Viewing her as a "reconciler of opposing states" and as his "rejuvenatrix" (81–82), he tries to sacrifice her on Mayday to ensure his own life and power. But Fevvers rejects the role of passive victim and male-constructed object and pulls out her own sword to save her life. She asserts her authority and subjecthood by matching his phallic power—located in his weapon rather that in his penis—sword for sword. The novel in this way emphasizes the violence that is part of male domination and that is tied to the realm of sexuality. As Michele Barrett argues, "sexual relationships are political because they are socially constructed and therefore could be different" and because of "the unequal power of those involved in sexual relationships."[18] Indeed, Christine Delphy explains that sexuality is "one of the fields of confrontation" or "struggle" between "social men and social women," so that oppression within the realm of sexuality is just "as material as economic oppression."[19] Later in the novel, a Russian grand duke attempts to cage her among his collection of exotic toys, but again Fevvers fights against objectification. After the Grand Duke breaks her sword, depriving her of phallic power, she resorts to feminine wiles to distract him: "a deep instinct of self-preservation made her let his rooster out of the hen-coop for him and ruffle up its feathers." She masturbates him and makes her escape at the moment "the Grand Duke ejaculated" (191–92). However, the novel does not jettison the conventions of realism, since it ultimately grounds seemingly extraordinary incidents—such as her narrow escapes from the wealthy gentleman and the Russian Grand Duke—in the daily victimization of women and thus challenges accepted notions of women as naturally and inevitably passive objects.[20]

Although Fevvers is presented as a fantastic being whose experiences encompass the extraordinary, the novel never severs the connection between her exploits and the material situation: Fevvers is fantastic but recognizable.[21] Her relationship with Lizzie is in this respect crucial, since Lizzie functions as the novel's didactic feminist voice. As a staunch Marxist feminist and former prostitute, Lizzie keeps the novel's focus from diverging too far from the economic aspects of material existence. In Hartsock's terms, Lizzie provides the novel with a "feminist standpoint [which] can allow us to descend further into materiality to an epistemological level at which we can better understand both why patriarchal institutions and ideologies take such perverse and deadly forms and how both theory and practice can be redirected in more liberatory directions."[22] Fevvers's story also indicates that Lizzie's politics have influenced her adopted daughter, particularly in the depiction of the whorehouse in which Fevvers was raised as "the common daughter of half-a-dozen mothers" (21) and which disrupts the nuclear family developed under capitalism. Since "the family" is at present "itself the site of economic exploitation: that of women"[23] and since "it is within the family that masculine and feminine people are constructed ... [and] that the categories of gender are reproduced," the production of new forms of subjectivity require new family structures and ideologies.[24]

Indeed, one of the means by which the novel begins to call into question the status quo and construct new notions of the subject is through its inversion of accepted norms in its treatment of prostitution and marriage. When Fevvers challenges Walser to print in his newspaper that she was raised by "women of the *worst class* and *defiled*," Walser's reply reveals his firm entrenchment in Western binary thought: "I myself have known some pretty decent whores, some damn' fine women, indeed, whom any man might have been proud to marry." Walser retains and even reemphasizes the dichotomy between good women and bad women, wives and whores, by asserting that some whores are good enough to become wives. The novel rejects these oppositions through Lizzie's voice, whose assertion that wives and whores have more in common than not undermines the Western ideology of marriage: "What is marriage but prostitution to one man instead of many" (21).

Lizzie's words echo not only Frederick Engels' discussion of bourgeois marriage in *The Origin of the Family* but also Carter's own discussion in her book-length essay, *The Sadeian Woman* (1978). *The Sadeian Woman* proposes that "sexual relations" are "necessarily an expression of social relations" and that, like prostitutes, "all wives of necessity fuck by contract." Carter undermines the conventional hierarchical opposition between wives and whores by stressing that "Prostitutes are at least decently paid on the nail and boast fewer illusions about a hireling status that has no veneer of social acceptability."[25] *Nights at the Circus* fictionalizes this criticism of the bourgeois notion of marriage and of the traditional dichotomy between wife and whore by using prostitutes as its positive female characters, reducing marriage to nothing more than an unquestioned custom grounded in a false ideology of happiness: "The name of this custom is a 'happy ending'." Lizzie cynically defines marriage as forcing a woman to give to a man both herself and her "bank account" (280–81), thus highlighting the economic exploitation of women within the institution of marriage that is covered over by fictions of romance.

The novel's Marxist feminism and its stress on the economic as well as ideological oppression of women surfaces in the descriptions of prostitutes as "working women doing it for money," as "poor girls earning a living" (38–39). Fevvers challenges the myths of whores as degenerates or nymphomaniacs by asserting that economics rather than pleasure informs the prostitute's work: "though some of the customers would swear that whores do it for pleasure, that is only to ease their own consciences, so that they will feel less foolish when they fork out hard cash for pleasure that has no real existence unless given freely—oh, indeed! we knew we only sold the *simulacra*. No woman would turn her belly to the trade unless pricked by economic necessity, sir" (39). In addition, the assumption that sexual favors can be both "real" and a *"simulacra"* of themselves calls into question the opposition between reality and fiction. Fevvers's words undermine the conventional association of sex with pleasure or desire by highlighting the contractual nature of all sexual relations. The novel designates sex as a business transaction rather than a moral category. Carter suggests that both the prostitute and the wife engage in sex as an economic exchange; the only difference lies in the prostitute's explicit acknowledgement of the contract. The prostitute comes out ahead in the novel, precisely because she is more aware of her position within an economic system in which all women necessarily participate.

Carter transforms the whorehouse into a "wholly female world," a "sisterhood" of active ambitious women, whose lives are "governed by a sweet and loving reason." The prostitutes are "all suffragists" (38–39)—*not* suffragettes—and professional women.[26] They engage in "intellectual, artistic or political" (40) pursuits before the whorehouse opens each evening and are thus active subjects as well as sexual objects. By making the prostitute its version of the feminist, the novel disrupts accepted norms and dualisms—including conventionalized notions of feminists. The term *whore* becomes ambivalent when it is dislocated from its position as polar opposite of wife, good woman, and even feminist. Furthermore, although her use of the term "honour" to denote selfhood is conventional, Fevvers's explicit questioning of the common reduction of women to their bodily orifices challenges traditional stereotypes: "Wherein does a woman's honour reside, old chap? In her vagina or in her spirit?" (230). Fevvers's words also emphasize the ways in which the biological body has been co-opted in the service of those in power.[27]

—————

Although some of the ideas Carter espouses in *The Sadeian Woman* find a voice within *Nights at the Circus,* the latter shapes Carter's ideas into a web of creative and overtly fictionalized narratives. In *Nights at the Circus,* Carter strengthens her feminist position through the use of various destabilizing aesthetic strategies. The novel's subversion of the notion of prostitution, for example, goes far beyond its overt analysis through the voices of Fevvers and Lizzie; it is reinforced by a thorough carnivalization of the whorehouse itself. Indeed, Carter's use of carnivalization and her creation of carnival spheres strengthen the novel's feminist impulses.

Mikhail Bakhtin describes the process of "carnivalization" as the "transposition of carnival into the language of literature" that brings to literary works the "carnival sense of the world [which] possesses a mighty life-creating and transforming power, an indestructible vivacity." The carnival attitude challenges the status quo by sanctioning unofficial behavior and by celebrating the "joyful relativity" of everything, so that the "behavior, gesture and discourse of a person are freed from the authority" of "the all-powerful socio-hierarchical relationships of non-carnival life." Bakhtin argues that this carnival attitude has been transmitted through the ages via various carnivalized genres, and in particular through Menippean satire.[28]

Literary critics engaging the postmodern have been quick to point out a connection between the carnivalization implicit in Menippean satire and postmodern literature. Brian McHale, for example, argues that "Postmodernist fiction is the heir of Menippean satire" and demonstrates ways in which postmodern literature appropriates processes of carnivalization. McHale maintains that postmodern fiction compensates for the loss of "the carnival context by incorporating carnival, or some surrogate of carnival, at the level of its projected world," so that "In the absence of a *real* carnival context, it constructs fictional carnivals."[29] An examination of the basic characteristics of Menippean satire as delineated by Bakhtin further suggests that carnivalization has overt political implications and might, therefore, be adapted as a feminist strategy. I am here arguing that *Nights at the Circus* utilizes a postmodern version of carnivalization as a vehicle for its more subversive feminist aims.

The political potential of Menippean and postmodern forms of carnivalization lies in what Bakhtin describes as its "*experimental fantasticality,*" its "creation of *extraordinary situations* for the provoking and testing of a philosophical idea." Carnivalized scenes of "scandal," "eccentric behavior," and other "violations" of "established norms" are used to create "a breach in the stable, normal ('seemly') course of human affairs and events," so as to "free human behavior from the norms and motivations that predetermine it." Bakhtin's further characterization of Menippean satire as having a "concern with current and topical issues" and as being "full of overt and hidden polemics" also points to the inherently political nature of this form of carnivalization.[30] Carter's *Nights at the Circus* is a prime example of a carnivalized novel, whose ultimate aim is to expose current feminist concerns and offer possibilities for change.[31] The novel's use of extraordinary and fantastic characters and situations and its creation of actual and surrogate carnivals begins to destabilize existing norms as well as the binary logic which undergirds Western culture.

By constructing the whorehouse, the museum for women monsters, the circus, and Siberia as versions of carnival, the novel disrupts and challenges traditional Western notions of reality and provides an aesthetic vocabulary for delineating possibilities of change. Since the carnival is a space within which the dominant hierarchical system and its laws and prohibitions are suspended, the carnival allows for ambivalence and relativity as well as for new forms of interrelationships—a primary feminist aim. The whorehouse in the "London" section of *Nights at the Circus,* for example, functions as a surrogate carnival and, as such, reinforces the novel's disruption of the accepted notion of prostitution and of the binary logic on which it depends. The novel's presentation of prostitutes in a positive light and of prostitution in non-moral terms, as well as its use of an extraordinary heroine with wings, are all carnivalesque disruptions of established norms. The physical description of the whorehouse itself further establishes its carnival status. The house's "staircase that went up with a flourish like, pardon me, a whore's bum" and its "drawing room [that] was snug as a groin" are comic touches that transform conventional imagery by inserting a whorehouse world view within a traditional descriptive style. Fevvers's outrageous depiction of the house as having an "air of rectitude and propriety" and as being "a place of privilege," in which "rational desires might be rationally gratified" (26–27), further challenges the status quo by deploying adjectives generally reserved for officially sanctioned institutions. The novel brings together high and low culture, destabilizing the distinction between them. The whorehouse of the novel's "London" section is a carnival sphere, in the sense that it defies established conventions and codes; it becomes other than what it is generally thought to be and thereby challenges the ruling order.

———

Fevvers is herself an ambivalent figure of carnival stature, disrupting established conventions of female characters. Not only are her identity and origins nebulous, but her reputation as "Virgin Whore" (55) defies the highly charged opposition between virgin and whore used by Western culture to name, objectify, categorize, and marginalize women. By claiming that she is the "only fully-feathered intacta in the history of the world" (294), Fevvers participates in her own social definition. Her admission at the end of the novel that she is after all not an "intacta" demonstrates that, in the absence of an essential self or soul, the possibility of self-construction exists alongside construction by others; Fevvers is able to create the being that others see her to be. Indeed, the outrageous nature of Fevvers as a character heightens the novel's challenge to Western culture's version of women as passive objects.[32]

The novel uses Lizzie's voice to reinforce didactically and theoretically the claim that selves are constructed rather than essential. Lizzie rejects the notion of "*soul*" as "a thing that don't exist" and asserts that it is history "that has forged the institutions which create the human nature of the present in the first place." In line with her staunch Marxism, Lizzie argues that the possibility of change rests on a thorough dismantling and restructuring of society: "It's not the human 'soul' that must be forged on the anvil of history but the anvil itself must be changed in order to change humanity" (239–40). Lizzie's declaration lends a Marxist tinge to the novel's feminism, with its implication that women's oppression will not end until social structures are radically altered. Carter uses the novel's two central female characters, Lizzie and Fevvers, to conjoin a material analysis of existing means of subject-construction and a carnivalized version of female self-construction as a way of exploring the possibility of new female subjectivities.

As a fantastic and indeterminate being, Fevvers can never be pinned down as a subject; her status is always in process of becoming other than itself.[33] Her identity is unstable, since she is a site of apparent contradictions: woman and bird, virgin and whore, fact and fiction, subject and object. Fevvers begins to lose her power and her subjecthood, however, when she questions her own status, "Am I what I know I am? Or am I what he thinks I am?", and regains it only when she reasserts her indeterminate identity by spreading her wings and recognizing herself through "the eyes that told her who she was" (290). Once again, she creates herself as the object of her spectators' desires and functions as both subject and object of desire.[34] Fevvers's subjectivity pushes toward the postmodern in the sense that her multifaceted and fluid identity destabilizes the rigid boundary between subject and object. Her indeterminate nature challenges these dichotomies and heralds the advent of new female subjectivities that are not grounded in binary logic and are released from the hierarchical relations implicit in binarism.

Desire is linked to a new version of subjecthood, as delineated by Fevvers, and to feminist liberating powers. By the end of the novel, Fevvers defines herself as a "New Woman" (273) in relation to—*not* in opposition to—both Walser, as the object of her desires, and desire itself. Her linking of Walser's "beloved face" to "the vague, imaginary face of desire" (204), suggests that the novel posits desire as an elusive but life affirming notion. The novel rejoins desire and love, which it depicts as divorced from sex in most instances—since it depicts sex as most often nothing more than pornography—and presents love and desire as containing emancipatory potentials. Carter ends *The Sadeian Woman* with the claim that "It is in this holy terror of love that we find, in both men and women themselves, the source of all opposition to the emancipation of women" (150). In *Nights at the Circus*, she takes a step further and creates a world in which human beings are freed through love and desire, by learning not to fear love and not to equate desire and sex with pornography. The novel's presentation of desire smacks of essentialism—desire as opposed to the culturally constructed pornographic *mise-en-scène* of desire—and yet, since desire functions on a utopian level and as carrying liberatory potential, it may be a utopian rather than essentialist reformulation of desire.

The novel distinguishes between pornography and desire. The pornographic nature of the "museum of woman monsters" (55), in which Fevvers is forced to work for a time, lies in its *mise-en-scène* of sexuality. As the Angel of Death, Fevvers claims that she does not engage in sexual intercourse itself; she merely poses as one of the *"tableaux vivants"* staged on "stone niches" in a "sort of vault or crypt" (60–61). The museum's male visitors indulge in a pornographic voyeurism; they don costumes and look at the female "prodigies of nature" (59) arranged as spectacle. The gentleman who favors Fevvers, for example, never touches her but, rather, looks at her while "playing with himself under his petticoat" (71). The male engages in sexual actions without the female in this pornographic situation and, as a result, remains in control; she serves merely as a visual stimulus. The novel's depiction of pornography as a staged representation of sexuality rather than as sexuality itself supports Marie-Françoise Hans and Gilles Lapouge's view of pornography as a "sexual spectacle, its reproduction or its representation, *the discourse on sexuality and not sexuality.*"[35]

The museum of women monsters in Carter's novel reinforces the notion that pornography is a representation of male domination.[36] The museum is an artificial arena, in which men occupy the position of dominance with no hindrances, since women are literally cast as museum objects to be viewed and consumed: Fevvers claims that the men visitors "hired the use of the idea of us [the women]" (70). Carter's depiction of the pornographic museum functions as a critique of male domination and the oppression of women; it supports her claims in *The Sadeian Woman* that pornography has a liberating potential, if it is used "as a critique of current relations between the sexes," and that "sexual relations between men and women always render explicit the nature of social relations in the society in which they take place and, if described explicitly, will form a critique of those relations, even if that is not and never has been the intention of the pornographer."[37] In other words, if pornography is a representation of male domination, then it is implicit that pornography can be used to criticize that very domination. As Susan Gubar points out, the divergent feminist arguments about pornography suggest that "an explicitly misogynist representation cannot automatically be equated with a sexist ideology."[38] Indeed, *Nights at the Circus* depicts the misogyny inherent in pornography as a means of criticizing male domination and its sexist ideology in general.

Fevvers's assertion that the women freaks in the museum had "hearts that beat like yours, and souls that suffer" (69) is an indictment of a society that objectifies women and treats them as less than human. The association of pornography and the dominant male-centered ideology surfaces through Fevvers' statement that "there was no terror in the house our [male] customers did not bring with them" (62). The novel depreciates male dominance with its depiction of men who are so fearful of losing their positions of mastery in the hierarchy of conventional heterosexual relationships that they are reduced to jerking themselves off while looking at women freaks in a damp basement. *Nights at the Circus'* strategy of turning pornography on its head manifests both feminist and postmodern impulses: feminist in the sense that it uses a conventionally misogynist discourse—pornography—to criticize the male-centered ideology that produces it; postmodern in its subversion of the supposed dichotomy established between pornography and daily life. Fevvers's assertion, for instance, that it was "those fine gentlemen who paid down their sovereigns to poke and pry at us who were the unnatural ones, not we. For what is 'natural' and 'unnatural', sir?" (61) both criticizes and calls into question the conventional dichotomy between that which is natural and that which is unnatural, exposing the opposition as an ideological construction. Within the world of the museum, sexual gratification occurs through staged means and is devoid of interpersonal connections or, in some cases, contacts. In the "Black Theatre," for example, the woman freak's task is to place "a noose around his [the client's] neck and give it a bit of a pull but not enough to hurt, whereupon he'd ejaculate" (61). The portrayal of the museum and its offerings demonstrates pornography's dehumanization of sex and sexuality.

The novel's depiction of pornography exceeds the bounds of the museum scenes, however, which heightens its criticism of male domination in its suggestion that sexual relations are for the most part pornographic in a culture that objectifies women. The attempted rape-murder by sword of Fevvers by a *gentleman* is a good case in point; it is a pornographic *mise-en-scène* of a sexual act. He makes her "Lie down on the altar" naked and approaches her with something that "was a sight more aggressive than his other weapon, poor thing, that bobbed about uncharged, unprimed," and that "*something* was—a blade" (83). This scene demonstrates the utter divorce between sexuality and interpersonal love and/or desire and the explicit link between sexuality and violence that exist in a male dominated world. Fevvers's description of the gentleman's useless and passive penis both ridicules the notion that man's dominating position is grounded in his *natural* aggressivity and exposes the means by which men dominate in actuality: through violence. The novel playfully reinforces the Lacanian notion that the privilege attributed to the male and the penis is grounded in "a confusion of the virile member with a phallic signifying function."[39] The gentleman dominates the situation only through his possession of a lethal sword, a phallic power that Fevvers appropriates—she has her own sword—to extricate herself from his power. Fevvers also uses her wings to escape the gentleman's grasp by simply flying out of his window and, therefore, uses a power that is not phallic in nature. The fantastic enables Carter to bypass and undermine phallic power and to posit other forms of power. Although flying away from an aggressor is not a practical solution for most women, Carter's use of the image indicates the liberating quality of strategies of empowerment that are not phallic and violent. Fevvers's use of her wings is a form of power similar to her use of storytelling, which she rids of its phallic associations—pen as penis—as well as of its reliance on strict distinctions between fiction and non-fiction; in both cases, self-empowerment is achieved through means that are nonviolent and that subvert Western binary logic.

The life stories of various abused women, which are retold by Fevvers within her own narrative, also contain depictions of events that are both part of everyday life and pornographic. Carter in this way makes explicit the link between pornography and the system that produces it. The story of the diminutive Wonder, one of the museum's women monsters, is punctuated by a description of how a company of comic dwarves mistreated her: "I travelled with them seven long months, passed from one to another, for they were brothers and believed in share and share alike. I fear they did not treat me kindly, for, although they were little, they were men." The dwarves' passing around of Wonder highlights the objectification of women inherent in Western culture. For the male dwarves, Wonder is a commodity to be used by all and then discarded, "abandoned" (68). Mignon's story is more explicit in its depiction of the violence inflicted on women by men to assert their authority. She is a battered circus wife, who is literally treated as an object: "the Ape-Man beat his woman as though she were a carpet" (115). She is also "abandoned to the mercies of a hungry tiger by her lover" (127), the Strong Man, when an escaped tigress intrudes upon their sexual encounter. Mignon's body itself, with its skin that was "mauvish, greenish, yellowish from beatings" and showed "marks of fresh bruises on fading bruises on faded bruises" (129), testifies to the horrifying violence that daily ensures male dominance.

The novel does not merely point out the oppression of women

by a male-dominated system, however; it offers potential solutions. Mignon, for example, acquires self-confidence and steps beyond her role as eternal victim. Fevvers and Lizzie help clean her up and find her a new position free of "The cruel sex [that] threw her away like a soiled glove" (155). Mignon is teamed up with the Princess in the dancing tigers act: the Princess plays the piano and Mignon sings. The two women quickly become friends and lovers, cherishing "in loving privacy the music that was their language, in which they'd found the way to one another" (168). Mignon is strengthened through the music that she believes they have "been brought together, here, as women and as lovers, solely to make" (275). The novel offers lesbian relationships as a possibility for women to find love and purpose in a world in which violence dominates heterosexual relations and women are kept from assuming control of their lives and talents. Fevvers reacts to this flowering of Mignon by asserting that "Love, true love has utterly transformed her" (276), in the sense that love has enabled Mignon to reject the role of victim and create herself as an active subject.

The transformative powers of love and the potential of lesbianism take on a larger and more fantastic force in the novel's depiction of a Siberian asylum for women who murdered their husbands and the revolt of these prisoners sparked by the vitality of desire. Designed and run by a Countess who "successfully poisoned her husband" and sought to assuage her conscience by serving as "a kind of conduit for the means of the repentance of the other murderesses," the prison is a *"panopticon"*: "a hollow circle of cells shaped like a doughnut, the inward-facing wall of which was composed of grids of steel and, in the middle of the roofed, central courtyard, there was a round room surrounded by windows. In that room she'd sit all day and stare and stare and stare at her murderesses and they, in turn, sat all day and stared at her" (210). As Michel Foucault has pointed out in *Discipline and Punish,* the panopticon prison design makes it "possible to hold the prisoner under permanent observation" by setting up "a central point from which a permanent gaze may control prisoners and staff." However, the cost of this system of surveillance by observation is that it also manages "to entrap the whole of penal justice and to imprison the judges themselves."[40] Carter playfully presents this paradox in the depiction of the Countess who is "trapped as securely in her watchtower by the exercise of her power as its objects were in their cells," since she must always keep watch over her prisoners: "the price she paid for her hypothetical proxy repentance was her own incarceration" (214). The wardresses are also imprisoned and watched, so that every one within the system of the asylum is, in effect, a prisoner regardless of her official position. Carter's depiction of the prison configuration implicitly serves as a parallel to the existing social structure, in which all human beings are effectively imprisoned.

In the prison chapter, the novel's omniscient narrative voice is totally separated from the voices of Fevvers and Walser, who are not present. Although the narrative does not condone murder, it analyzes the murderesses' acts as responses to the historically specific condition of women: "There are many reasons, most of them good ones, why a woman should want to murder her husband; homicide might be the only way for her to preserve a shred of dignity at a time, in a place, where women were deemed chattels, or, in the famous analogy of Tolstoy, like wine bottles that might conveniently be smashed when their contents were consumed" (210–11). The narrative voice's feminism surfaces in this discussion of the murderesses as victims of an inequitable system. The mock-rational tone emphasizes the absurdity of a world in which violence is the only recourse for women, since they are dominated and oppressed by men through violence. The narrative zooms in on one of the inmates, Olga, "who took a hatchet to the drunken carpenter who hit her around once too often" (211). Having "rehearsed in her mind the circumstances of her husband's death" and attributed them to things outside of her control, Olga "exonerated herself" (214–15) and set out to communicate with the wardress who brought her food daily. The relationship between Olga and her guard, Vera, quickly moves from a touch of the fingers, to "a free if surreptitious exchange of looks," to an exchange of notes. Having no pen or pencil, Olga "dipped her finger" in "her womb's blood" to write an answer to Vera's "love-words" (216).

Olga's use of her menstrual blood to assert herself as an active subject challenges the traditional association of menstrual blood with dirtiness and inferiority to men. Later in the novel, Carter provides evidence of this conventional devaluation of anything to do with women's reproductive selves in the depiction of a tribal woman banished to a "primitive hut" outside the village to give birth to her child. Lizzie aptly describes the scene, with the submissive "prone woman" and her baby alone in the freezing hut, as a "tableau of a woman in bondage to her reproductive system" (280–81).[41] Olga uses one of the most overt emblems of femaleness, traditionally used to set women apart as inferior to men, as a means of empowerment; she literally writes herself into subjecthood with her menstrual blood. This specific instance of a woman's assertion of power through an innovative writing process is linked to the novel's general presentation of creative story-telling as a strategy for empowerment and self-construction that challenges the established order.

Moreover, desire has generative powers within the world of the prison. It engenders love, which in turn feeds desire. The desire and love that develop between Olga and Vera spread to the other inmates of the asylum: "Desire, that electricity transmitted by the charged touch of Olga Alexandrovna and Vera Andreyevna, leapt across the great divide between the guards and the guarded. Or, it was as if a wild seed took root in the cold soil of the prison and, when it bloomed, it scattered seeds around in its turn. The state air of the House of Correction lifted and stirred, was moved by currents of anticipation, of expectation, that blew the ripened seeds of love from cell to cell" (217). The novel depicts desire as a force strong enough to destroy the artificial divisions that culture establishes between human beings to uphold a given hierarchical social order. Desire and love become agents of hope that have potential liberating powers. Within the world of the prison, that potential is actualized when the women prisoners and guards rise up against the countess and escape the asylum.

The image of "an army of lovers" striking out on foot across the Siberian tundra to "found a primitive Utopia" is both fantastic and freeing. Carter's novel uses this extraordinary situation to assert the possibility of change: "The white world around them looked newly made, a blank sheet of fresh paper on which they could inscribe whatever future they wished" (217–18). The new sisterhood of women sets out to forge a new social order that excludes men and rejects the notion of "fathers" and "the use of the patronymic" (221). This new "republic of free women" is not totally independent of men, however, since they are forced to ask a passing male traveler for "a pint or two of sperm" to ensure their community's survival. When Lizzie hears the traveler recount his meeting with the women, she sarcastically asks what they will do if they give birth to baby boys: "Feed'em to the polar bears? To the *female* polar bears?" (240–41). Lizzie's question highlights the impossibility of severing ties between the sexes if humanity is to continue, since both sexes are necessary for reproduction. While the narrative voice cannot be equated with Lizzie's specific words, Lizzie's challenging of the female utopia indicates that the novel does not view a separatist lesbian community as a final answer to the problems faced by women within a male-centered culture. The novel clearly seeks to go beyond separatism to a restructuring of the whole system in such a way that men would no longer dominate and oppress women.

Although the novel depicts love and desire as they manifest themselves between women on the margins of accepted institutions or norms of behavior, such as prostitutes, freaks, battered women, and murderesses, *Nights at the Circus* also delineates the transformations necessary to achieve love and desire within heterosexual relationships. Carter's novel asserts that changes in the status of women and the relations between the sexes require the formation of "New Men" alongside "New Women." As in the novels of Lessing, Piercy, and Atwood, *Nights at the Circus* implicitly calls for a restructured society in which the quality of life would improve for both women and men. Fevvers proposes to "mould" and "transform" Walser "into the New Man, in fact, fitting mate for the New Woman, and onward we'll march hand in hand into the New Century" (281). She has a utopian vision of the future as a "new dawn": "all the women will have wings" to escape their "mind forg'd manacles" and to "rise up and fly away." At the same time, the novel grounds this utopian dream and fantastic images in the material situation, through Lizzie's retort that "It's going to be more complicated than that" with plenty of "storms ahead" (285). Lizzie's words do not negate the novel's utopian impulses so much as refuse to disconnect them from material practice. The novel offers possibilities for the future while highlighting the extensive struggles that will be necessary to achieve the kind of feminist utopia Fevvers imagines.

Despite Lizzie's skepticism about the future, *Nights at the Circus* does contain two male characters who undergo significant changes that move them closer towards Fevvers's notion of the "New

Man" by the novel's end. The Strong Man begins as an abusive male who uses his physical strength to dominate and oppress women such as Mignon. His lust for her is slowly transformed, however, into a love for Mignon and the Princess as a pair. He grows "stronger in spirit," and his new hope is to become worthy of the two women's love of him as "a brother": "I abused women and spoke ill of them, thinking myself superior to the entire sex on account of my muscle, although in reality I was too weak to bear the burden of any woman's love" (276). Through its depiction of the Strong Man's metamorphosis from a caricature of a misogynist he-man to a complex caring "New Man," the novel exposes self-indulgent lust as a form of desire that is nothing more than power-play, while highlighting the transformative potential of desire that grows into selfless love.

Walser also undergoes great changes, which the novel delineates in much greater detail than in the case of the Strong Man—a relatively minor character. The novel traces Walser's transformation from a skeptical man of action who tries to establish and co-opt Fevvers' identity to a man who accepts indeterminacy and seeks to explore the complexities of humanity itself. His questions shift from a disengaged "Is she fact or is she fiction?" (7) to an intense "Have you a soul? Can you love?" (291). While fashioning Walser into a suitable companion for the "New Woman" demonstrates feminist impulses, the novel uses the carnivalesque and fantastic, strategies often associated with postmodern fiction, to disrupt traditional linear time and notions of an essential core self as well as the rigid distinctions between reality and fiction, civilization and nature, self and other. Although the novel initially presents Walser as a polished and skeptical man of the world, the narrative also specifies that he is "unfinished" and that "his inwardness had been left untouched" (10) by his experiences. This "unfinished" quality implies that Walser is neither fixed nor static, that he is malleable, that he is a subject in process. Walser's decision to join the circus to follow up his story of Fevvers functions as a step into the realm of the fantastic. The novel's central section focuses on the world of the circus, a more overt form of the carnival than the whorehouse of the preceding section. The depiction of the circus performers both in and out of the ring challenges the conventional opposition between reality and fiction. Although illusion is sought within the ring, the novel indicates

that illusion exists outside of it as well. The carnivalesque repudiation of the established hierarchical order filters out from the circus
ring into the personal lives of the performers. The novel extends the
boundaries of carnival well beyond the physical circus ring, thus
extending the carnival's transformative powers to life itself.[42]

Fantasy and the material situation meet head on in the world
of the circus. The set divisions and hierarchies between humans and
animals and between men and women in the Western world at large
break down in Carter's circus. The ringmaster is a caricature of the
American capitalist and patriot with his belt "buckle, in the shape of
a dollar sign" and his "tightly tailored trousers striped in red and
white and a blue waistcoast [sic] ornamented with stars" (99). He
uses his pet pig, Sybil, to make his decisions for him, so that, when
Walser asks for a job with the circus, the ringmaster invites "his pig
to tell him whether to hire the young man or no" (98) and to tell him
how Walser should be used. Sybil proceeds to nod her approval and
to spell the word "C-L-O-W-N" (102) out of a pile of alphabet cards.
The ringmaster as an incarnation of Uncle Sam both in and out of
the limelight disrupts the distinction between illusion and reality:
he is a fantastic absurd figure and yet occupies a tangible position of
power, since he actively manages a circus and controls the fates of
his employees. Moreover, Sybil's decision-making skills and responsibilities not only reinforce the ringmaster's extraordinary nature
but also undermine the conventional division between humans and
animals, based on the posited opposition between civilization and
nature.

The circus not only actively brings together the civilized and
natural worlds, by placing under the same roof "lovely ladies" with
their "French perfume" and hairy beasts with their "essence of
steppe and jungle" (105), but also explodes the hierarchical opposition
between civilized humans and primitive animals. The chimpanzee
act parodies a classroom scene, with a Professor chimp writing on
the blackboard and the student chimps busy over their slates.
Walser "knew he had stumbled on a secret when the lesson immediately stopped" after he attempted to get a closer look at the
Professor's "mysterious scholarship." After Walser's and the
Professor's eyes meet in a nonverbal but "intimate exchange," a
"meeting across the gulf of strangeness," Walser recognizes that the
chimp is "unreachable … but not unknowable." This unusual contact

allows Walser to ascertain that the chimps take no pleasure in the forced play of their comic monocycle routine, "going through the motions with a desultory, mechanical air, longing perhaps, to be back at their studies." When the Professor uses Walser as a model for an anatomy lesson, Walser is left with "a dizzy uncertainty about what was human and what was not" (108–10). The irony of the episode lies in the contrast between the studious chimps and the trainer's woman, Mignon, who is copulating with the Strong Man on the side of the ring during the anatomy lesson. This overt reversal, in which the chimps are engaged in civilized behavior while the humans have descended into brute animalism, challenges the established order. The Professor even negotiates his own contract with the ringmaster, on the grounds that "Nature did not give me vocal cords but left the brain out of Monsieur Lamarck," the Ape Man (169). The novel's comic and fantastic treatment of the chimps exposes the indeterminacy inherent in concepts such as humanity and civilization as well as in the dichotomies used to anchor them. Moreover, the Professor's rejection of the Ape Man's humanity and authority reinforces the novel's feminist stance by challenging man's place at the top of the hierarchy of existence. Like the chimps, the women circus performers rebel against the men that dominate them: Fevvers foils the ringmaster's advances, Mignon rejects both the Ape Man and the Strong Man in favor of the Princess, and the Princess keeps aloof of human beings altogether.[43]

The circus scenes not only break down the conventional hierarchical order in which man rules over women and animals but also challenge the notion of *Being* itself. The figure of the clown functions as a locus of indeterminacy that threatens Western metaphysics. While the clown's makeup and costume are a mask, this mask takes on a life of its own and as such has a liberating potential: it undermines notions of the self as predetermined, fixed, unitary, and centered. When Walser is transformed into a clown for the first time, he feels "the beginnings of a vertiginous sense of freedom," "the freedom that lies behind the mask, within dissimulation, the freedom to juggle with being" (103). The clown's mask unsettles *Being* by calling into question notions of origin and selfhood. The mask disrupts the Western concept of the essential self by reducing identity to an explicitly artificial mask. As the clowns sit together eating a meal, their white faces "possessed the formal lifelessness of death masks, as if, in some essential sense, they themselves were absent from the repast and left untenanted replicas behind" (116). If there is merely "An absence. A vacancy" (122) beneath the mask, then the mask is merely an empty signifier, an illusion of a stable identity. However, while the clown scenes present the self as nothing more than a constructed shell, this self is neither powerless nor static. Clowns have the privilege of self-construction: "We can invent our own faces! We *make* ourselves" (121). Their freedom to choose the self they wish to become undermines the Western concept of an essential self or soul that exists prior to socialization. The political potential of a conception of the self as constructed rather than essential is great, since it allows for the creation of new versions of the self. Once Walser dons the clown mask, for example, he becomes other than he has been. The novel's attempt to conceive a "New Woman" and a "New Man" depends on this possibility of creating the self as other than it has been constructed by and through a male-centered culture.

The clown also challenges the traditional Western opposition between subject and object by being both the subject and the object of laughter. In this respect, the novel's version of the clown is similar to its version of the prostitute. Clowns are "whores of mirth" whose chosen means of economic survival entail giving pleasure to others; they are subjects who consciously make themselves into objects. Like the prostitutes, the clowns defy the conventional opposition between work and play: "Our work is their pleasure and so they think our work must be our pleasure" (119). It is the clown's job to foster illusions by suspending the distinction between reality and fiction. The novel goes one step further, however, in its depiction of the clowns' final performance, during which the head clown, Buffo, goes raving mad and attempts "*real* manslaughter" on Walser. This scene totally breaks down the hierarchical opposition between reality and fiction, as the clowns pretend that Buffo is only pretending to try to kill Walser. The clowns attempt "to give the illusion of *intentional* Bedlam" (177) to a scene that *is* Bedlam. What is real or true and what is fiction or illusion are so completely intertwined that they can no longer be distinguished. The narrative's claim that "the circus could absorb madness and slaughter" (180) emphasizes the subversive potential of carnival, with its power to challenge and break down the binary logic that undergirds Western culture. In

Carter's novel, the carnivalesque infects everything, so that its subversive impulses are not contained within any artificial boundaries such as the circus ring.

The collapse of the rigid opposition between reality and fiction in the depiction of the clowns renders the laughter they engender ambivalent. This ambivalence is a function of the uncertain object of the laughter: is it the clowns' antics or the established order they are parodying? The ambivalent laughter they have induced has a liberating potential, since it creates a space for overtly criticizing the dominant system through ridicule. Although this space has the potential of being harnessed for specific political purposes, the narrative is seduced at times into a nihilistic descent into chaos. When they perform outside the circus ring in their Russian lodging and, later, out on the tundra, the clowns' dance becomes a "savage jig" that mimes "beastly, obscene violence." Rather than an affirmation of life or a parody of established order, it becomes a "Dance of disintegration; and of regression; celebration of the primal slime" (124–25). The clowns' "dance of death" literally ends in death when a snow blizzard hits the site of their performance in the Siberia section, blowing all the clowns "off the face of the earth" (242–43). The novel's emphasis on chaos and disintegration in some of the clown scenes veers away from either a criticism of the dominant system or an offering of new possibilities. At those points where a movement toward unrestrained deconstruction and chaos surfaces, the narrative severs its connection to the novel's feminist reconstructive aims.

Carter's novel as a whole avoids this tendency towards excessive chaos, however, through its periodic re-anchoring of chaos and the fantastic in the historical and material situation, and thus implicitly exposes the limits of the postmodern tendency toward chaos. The world of the circus, for instance, is firmly grounded in its physical locale, in the daily lives of its performers, and in the hierarchies of Western culture at large. The luxury of the "Imperial Circus," with its "red plush boxes trimmed with gilding," cannot escape "the aroma of horse dung and lion piss that permeated the building" (105), so that the circus' illusion of grandeur and magic is always in the process of being challenged. Outside the ring, the performers must take part in the daily tasks that ensure survival, as evidenced by the "row of freshly washed white muslin frocks pegged out on a clothesline," Lizzie "carrying a tray covered with a white cloth" (106) for Fevvers' lunch, and the Princess filling "her arms with bleeding meat" to feed the lions (148).

The link between power and material conditions that prevails in Western culture finds its parallel in the world of the circus. The ringmaster and the star, Fevvers, stay in a luxurious hotel, filled with "the dazzle of electricity, the furry carpets, the fine ladies" (126–27), while Walser and the "clowns were lodged among the poorest" (98) people in St. Petersburg's "rotten wooden tenement" (116). The narrative further highlights the inequities inherent in hierarchical positions through its depiction of the different cities that Walser and Fevvers experience: Walser has "seen only the beastly backside" of St. Petersburg, while "Fevvers, nestling under a Venetian chandelier in the Hotel de l'Europe has seen nothing of the city in which Walser lodges" (104). All of these physical details strengthen the novel's socio-historical grounding and prevent its disruptive postmodern tendencies from falling into an overly aestheticist or theoretical realm divorced from the material situation. Although the novel uses the circus to expose the artificiality of the traditional dichotomy between reality and fiction, the novel does not collapse the two terms. Instead, the fantastic stands side by side with the details of daily human existence, so as to emphasize their necessary interrelatedness; ultimately, everything—including the fantastic—exists within the context of the material situation and the relations of power that structure it. The novel not only makes use of the carnivalesque and fantastic to disrupt Western meta-physics as a means of creating a space for reconstruction but also highlights the carnivalesque and fantastic as aesthetic modes constructed within and intricately tied to material contexts.

As the narrative progresses into the Siberia section, temporal and spatial logic break down more radically, and the fantastic becomes more prominent. The circus segment ends with Fevvers's escape from the Grand Duke's attempt to objectify her literally, as a bird in a gilded cage to stand among his collection of toys. Her method of escape, however, transgresses all established notions of time and space. Fevvers jumps onto the Grand Duke's toy train, which immediately becomes the Siberian Express on which the circus company is traveling:

She dropped the toy train on the Isfahan runner—mercifully, it landed on its wheels—as, with a grunt and whistle of expelled breath, the Grand Duke ejaculated.

In those few seconds of his lapse of consciousness, Fevvers ran helter-skelter down the platform, opened the door of the first-class compartment and clambered aboard.

"Look what a mess he's made of your dress, the pig," said Lizzie. (192)

Not only does Fevvers shrink to the size of the toy train, but the toy train is then transformed into the life-size train carrying the circus across Siberia. Consequently, she travels from the Duke's home to the Siberian Express instantaneously. This episode totally disrupts Western temporal and spatial laws, which view time as linear movement and duration and space as a fixed three-dimensional entity, and thus steps decisively into the realm of the fantastic. The narrative does not differentiate between the reality status of the toy train and the Siberian Express, so that distinct levels of narrative merge and the opposition between reality and fiction becomes meaningless.

Postmodern fiction often engages the fantastic as a means of making visible "the unsaid and the unseen of culture." Rosemary Jackson's argument, in *Fantasy: The Literature of Subversion*, that fantasy "reveals reason and reality to be arbitrary, shifting constructs, and thereby scrutinizes the category of the 'real'" suggests that fantasy and postmodern fiction have some common grounds.[44] Indeed, McHale claims that postmodern fiction has "co-opted" the fantastic as one of several strategies that "pluralizes the 'real' and thus problematizes representation."[45] Fantasy's subversive potential is postmodern in the sense that fantasy continuously questions the reality status of what is being presented, thereby creating a climate of perpetual indeterminacy that threatens the established order. Moreover, Jackson's assertion that fantasy does not "construct alternative realities" but rather focuses on "absence, lack, the non-seen" and "moves into, or opens up, a space without/outside cultural order" points to a possible use of fantasy as a strategy to fulfill feminist aims.[46] Since most of the absences and silences in Western culture stem from that which threatens the male dominant order, a genre that highlights these spaces has feminist potentials.[47]

The novel's last section is significantly positioned in what is essentially a non-location. As a vast, seemingly boundless, empty expanse, Siberia is an ideal context for fantastic occurrences. The tundra is literally a "white world," a "blank sheet of fresh paper" (218), a "limbo to which we had no map" (225), an "empty horizon" (236). Unlike the whorehouse, the museum for women monsters, and the dressing room in the first section and the circus in the second section, Siberia is neither an enclosure nor a cultural artifact. It is an open space that dissolves the very notion of limits and boundaries that structure Western thought. Like the whorehouse and the circus, however, Siberia becomes a carnivalized realm. After the Siberian Express crashes, the characters are set wandering about the tundra and encountering extraordinary situations and persons.[48]

The novel does not lose sight of material conditions, however; the fantastic quality of the events that follow the train's derailment stands side by side with the mundane details of daily life. The immediate consequences of the crash include both the extraordinary fate of the circus' tigers and the basic physical harm suffered by various characters: the "tigers were all gone into the mirrors," having "frozen into their own reflections," while Fevvers has broken her "right wing" and Walser has been knocked unconscious. The performers are kidnapped by "a band of rough-looking coves in sheepskins, armed to their teeth" (205–07), with the exception of Walser, who remains hidden under a pile of debris in a comatose state. Walser is later unearthed but left behind by the escaped murderesses. Beset by amnesia, Walser subsequently wanders around in the tundra until he is taken up and apprenticed by a tribal Shaman. When Walser and Fevvers meet again, the time span that has elapsed is not the same for each of them. Although this string of events is fantastic and absurd in the sense that it flaunts the conventions of realism, the implausibility or strangeness of the various incidents do not sever them from their sociohistorical grounding. For instance, the bandits who derail the train and kidnap its passengers are outlaws as a result of the vengeance they sought against the "minor officials, army officers, landlords and such like petty tyrants, who forcibly dishonoured the[ir] sisters, wives and sweethearts." Having read a newspaper headline claiming that Fevvers is "the intimate of the English royal family," the bandits blow up the railroad track in an attempt to get Fevvers to intercede in their favor with "Queen Victoria." The extraordinary nature of the bandits' actions and motives are linked to unjust class relations and to their idealistic vision of the ruling class. Fevvers shatters the bandit chief's illusions by informing him that it is "idle folly" to "fancy these great ones care a single jot about the injustice you suffer," since they "themselves weave the giant web of injustice that circumscribes the globe" (230–32). Although the narrative's tone is ironic and the bandits appear overly naive, these absurd fantastic events have a firm basis in the material situation. The fantastic plot here functions as a means of exposing sociohistorical inequities.

Walser's amnesia, his aimless wanderings through the snow without freezing to death, and his adoption by a Shaman are similarly ludicrous and fantastic in nature. In the world of the Shaman and his tribe, reality and dream-vision are not distinct. Indeed, the Shaman valorizes dreams as that which "dissolved the slender margin the Shaman apprehended between real and unreal." For the tribesmen, "there existed no difference between fact and fiction; instead, a sort of magic realism" (260). This notion of "magic realism" is appropriate to the novel as a whole, since the novel is intent on bringing together realism and fantasy. Unlike the tribesmen, however, Carter's novel does not collapse fact and fiction but rather disrupts the Western hierarchical opposition between the two to reveal the constructed and artificial nature of Western binary logic. Since the tribesmen value dreams and hallucinations as communication with the world of spirits, they respect Walser's amnesiac ravings. As he slowly recovers from his amnesia, Walser views his memories as dreams or products of his trances or hallucinations. Although others eventually substantiate some of his memories, the distinction in his mind between fact and fiction remains fluid after his sojourn within the tribe.

Walser's developing self is as a result no longer firmly grounded in binary logic. The first thing Fevvers notices about Walser when they are finally reunited is that his eyes contained "no trace of scepticism at all" (289), a striking reversal from the novel's initial description of Walser as having "eyes the cool grey of scepticism" (10). Fevvers instantly recognizes that "he was not the man he had been," that he was a "reconstructed Walser." When he asks Fevvers about her soul and her ability to love, she is "exuberant" and assures him that "That's the way to start the interview" (291). No longer bound by and trapped within binary logic, which the novel early on exposes as male-centered, Walser moves toward Fevvers's ideal of the "New Man." While Walser's development into this "New Man" fulfills the conventions of romance narratives, in that he becomes a "fitting mate for the New Woman" (281), the novel simultaneously disrupts the very conventions of romance fiction, which are based on a binary logic that posits men as dominant over women. Free of his initial skepticism, Walser is no longer interested in whether Fevvers is fact or fiction, a question that has little meaning or relevance after he experiences and acknowledges the arbitrary and artificial nature of such an opposition. Although Walser's new concern with Fevvers's identity and soul would seem to revert back to an essentialist viewpoint, these notions lose their essentialism, since they are no longer grounded in binary logic or in any belief in origins. Walser has learned to accept Fevvers as an indeterminate being; he is no longer interested in drawing "any definite conclusions" from the fact that "she indeed appeared to possess no navel" (292). Moreover, the subversive carnivalesque nature of Fevvers, her life-story, and the laughter with which the novel ends inherently disrupt essentialist positions.

Before Walser and Fevvers are reunited at the end of the novel, the fantastic forcefully rears its head when Fevvers gets a momentary glimpse of Walser with the tribesmen. She is startled by his long beard and wild appearance: "But it's not a week since we all parted company! You can't go native in a week." Lizzie reminds Fevvers that they have lost their clock and therefore have no control over time: "Remember we have lost our clock; remember Father Time has many children and I think it was his bastard offspring inherited this region for, by the length of Mr Walser's beard and the skill with which he rode his reindeer, time has passed—or else is passing—marvellous swiftly for these woodland folk" (272). Moreover, the narrative asserts that "Time meant nothing" to the tribesmen and that, if a "global plebiscite" had been taken, "the entire system of dividing up years by one hundred would have been abandoned" (265). The novel uses the fantastic to disrupt the Western notion of time as a linear and absolute dimension. The power with which the lost clock is imbued serves as a means of high-lighting the notion that clocks, a product of Western rationalism, construct and control time. However, Lizzie's comment is also ironic, since the old clock, taken as souvenir from the whorehouse, is permanently stopped at midnight or noon; the dysfunctional clock suggests the precariousness of a concept (time) that depends on a mechanical, physical, and thus breakable object. That Lizzie and Fevvers choose to carry around a stopped clock indicates their rejection of Western conceptual modes. Indeed, from the beginning of the novel, Fevvers and Lizzie are involved in disruptions of linear time. During the initial interview scene, for instance, Walser becomes "seriously discomposed" (42) after he hears Big Ben strike midnight three separate times while Fevvers tells her story. The literal suspension of time, which renders Fevvers' dressing room into a place "plucked out of its everyday, temporal continuum" (87), defies the linear movement attributed to it by Western culture and poses a threat to Walser, whose very being is defined by that culture.

The difference in the time periods lived by Walser and Fevvers under divergent systems of thought and beliefs exposes time as a relative concept rather than a series of fixed quantitative increments. The novel goes beyond the modernist incorporation of Einsteinian relativity, which focuses on the position of the observer, by flaunting its transgression of established temporal boundaries. The length of Walser's beard indicates a time span that is incommensurable with the week that Fevvers claims has passed, regardless of perspective. Traditional Western logic cannot reconcile this lack of agreement and symmetry. The gap between the two divergent temporal experiences, which remains open and unresolved, disrupts one of the West's central points of reference. Crucial to my argument is that the novel's emphasis on temporal indeterminacies through fantasy serves a practical function linked to its feminist impulses. It allows Walser a significant time span to recover from his amnesia and reshape himself under the influence of a culture that is not grounded in binary logic and values the world of the irrational, such as dreams and hallucinations. Unlike Fevvers, who is already moving toward being a representative of the "New Woman" from the novel's start, Walser needs time to develop a self that moves toward Fevvers's utopian image of the "New Man." Fevvers's wanderings through Siberia need not include the same number of experiences as Walser's for them to meet on a more equal footing when they are reunited. The novel's transgression of temporal boundaries functions as a means of both disrupting confining Western conceptual modes and fulfilling asymmetrical narrative needs.

Although Walser undergoes a more extensive transformation, Fevvers's experiences in Siberia also shape her. Having lost both her sword and her clock, Fevvers no longer possesses the tools she has usurped from the dominant order to wield her own power and control. She feels "herself diminishing" (273) and must seek new ways of empowerment that are neither male-centered nor male-defined. Lizzie explains to Fevvers that, since she exists as a recent untried phenomenon, she must shape the form this "New Woman" will take: "You never existed before. There's nobody to say what you should do or how to do it. You are Year One. You haven't any history and there are no expectations of you except the ones you yourself create" (198). Fevvers has created herself as an indeterminate being, hovering between fact and fiction, with the help of her extraordinary wings. With one wing broken and the dye in her hair and on her wings fading, however, her explosive singularity diminishes; she feels reduced from a "tropic bird" to a "London sparrow" (271). Furthermore, the tundra affords her no audience to view her as a marvel and value her as a new being. Fevvers feels renewed only when she spreads her wings in front of Walser and the tribesmen and feels "the wind of wonder" from "their expelled breaths." Her power and strength as a "New Woman" requires others whose "eyes fixed upon her with astonishment, with awe, the eyes that told her who she was" (290). The novel's notion of the "New Woman" thus retains the concepts of subject and object and of self and other at the same time as it challenges the hierarchical oppositions within which these concepts have traditionally been positioned by Western culture. Fevvers's existence as a subject is dependent on both her own self-construction and the acknowledgment of that construction as read in the eyes of others, which indicates that subjecthood is a continuous process rather than a static position (see discussion earlier in the chapter).

Nights at the Circus also posits another dimension to the formation of new women and men subjects: romantic love. Contemporary fiction has tended to focus on the absence or death of love rather than on its presence. Carter revives the notion of love by redefining it and asserting its liberating potential. Love replaces the sword, or violence in general, as a means of self-empowerment. All of the novel's characters who undergo transformations toward the ideal of the "New Woman" or the "New Man" are also in love:

Fevvers, Mignon, the Princess, the murderesses, Walser, and the Strong Man. Although the novel depicts love between women, its focus is on exploring the possibility of a strong heterosexual love. Fevvers and Walser fall in love fairly early in the novel, but only when they are separated in Siberia and undergoing transformations does their love surface and grow. On one level, the novel is a romance, although it is a literary rather than a realistic romance. Carter's novel asserts that the recognition of "fear of the death of the beloved, of the loss of the beloved, of the loss of love" (292–93) helps to shape a self that is engaged and open to change. The love proclaimed by the novel as liberating is a form of love that has been released from culturally imposed prescriptions and from oppressive relations of power. The novel seeks to get beyond the "popular ideology of romantic love," which, as Barrett argues, coexists with "the brutal facts of rape, domestic violence, pornography, prostitution, a denial of female sexual autonomy."[49] Walser's initial hopes for the future with Fevvers are marked by his dream of making her his "wife, Mrs Sophie Walser," and thus occur within the context of male domination and ownership of women. By the end of the novel, however, Walser recognizes that he must rewrite his hopes for the future, which now focus on "busily reconstructing" a "self": "Walser took himself apart and put himself together again"; he has "to start all over again" (293–94). Content to be Fevvers's lover, Walser no longer seeks ownership of her; and she, in fact, remains in control of their relationship to the novel's last line.

Although the novel ends with the bringing together of the "New Woman" and the "New Man," the utopian quality of the ensuing bedroom scene between the two reunited lovers is firmly grounded in details of material existence. For example, Fevvers insists on "washing herself piece by piece in a pot of water" before consummating their relationship. Romance is brought down to the realm of practical considerations that is a vital part of human daily life. As he watches Fevvers wash with her feathers released, Walser also focuses on practical physical details by reflecting on "how nature had equipped her for the 'woman on top' position." Moreover, the utopian union of Fevvers and Walser exists side by side with Lizzie's active feminist practice, as she sets up an "improvised maternity ward" for the Shaman's tribe and embarks "on the elaboration of an extensive ritual of mother-and-baby care" (292–93).[50] Carter's novel retains its political impetus by offering both possibilities for change and practical examples of how change can be brought about.

The novel ends on the rejuvenating and liberating note of Fevvers's carnivalesque laughter, brought on by Walser's question as to why she went "to such lengths" to convince him that she was the "only fully-feathered intacta in the history of the world?" She is delighted by this question, to which she gleefully retorts, "Gawd, I fooled you." Fevvers's subjecthood is assured through Walser's question, since it proves that she has the power to construct her own version of herself. She attributes her ability to fool even a skeptic, such as Walser was at the start of the novel, to her spirited determination to define herself: "'To think I really fooled you!' she marvelled. 'It just goes to show there's nothing like confidence'" (294–95). Along with love, then, laughter functions as a liberating strategy that is useful in the process of developing new versions of the subject.

Fevvers's loud uncontrollable laughter problematizes the meaning of the novel's ending at the same time as it releases a liberating energy. It is an ambivalent form of laughter, in that it exceeds its context and in that its meaning is plural and dynamic. Ambivalent laughter is a vital element of the carnival, described by Bakhtin as embracing both "death and rebirth" and as "directed toward something higher—toward a shift of authorities and truths, a shift of world orders."[51] Fevvers's laughter salutes the end of Walser's skepticism and disengagement, as well as her feelings of diminishment, and welcomes the fresh winds of change. The laughter that physically ends Carter's novel creates a sense of beginning. Uncontained, it "spilled out of the window" and infected everyone and everything: "The spiralling tornado of Fevvers' laughter began to twist and shudder across the entire globe, as if a spontaneous response to the giant comedy that endlessly unfolded beneath it, until everything that lived and breathed, everywhere, was laughing" (294–95). This ending, which is also a beginning, offers ambivalent laughter as a means of approaching twentieth-century life, since Fevvers's laughter rings out as midnight passes and ushers in a new century.

Carter's exploration of carnivalistic laughter also indicates that it can help propel feminist aims. Fevvers's laughter over her ability to fool Walser into believing that she is a virgin bird-woman challenges male domination as well as Western binary logic. Fevvers resists male-centered definitions of her by assuming control of her own self-construction and undermining the conventional opposition between reality and fiction. Her laughter disrupts the male-centered established order; it is a manifestation of release from the status quo that is directed toward an as yet undelineated feminist version of a new and better world. Ending the novel on a note of carnivalistic laughter does not diffuse the subversive nature of *Nights at the Circus;* rather, it provides a vital image, one that is divorced from Western rationality and logic, to carry the potential for change that the novel urges. Bakhtin's claim that carnivalistic laughter can "grasp and comprehend a phenomenon in the process of change and transition" helps to explain why it is a useful vehicle for feminist fiction seeking not only to expose the ills of the established order but also to posit ways in which that order is being undermined and changed. The novel's ending with laughter also anticipates potential new forms for feminist fiction. Bakhtin's argument that carnivalistic laughter possesses "Enormous creative, and therefore genre-shaping, power" supports my argument that a feminist appropriation of carnival laughter opens up the way for the formation of new types of feminist fiction that would be subversive and liberating both at the level of narrative and of politics.[52] Since ambivalent laughter and the carnivalesque in general bring together the ordinary sensory physical world and the visionary, and thus allow a space for change and for the future without divorcing themselves from the material situation, they make ideal strategies for the furthering of subversive feminist aims.

Although Carter uses a variety of strategies to strengthen and propel the novel's feminist aims, her use of postmodern adaptations of fantasy and carnivalization, with its ambivalent form of laughter, dominates. Like madness in Lessing's *The Golden Notebook* and Piercy's *Woman on the Edge of Time,* fantasy and carnivalization perform disruptive functions within Carter's *Nights at the Circus.* By subverting expectations, these strategies both expose and challenge the established male-centered order and offer possibilities for change. But Carter is careful to keep her narrative grounded in the material situation by maintaining a balance between depictions of daily life and fantastic occurrences, even if they are intermingled.

As in the case of the other novels discussed, *Nights at the Circus* delineates a new female subject that exists as a process or a becoming other than itself rather than as a fixed and centered entity. Unlike the other novelists, however, Carter emphasizes the liberating potential of love and desire.[53] She revolutionizes the conventional notion of love by separating it from social contracts and reuniting it with desire, and she offers love and desire as alternate means of empowerment and subject formation. The novel also makes more explicit the claim that men as well as women must be transformed if a new world free of oppression is to be created. Carter's novel demonstrates how fantasy and carnivalization can be mobilized as aesthetic means of depicting the possibility of such transformations, since these strategies sever the characters from the Western laws of binary logic and rationality.

While fantasy and carnivalization propel forward the novel's more utopian feminism, other strategies, such as embedded stories-autobiographies and inverted norms, also serve subversive functions, notably as vehicles for the novel's Marxist feminism. A variety of strategies usually associated with postmodern fiction enable Carter to bring the two strands of subversive feminism together and to posit a feminism that blends their best qualities and avoids their pitfalls: *Nights at the Circus* adopts Marxist feminism's emphasis on the material situation, which utopian feminism tends to ignore; and it adopts utopian feminism's creative and hopeful dynamism, which Marxist feminism often lacks. By establishing a materialist socio-historical grounding for its utopian vision, of new women and men creating a world that would be better in feminist terms, the narrative explains why the present world is still far from being a feminist utopia and yet still offers some hope for the future.

7. FEMINIST-POSTMODERN FICTION

In this study, I demonstrate that an active and potentially productive area of intersection exists between recent fiction with feminist impulses and postmodern forms of subversive aesthetic strategies. While postmodern theories and aesthetics lack the specific activist political engagement of feminism, they can offer feminism strategies for challenging the conceptual modes of a male-centered Western metaphysics. Indeed, I argue that much feminist fiction since the early 1960s co-opts and transforms disruptive postmodern strategies to satisfy specifically feminist aims. The impulse away from both realism and high modernism that emerges from post-World War II feminist fiction is grounded both in the recent cultural and intellectual context and in the experimentation of women writers' version of modernism earlier in the century. As women modernist writers sought to depict a specifically female subject and consciousness, their fiction tended to undermine traditional narrative and accepted notions of gender and sexuality in ways that began the challenge to Western binary logic that recent feminist fiction takes up more fully and radically. My in-depth analyses of Doris Lessing's *The Golden Notebook,* Marge Piercy's *Woman on the Edge of Time,* Margaret Atwood's *The Handmaid's Tale,* and Angela Carter's *Nights at the Circus* develop and reinforce my claim that postmodern aesthetic strategies emerge from many contemporary novels as means of propelling forward specifically feminist aims. However, the feminist politics within these novels refocus the postmodern strategies to emphasize reconstructive rather than deconstructive processes. Challenging the status quo serves as a means of opening the way for new social and thought structures as well as for new conceptions of the subject that are compatible with feminist aims to eradicate the oppression of women. The novels I explore appropriate and develop the utopian potential within postmodernism while jettisoning its tendencies toward overdetermination and underdetermination, neither of which leads to specific political engagement.

The four novels by Lessing, Piercy, Atwood, and Carter differ substantially: *The Golden Notebook* explodes the novel form by physically fragmenting its structure and thematizing this structural change, as an attempt to account for post-war fragmentation, violence, and multiplicity; *Woman on the Edge of Time* places two temporally discrete worlds in confrontation as a means of delineating the vast changes in societal and thought structures that must occur before a feminist utopia can be created; *The Handmaid's Tale* questions the status of official history by highlighting the gaps that exist between an unnamed narrator's lived experiences, her oral tale, and its written version; *Nights at the Circus* mobilizes fantasy and the carnivalesque as aesthetic means of depicting possibilities of transformation, including new forms of feminist fiction. At the same time, these novels have much in common in that they all challenge from a feminist perspective the system of binary hierarchical oppositions at the root of Western culture, the humanist subject with its integrated essential self, the possibility of mimetic representation, the effectiveness of traditional narrative, the stability of language, and notions of origin and authorship. Through their use of a variety of disruptive postmodern strategies to effect these challenges, the novels display the potential breadth of the area of intersection between feminist and postmodern theories and aesthetics.

While undermining the hierarchy inherent in binary oppositions, these novels reject the chaos or obsessional structures that accompany breakdown in much postmodern fiction and, instead, immediately move toward the delineation of new non-binary structures, using a variety of subversive aesthetic strategies: narrative and temporal disruptions as well as metafictional devices in all four novels, explorations of madness in Lessing and Piercy, co-optations of popular forms such as the utopia in Piercy and the dystopia in Atwood, linkages of sexuality-desire to power in Atwood and Carter, and appropriations of fantasy and carnivalization in Carter. Moreover, these texts undermine Western binary logic without doing away with notions of difference. Their challenges to the humanist subject, for example, focus not so much on its breakdown as on the construction of new versions of the subject independent of the traditional male-centered hierarchical oppositions between subject and object, self and other, man and woman, male and female, masculine and feminine. Through a continual process of difference and deferral, this new subject is both and neither subject and object, self and other; it is always in process of becoming other than itself. The novels present the new subject as a multiplicity of socially constructed roles or selves. They expose naming and notions of unified centered identity as artificial means of fixing and oppressing individuals, and they deliberately avoid fixing their protagonists in static subject positions: Lessing disperses identity by presenting a multiplicity of Annas; Piercy destabilizes Connie's *Being* by placing her simultaneously in two temporally disparate worlds; Atwood refuses to name her protagonist and thus provide her with a stable origin; and Carter problematizes Fevvers's origins by making her an orphan woman with wings. In addition, this new centerless and dispersed subject neither disintegrates nor loses individual agency within the novels by Lessing, Piercy, Atwood, and Carter. The feminist impulses within these texts create a subject that has no fixed essence but is still capable of focused political action. Although various historical and sociocultural forces and power relations limit available subject positions, a range of subject positions does exist at any given time, including positions that have been marginalized and rendered powerless because they threaten the status quo.[1] All four novels assign their protagonists to such traditionally marginalized positions as means of both challenging the humanist subject and fictionally creating new subjects: Anna is a divorced, left-wing, single-parent, and at times mad woman; Connie is an aging, lower-class, man-less, Chicana, mad woman; Offred is an enslaved baby-maker, a walking womb; Fevvers is a lower-class, whorehouse-bred, circus-star, orphaned, monster woman. All these subject positions have strong ties to the material situation, as feminism demands. The novels' feminist politics lead them to move toward new notions of the subject as socially constructed and yet overtly connected to the concrete physical and psychic experiences of human beings within inequitable material conditions.

Similarly, these novels challenge the possibility of mimetic representation while retaining a firm grounding in the material situation. They depict women's daily lived oppression and yet refuse to assume that these illustrations are exact copies of an objective reality. The novels internalize the postmodern insistence that reality is always already represented, which does not so much deny the value of representation as situate representation within its particular historical, geopolitical, and sociocultural context. The four novelists in question appropriate non-realist modes such as dreams, utopia, dystopia, fantasy, and carnival to both criticize the present world and move toward delineations of new social and thought structures. More specifically, the novels engage disruptive narrative strategies that problematize the rigid distinction between reality and fiction while creating a new space for depicting women's previously silenced or marginalized stories-histories. Lessing posits a plurality of realities—a realist novella, five notebooks that focus on different aspects of her protagonist's life (and include recollections, parodies, experiments in style and form, dream visions), and a fragmented novel—to counter the notion that one objective reality dominates; she offers a mode of representation that accounts for fragmentation, multiplicity, and violence as well as for identity as a composite of ever-shifting roles. Piercy's feminist utopia implicitly criticizes the existing state of culture while presenting possibilities for change, by superimposing temporally discrete worlds and in so doing challenging Western rationality as well as linear narrative. The metafictional structure of Atwood's novel highlights the gap that exists between official history, women's oral stories-histories, and women's lived experiences, revealing the inevitability of strategic/biased fictionalization in all modes of representation; consequently, the novel opens the way for a multiplicity of histories that includes women's personal stories-histories. Carter constructs a fantastic heroine and carnivalizes her characters' exploits and settings to simultaneously depict and criticize the inequities faced daily by women and offer possibilities for change. While the novels challenge mimetic representation, however, they retain narrative: a narrative structured by disruptions, which allows for the construction of something new. Lessing's presentation of a formally fractured narrative that defies notions of beginning and ending enables the novel to offer women new and multiple roles and endings and to include the plurality of public and personal realities that make up individual existence. The temporal shifts that disrupt Piercy's narrative make possible the depiction of Connie's life story-history as well as the presentation of a blue-print for a new society free of human oppression. Breaking her novel into two distinct pieces that challenge each other enables Atwood to offer history as a multiplicity of versions of lived experiences. Carter's temporal and spatial disruptions enable the narrative to account for different realities and for different rates of change in the two central characters, Fevvers and Walser, as the novel moves toward the creation of a New Woman and a New Man.

Not only do these novels both destabilize and retain traditional narrative, but they also call into question language while acknowledging their dependence on language. They challenge the stability of language while usurping language for their own political purposes; after all, if language is unstable, it is also malleable. Lessing literally fragments language and grammar, while Piercy degenders language; and both Lessing and Atwood question the expressive potential of language by emphasizing that words can never adequately represent or recapture a given experience. The novels of Lessing, Atwood, and Carter also stress the connection between language and power by presenting women characters who author their own subjecthoods and challenge traditional male-centered authority. Although they are unconventional authors, the protagonists of these novels tell their own versions of their personal stories-histories and as a result move toward constructions of themselves as decentered and dispersed subjects. Lessing's Anna attempts to represent her life through various forms of writing and eventually creates herself as the author of a fractured novel, *The Golden Notebook,* which encompasses all these forms. By recording her story on cassettes, Atwood's Offred assumes control of an oral version of her life experiences; and, without a name other than the indeterminate one the Gileadean regime imposes on her, she remains in part an active subject who will not be fixed by others—particularly the scholars who attempt to appropriate her story two centuries later. Carter's Fevvers similarly appropriates her own story-history and strategically constructs the indeterminate identity she presents to the world in order to avoid being constructed by that world. While the novels challenge the stability of language and traditional notions of story-telling, they nevertheless offer their own language usage and story-telling modes that push toward creating new subjectivities and representing women's previously marginalized stories-histories.

Moreover, all four novels retain the concept of the author as they posit female protagonists who tell their own stories; yet their narratives question Western notions of authorship and origin, if only in limited ways. By undermining the stability and even the possibility of a definitive author or origin, they challenge the institutionalized accounts of women's stories-histories that work to fix women in marginalized roles. The ambiguity of voice and the overlapping of narrative levels in the various fragments of *The Golden Notebook* problematize authorship and undermine any notion of original or ultimate meaning, so that Anna can only be approximated but never pinned down. By offering a scholar's version of an oral tale tape-recorded by an unnamed woman, *The Handmaid's Tale* opens a wide gap between the experiences of the teller of the tale and its written version and thereby undermines notions of authorship and origin. In *Nights at the Circus,* Fevvers's indeterminate identity and her creative or fantastic story-telling, with various imbedded narratives, also threatens notions of absolute authorship and origins. Although Connie does not narrate and thus construct her own story, *Woman on the Edge of Time's* sympathetic version of Connie's life challenges the authority and veracity of the state records of her psychiatric institutionalizations presented in the last chapter.

As this brief summary of my analyses of the novels by Lessing, Piercy, Atwood, and Carter indicates, these texts appropriate a variety of disruptive postmodern strategies specifically to challenge the binary logic and hierarchical structures endemic to Western culture so as to create a space for transformations in feminist terms. Lessing offers a new, fractured novel form that tries to account for the fragmented, dispersed, centerless post-World War II subject and world. Piercy presents a blueprint for a new, qualitatively better society free of human oppression and social hierarchies. Atwood replaces official history with a notion of history as a multiplicity of histories, each of which is only one version of lived experiences. Carter's proffered carnival laughter anticipates new forms of subversive feminist fiction. These novels' attempts to create anew the subject, the novel form, visions of social structures, and notions of history are all constructive moves that push beyond the tendency within postmodern theories and fiction to call into question elements of Western culture without offering replacements for them. As I have argued, the reconstructive tendency within these particular novels is inextricably linked to their more subversive feminist impulses not only to expose and challenge the means by which Western culture retains male-dominated power relations but also to offer potential new structures and notions that are not governed by hierarchical power relations (see Chapter 1). None of these four texts totally subverts existing culture or creates completely new concepts or systems, since they cannot escape their own cultural contexts; but they nevertheless demonstrate a movement *toward* such new structures and concepts as they seek to transform the consciousness of their readers.

Indeed, disruptive strategies exist side by side with conventional ones in these novels, which are in some ways stylistic hybrids. Their narrative modes, for example, are familiar—chiefly realism and stream-of-consciousness—and yet include elements that radically disrupt these otherwise conventional narratives. Lessing's novel simultaneously holds on to and moves beyond traditional narrative by including both the conventional "Free Women" sections and the longer fragmented "Notebook" segments. Piercy's superimposition of temporally discrete worlds explodes realism in its bold disregard for the linear conception of time, and her final chapter written from the perspective of the state psychiatric institution unveils the inherent biases in the supposed objectivity of Western scientific discourses. Atwood's metafictional ending not only calls into question the conventional narrative that precedes it but also points to the gaps that realism masks. Carter's fantastic and carnivalesque elements temper and disrupt the realist feminist didacticism that surfaces in the dialogues of Lizzie and Fevvers. By both engaging the conventions of realism and highlighting their contradictions, these novels appear to be both reformist and revolutionary. Although they co-opt established and familiar narrative strategies (particularly realist ones), the intrusion of disruptive elements testifies to their internalization of the contemporary crisis of representation. Moreover, by combining recognizable modes and subversive ones, these novels can reach a wider audience of readers trained in traditional modes (chiefly realism) while still creating the possibility that some of these readers will acknowledge the problems inherent in conventions conditioned by conceptual modes that also lead to inequitable relations of power.

Nights at the Circus contains the most overtly disruptive and most pervasive postmodern strategies of the four novels. Fantasy, carnivalization, and both spatial and temporal narrative disruptions structure Carter's novel, even though pockets of realism remain.

The various realist depictions of women's lived oppression imbedded within the narrative indicate, however, that feminist politics ground the novel in the ordinary physical world. Yet the novel's postmodern strategies also serve feminist aims by creating a space and providing an artistic vocabulary for delineating possible changes or transformations. Carter posits a feminism that is both potentially liberating and still anchored in the material situation. However, because *Nights at the Circus* problematizes realism more overtly than the other novels, it appears more experimental. As a result, it may be less readable and coherent to the majority of readers schooled in realist modes of fiction, which may help to explain why Carter's novel has not enjoyed the same popular success as the other three texts.[2] The novels by Lessing, Piercy, and Atwood have appealed primarily, although not exclusively, to women readers. That this mass appeal has included feminists and non-feminists alike indicates that these novels contain familiar representations that women can identify with as women, regardless of political allegiances. The same impulse may be at work here as the one that motivates liberal feminists to view women's fiction as a reflection of women's lives: women want to see and find solace in familiar representations of themselves and of their own lives in the fiction they read. Yet, while realism offers the reader a level of familiarity, what is intelligible as realism is nothing more than an established set of conventions.[3] Carter's novel does not play to the demands of familiarity; rather it undermines the conventions of realism. Fevvers is a difficult female protagonist for women to identify with, since she is a fantastic figure with an equally fantastic life story-history. In contrast, women readers can readily identify with the protagonists of the other three novels, whose more realist representations are more familiar. However, although *Nights at the Circus* might appear more experimental on a first reading than the other three novels, it does not greatly differ from them. The disruptive strategies in the novels by Lessing, Piercy, and Atwood are merely less overt or pervasive than in Carter's novel and are thus easier to ignore, as many readers and critics have done. *Nights at the Circus* may not be as much of a woman's novel as the others, but it stands side by side with them as a subversive feminist text. The novels by Lessing, Piercy, and Atwood are in a sense more effective than Carter's on a thematic level (even if their postmodern subversions are often overlooked), since their politics are feminist but their recognizable realist aesthetics appeal to women at large and therefore provide their novels with a larger readership; yet Carter's novel is more forcefully subversive in its refusal to allow passive or neutral readings. Fevvers disrupts traditional gender and sex divisions more thoroughly than any of the other protagonists; that she is not a reflection of *real* women is in itself subversive and liberatory.

Although *The Golden Notebook, Woman on the Edge of Time, The Handmaid's Tale,* and *Nights at the Circus* are strong and varied examples of the active intersection of feminist and postmodern strategies that manifests itself in fiction written during the last three decades, choosing to analyze these specific novels was arbitrary in the sense that a great number of recent novels testify to such an intersection. In other words, I am arguing that these four novels represent a prevalent trend rather than an exception. They exhibit a conjoining of feminist politics and postmodern aesthetic strategies that are to be found in many other novels, such as Maxine Hong Kingston's *The Woman Warrior,* Toni Morrison's *Beloved,* Marilynne Robinson's *Housekeeping,* Alice Walker's *The Color Purple,* Fay Weldon's *The Life and Loves of a She-Devil,* Christa Wolf's *Cassandra,* as well as in the more overtly experimental fiction of writers like Kathy Acker and Christine Brooke-Rose. Although the latter group is the only one that (chiefly male) critics have consistently associated with postmodernism, I deliberately chose not to focus on these more experimental and less widely read texts to emphasize my argument that the use of postmodern strategies for feminist purposes is so widespread that it manifests itself in bestsellers as well as in more literary novels, including more fully experimental ones published by smaller independent or even underground presses.

Fiction that combines specific feminist politics and postmodern aesthetic strategies testifies to the political potential of postmodernism for feminism, particularly the postmodern emphasis on things as non-eternal and non-universal. As exemplified through my analysis of the four novels by Lessing, Piercy, Atwood, and Carter, fiction that appropriates postmodern strategies to enact its feminist politics tends to focus on the radical transformations that challenges to the status quo make possible, while remaining intimately linked to the material situation. Such fiction has much in common with other politically motivated postmodern fiction. For instance, Larry

McCaffery suggests that, in *One Hundred Years of Solitude,* García Márquez combines postmodern "experimental impulses with a powerful sense of political and social reality" and thus "uses experimental strategies to discover new methods of reconnecting with the world outside the page, outside of language."[4] McCaffery's discussion could just as well be directed at the four novels by Lessing, Piercy, Atwood, and Carter. The political potential of postmodernism has in fact been exploited by a variety of politically engaged novels in the service of specific feminist, cultural, and racial politics.[5] This is not to say, however, that all postmodern fiction is motivated by an engaged and focused politics firmly anchored in the material situation. For instance, many recent novels (particularly American ones) that directly address history and politics have a tendency to dwell on the chaos or obsessive structures that follow challenges to existing culture and its structures. Novels like Pynchon's *Gravity's Rainbow,* Coover's *The Public Burning,* and DeLillo's *Libra* are permeated with politics that are so diffuse and impersonal that overdetermination or underdetermination in the end overshadows and blunts the subversive potential of their politics (see Chapter 1). Indeed, as I have argued, the key to a postmodernism that remains connected to the ordinary material world, and that is constructive or utopian rather than focused solely on the collapse of Western culture, is directly related to the level of focused political engagement that anchors it. The specificity of feminist commitment brings a level of direct engagement to postmodern aesthetic strategies that makes them potentially more effective in transforming the reader's consciousness than when tied to the more detached politics of much (white male) postmodern fiction.

In contrast to the novels of DeLillo, Pynchon, and Coover, the four novels by Lessing, Piercy, Atwood, and Carter investigate the radical possibilities of indeterminacy as a challenge to the status quo while simultaneously keeping a tight rein on the potentially chaotic or overstructured outcome. *The Golden Notebook's* assertion that "out of the chaos, a new kind of strength" will emerge effectively captures the impulse and direction of postmodern strategies motivated by feminist aims.[6] As a politics inextricably tied to the daily lived experiences of individuals, feminism aims toward the creation of new social structures devoid of hierarchical power relations. The utopian element within feminist fiction has no use for underdetermination or overdetermination as ends in themselves; chaos and obsessive structures serve merely as spaces from which to effect radical transformations. In Lessing's novel, for example, Anna plunges into the chaos of madness only to reemerge as a new subject that is not dependent on hierarchical oppositions between madness and sanity or subject and object. Feminist texts recognize chaos not only as a means of calling into question certain oppressive aspects of Western rationality but also as a springboard for delineating new structures and formulating new conceptual modes. Moreover, rather than adopting a grand scale that includes major historical events and figures, as in the cases of DeLillo, Pynchon, and Coover, the four novels by Lessing, Piercy, Atwood, and Carter focus specifically on the personal stories-histories of unknown women. These latter texts not only illustrate the details of women's daily existence within a culture that has traditionally oppressed and marginalized women but also challenge the cultural structures that maintain inequitable relations between men and women. The novels contain utopian elements that are simultaneously grounded in the material situation and propelled by disruptive postmodern strategies. While they often remain undefined or untried, the utopian impulses of these narratives nevertheless underscore the specific political agenda and potential of feminism.

The utopian impulses within the novels by Lessing, Piercy, Atwood, and Carter further testify to the sense of collective values implicit in all forms of feminism—and of engaged politics in general—but absent from much postmodern fiction.[7] Many postmodern novels' movement toward indeterminacy and chaos has a tendency not only to neutralize their own political implications but also to negate cultural standards without ever totally escaping the trappings of the thought system from which those standards evolved. While feminists have joined in the enterprise of challenging Western culture's male-centered, and thus biased, value systems, they nevertheless refuse to take refuge in a world supposedly free of social norms or values—close scrutiny of many (male) postmodern novels indicates that their versions of chaos often remain very much male-centered. In contrast, the feminist utopian impulse envisions new, more equitable social structures, in which power relations are no longer hierarchical and oppressive and in which quality of life is better for all human beings. Notions of equality and a better quality of life are anything but value-free and in fact demonstrate some degree of continued allegiance to Enlightenment ideals. Feminist and postmodern theories and aesthetics are in this sense worlds apart; and yet postmodern aesthetics offers feminist fiction disruptive strategies with which to effect the continual challenge that collective values need if they are to remain dynamic rather than become fixed dogma. Indeed, references to *values* have become taboo in a critical climate dominated by poststructuralist theories. However, specific politics such as forms of feminism require some sort of shared system of values. What postmodern theories bring to feminist politics is the recognition not that values are non-existent but rather that these values are temporary, contingent, subject to change.

While literary critics such as Felski, Hite, and Greene have recently distanced feminist from postmodern fiction, I am arguing that feminist politics and postmodern aesthetics complement each other within much recent fiction.[8] One of the problems with severing feminist from postmodern fiction is that it marginalizes feminist texts from the dominant culture and its cultural products. Not only is the separation of feminist from postmodern fiction artificial in the sense that both are, at least in part, products of the same historical, cultural, intellectual context (see Chapter 1), but the separation obscures the potential of feminist fiction to effect changes in the direction of fiction in general. Since the intent of subversive forms of feminism is to restructure existing social and thought structures, feminism cannot marginalize itself if it is to be effective at the level of praxis. It would seem more productive from a feminist perspective to nurture and develop the influence that feminist fiction is generating. Indeed, fiction that combines feminist politics and elements of postmodern aesthetics signals a more engaged version of postmodern fiction, which might conceivably influence the general direction of fiction. Moreover, the recognition of what I will tentatively call feminist-postmodern fiction opens up the category of postmodern fiction to a variety of previously marginalized aesthetic practices. Although for practical reasons I have limited my study to recent white Anglo-American women writers, analyses of texts written by writers of various ethnic origins, class positions, and sexual orientations would continue to expand and complicate the arena of postmodern fiction. The delineation of *other* postmodern practices is crucial not only to expand notions of postmodern fiction but also to promote these politically motivated practices.

As my particular (and limited) study indicates, while much postmodern fiction anticipates the end of Western civilization, novels such as Lessing's *The Golden Notebook,* Piercy's *Woman on the Edge of Time,* Atwood's *The Handmaid's Tale,* and Carter's *Nights at the Circus* anticipate and celebrate possibilities for a new, restructured culture and new forms of feminist aesthetics. The feminist utopian impulses within these novels reject chaos and total indeterminacy as an alternative to the status quo and instead move toward creative reconceptualizations of existing social and thought structures. Although these texts appropriate disruptive postmodern aesthetic strategies to challenge Western culture on the level of narrative, they ultimately emphasize reconstructive processes. These novels testify to the necessity of engaging in both deconstruction *and* construction if radical transformations are to be effected; and, in so doing, they signal the potential transformation of Western civilization and its products, including aesthetics, rather than their demise. The widespread use of disruptive strategies usually associated with post-modernism to propel feminist aims within recent fiction signals a move toward new forms of feminist aesthetics, ones that would be rigorously critical as well as radically constructive, creative, celebratory, and perhaps toward changes in aesthetics in general.

NOTES

Chapter 1: Feminism and the Postmodern Impulse

1. DeLillo, *Libra,* p. 441. All subsequent references to this novel will be placed within the text itself.

2. Similarly, Felski "defines as feminist all those forms of theory and practice that seek, no matter on what grounds and by what means, to end the subordination of women" *(Beyond Feminist Aesthetics,* p. 13). As Fuss suggests, "it is difficult to imagine a *non-political* feminism" so that "politics emerges as feminism's essence" *(Essentially Speaking,* p. 37).

3. Jameson, *The Political Unconscious,* p. 20.

4. Wolff, *Feminine Sentences,* p. 89.

5. Hutcheon, *A Poetics of Postmodernism,* pp. 100–01.

6. My article, "The Political Paradox in Don DeLillo's *Libra,*" engages in a more in-depth analysis of Libra in the terms I have outlined here.

7. Critics of *Gravity's Rainbow* have argued that the novel is not as negative as it initially appears and that it offers positive as well as negative possibilities for the world. But none of these critics seem to be able to pinpoint these positive possibilities; instead, they only hint at the redeeming potential of features such as the novel's humor and mysticism, as well as its examination of probability. See Hite's *Ideas of Order in the Novels of Thomas Pynchon,* Moore's *The Style of Connectedness: "Gravity's Rainbow" and Thomas Pynchon,* and Siegel's *Pynchon: Creative Paranoia in "Gravity's Rainbow".*

8. I have chosen to use terms such as "problematize" because, as Hutcheon argues, "-ize" forms "underline the concept of *process* that is at the heart of postmodernism" *(A Poetics of Postmodernism,* p. xi).

9. Ross similarly avoids making postmodernism into a distinct thing, by referring to postmodernism as "the collection of practices that call themselves postmodern" ("Introduction," *Universal Abandon?,* p. xi).

10. Acker and Brooke-Rose are two of the few women writers regularly cited as producers of postmodern fiction (at least when women writers are cited at all).

11. Felski, *Beyond Feminist Aesthetics,* pp. 7–8.

12. Barrett, *Women's Oppression Today,* pp. 97–98. Barrett defines ideology as "the processes by which meaning is produced, challenged, reproduced, transformed" (97).

13. Felski, *Beyond Feminist Aesthetics,* pp. 5–6.

14. Wolff, *Feminine Sentences,* p. 6. Although Wolff attributes this linkage of "the textual and the social" to feminism rather than to postmodernism, I am arguing that her claim is valid for both feminism and postmodernism.

15. Foster, "Postmodernism: A Preface," p. xii.

16. See *Aesthetics and Politics* for a selection of essays by the debate's principal participants: Ernst Bloch, Georg Lukacs, Bertolt Brecht, Walter Benjamin, Theodor Adorno.

17. Brecht, "Popularity and Realism," pp. 81–82.

18. Jameson, "Reflections in Conclusion," pp. 203–06.

19. See Adorno's "Commitment" for a lengthier discussion.

20. Belsey, *Critical Practice,* pp. 46–47. Belsey's book provides an in-depth discussion of the problems with what she calls "expressive realism" and of some recent theoretical responses to that problem.

21. Wolff, *The Social Production of Art,* p. 93.

22. Belsey, *Critical Practice,* p. 51.

23. Both Lukacs and Brecht speak of the didactic potential of art, although they admit that art cannot teach directly *(Aesthetics and Politics).* Schweikart argues that feminist criticism is "a mode of *praxis*" whose aim "is not merely to interpret literature in various ways" but "to *change the world*": "Literature acts on the world by acting on its readers" ("Reading Ourselves," p. 531).

24. Belsey, *Critical Practice*, pp. 92, 103.

25. I here agree with Felski's call for a shift away "from the pursuit of a single 'feminist aesthetics'" (181), in *Beyond Feminist Aesthetics.* However, although I agree with her rejection of the claim that "there is anything inherently feminine or feminist in experimental writing," I disagree with

her insistence that it is content rather than form that establishes a link between literature and feminism (5–7). Felski sets up an opposition between popular and experimental writing, writing that uses realist forms and writing that uses non-realist forms; instead, I argue that much popular fiction with feminist impulses combines realist and non-realist forms.

26. I will assume that *feminism* and *postmodernism* are plural in nature throughout the book, although for the sake of convenience I will not add the "s" each time I come upon these terms.

27. Hassan, "Postface 1982," p. 266. Similarly, Calinescu argues that "postmodernism designates at once a historical category and a systematic or ideal concept" ("Introductory Remarks," p. 4).

28. Hutcheon, *A Politics of Postmodernism,* p. 23. She further asserts that "postmodernism" and "postmodernity" must be kept separate since "critique is as important as complicity in the response of cultural postmodernism to the philosophical and socio-economic realities of postmodernity" (26).

29. Wolff also suggests that "postmodernism as cultural practice" should not be collapsed with "postmodern philosophy" and that "Many so-called postmodern art forms ... are far removed from, and indeed hostile to, the philosophically radical project of postmodern philosophy" (*Feminine Sentences,* p. 91).

30. McHale, *Constructing Postmodernism,* pp. 1–3. McHale does not seem to distinguish between postmodern culture, theory, and aesthetics.

31. Morris, "Feminism, Reading, Postmodernism," pp. 378, 381.

32. Mouffe, "Feminism, Citizenship and Radical Democratic Politics," p. 370.

33. Butler, "Contingent Foundations," p. 5.

34. Mouffe, "Feminism, Citizenship and Radical Democratic Politics," p. 370.

35. Singer, "Feminism and Postmodernism," p. 470.

36. Felski, *Beyond Feminist Aesthetics,* p. 74. Although Felski's discussion is directed at the cultural context of feminism, her comments are applicable to postmodernism as well, since feminism and postmodernism share the same cultural context.

37. Clearly, feminism has historically been engaged in an assault on cultural practices, so that recent forms of feminism are shaped by both their

specific historical and cultural contexts and a history of challenging cultural structures and practices.

38. Hassan, *The Postmodern Turn*, pp. xvi–xvii.

39. Singer, "Feminism and Postmodernism," p. 469.

40. Wolff asserts that "the radical task of postmodernism is to deconstruct apparent truths, to dismantle dominant ideas and cultural forms, and to engage in the guerilla tactics of undermining closed and hegemonic systems of thought. This, more than anything else, is the promise of postmodernism for feminist politics" *(Feminine Sentences, p. 87)*.

41. McCaffery suggests, for example, that the "impulses behind the experimentalism of, say, Latin American or East European fiction are clearly different from those that motivated U.S. authors in the 1960's" *(Postmodern Fiction, p. xiv)*. Huyssen maps the trajectory of postmodernism from the 1950s to the early 1980s in "Mapping the Postmodern."

42. Hassan, "Toward a Concept of Postmodernism," pp. 91–92. Hassan follows his list with the admonition that "the dichotomies [between modernism and postmodernism] this table represents remain insecure, equivocal. For differences shift, defer, even collapse; concepts in any one vertical column are not all equivalent; and inversions and exceptions, in both modernism and postmodernism, abound."

43. Hassan, "Pluralism in Postmodern Perspective," pp. 170, 169.

44. See Bertens's "The Postmodern *Weltanschauung.*"

45. Hutcheon, *The Politics of Postmodernism*, p. 26.

46. Huyssen, "Mapping the Postmodern," pp. 185–90. Other critics have commented on the relationship between modernism and postmodernism. For example, Kaplan argues that the "word 'postmodern' is then useful in implying the links with modernism, while at the same time indicating a substantial move beyond/away from it" ("Introduction," *Postmodernism and Its Discontents*, p. 1), and Hassan argues that postmodernism both challenges and contains modernism, that it "must be perceived in terms *both* of continuity *and* discontinuity" ("Postface 1982," pp. 263–64; also see pp. 267–68). Also, see Jameson's "Postmodernism, or The Cultural Logic of Late Capitalism," for a discussion of the relationship between modernism and postmodernism.

47. Hutcheon argues that works of surfiction are not examples of postmodernism since they do not fit her definition of postmodernism as "historiographic metafiction," but this distinction limits the notion of postmod-

ern fiction she presents (*A Poetics of Postmodernism*, p. 40). My project entails expanding notions of postmodern fiction.

48. McCaffery, *Postmodern Fiction*, p. xxii.

49. Huyssen, "Mapping the Postmodern," pp. 183, 188, 198. Although he uses the inclusive term postmodernism, he seems here and elsewhere in the essay to be referring to forms of postmodern aesthetics.

50. Although I am focusing my discussion on the exclusion of feminist texts from the canon of postmodern fiction, it is clear to me that the fiction of minority writers has similarly been excluded. To keep this project manageable, however, I cannot here deal with the specific kinds of postmodern strategies that emerge from the latter texts.

51. Hite, *The Other Side of the Story*, pp. 1–2. Another recent book, Greene's *Changing the Story*, implicitly rejects the possibility of postmodern feminist fiction. Greene designates postmodernism as a male domain in her passing reference to "postmodern (i.e., male) writers" (1–2), and she distances recent feminist fiction from postmodernism by arguing that recent feminist fiction is closer to modernism: "Growing out of a sense of the unprecedentedness of contemporary experience, feminist fiction seeks new forms to express change, which is why it is often—like Modernist fiction—self-reflexive" (35).

52. Moi, *Sexual / Textual Politics*, pp. 69, 8. Moi's book provides good summaries and critiques of the main arguments and positions of Anglo-American feminist literary critics such as Millett, Ellmann, Moers, Jehlen, Gilbert and Gubar, Kolodny, and Showalter, which clearly back up this argument. However, Moi's book was one of the first to examine both Anglo-American and French feminism and is thus necessarily dated. Many critics have since questioned the dualistic structure she constructs, which opposes these two strands of feminism. I find it more appropriate to distinguish the feminisms she discusses in terms of philosophical approach rather than in terms of the author's national origin, especially now that many so-called Anglo-American feminist critics champion and practice so-called French feminism. In addition, Moi's use of the term *patriarchal* is problematic in that it places all forms of male dominance under a very specific and limited term—see Fox-Genovese's *Feminism without Illusion* (142–45). I would replace *patriarchal* with *male-centered*.

53. Scott, "Experience," pp. 25–26.

54. Hite, *The Other Side of the Story*, p. 13.

55. See Gilbert and Gubar's *The Madwoman in the Attic* and the more recent *No Man's Land* series.

56. Barrett further argues that it is impossible "to take literary texts, or any other cultural products, as necessary reflections of the social reality of a particular period. They cannot even provide us with a reliable knowledge of directly inferable ideology" (*Women's Oppression Today*, p. 107).

57. Hutcheon suggests that one of the things that "feminisms have brought to postmodernism" is "an increased awareness of gender differences" (*The Politics of Postmodernism*, p. 167).

58. Along with a variety of feminist critics and theorists, Hartsock has argued convincingly that dualisms in Western culture are "overlaid by gender" and that "Dualism, along with the dominance of one side of the dichotomy over the other, marks phallocentric society and social theory. These dualisms appear in a variety of forms—in philosophy, sexuality, technology, political theory, and in the organization of class society itself" (*Money, Sex, and Power*, p. 241).

59. *In The Politics of Postmodernism*, Hutcheon similarly notes the "shared deconstructing impulses" (23) of both feminism and postmodernism as they participate in "the same general crisis of cultural authority," and yet she also emphasizes the difference in their orientations: "postmodernism is politically ambivalent for it is doubly coded—both complicitous with and contesting of the cultural dominants within which it operates," while "feminisms have distinct, unambiguous political agendas" (142). However, she limits the scope of her project by working with "one particular definition of postmodernism from the point of view of its politicized challenges to the conventions of representation" (17), which she derives "from a model based on architecture" (119), and centering her discussion of postmodern fiction on parody. While her discussion of postmodern parody is useful and valuable, I will argue that other postmodern strategies surface in recent feminist fiction.

60. In a similar vein, Fraser and Nicholson argue that "Post-modernists offer sophisticated and persuasive criticisms of foundationalism and essentialism, but their conceptions of social criticism tend to be anemic," while "Feminists offer robust conceptions of social criticism, but they tend at times, to lapse into foundationalism and essentialism." Moreover, they assert that "the ultimate stake of an encounter between feminism and postmodernism is the prospect of a perspective which integrates their respective strengths while eliminating their respective weaknesses" ("Social Criticism without Philosophy," p. 20). I see Fraser and Nicholson's essay as the most balanced, incisive, and rigorous discussion to date of the relationship

between feminism and postmodernism and its potential; and their discussion firmly supports my arguments. However, Hutcheon makes a similar claim when she suggests that there is "a two-way involvement of the postmodern with the feminist: on the one hand, feminisms have successfully urged postmodernism to reconsider—in terms of gender—its challenges to that humanist universal called 'Man' and have supported and reinforced its de-naturalization of the separation between the private and the public, the personal and the political; on the other hand, postmodern parodic representational strategies have offered feminist artists an effective way of working within and yet challenging dominant patriarchal discourses" (*The Politics of Postmodernism,* p. 167).

61. Felski refers specifically to two anthologies, Cornillon's *Images of Women in Fiction* (1972) and Donovan's *Feminist Literary Criticism* (1976), as examples of "the earliest feminist writings on literature" (*Beyond Feminist Aesthetics,* p. 22).

62. Hartsock, "Foucault on Power," p. 163.

63. Waugh, *Feminine Fictions,* p. 6.

64. Felski, *Beyond Feminist Aesthetics,* pp. 13, 71, 15.

65. Showalter, *A Literature of Their Own,* p. 118. Certainly, neither poststructuralists nor postmodernists would claim the notion of transcendence that Showalter attributes to them.

66. Showalter, "A Criticism of Our Own," p. 186.

67. See Kristeva's "Postmodernism?" and Jardine's *Gynesis.*

68. See Harari's "Preface" (12) and "Critical Factions/Critical Fiction" (29) for more in-depth discussions of poststructuralism. In addition, see Jameson's "Postmodernism, or The Cultural Logic of Late Capitalism" (55, 61) and Huyssen's "Mapping the Postmodern" (36) for two strong essays on postmodernism.

69. Hassan, *The Postmodern Turn,* p. xvi.

70. Huyssen, "Mapping the Postmodern," p. 213. I would stress, however, that this is not valid for all forms of postmodernism.

71. Hite similarly notes that "Theorists of postmodernism on both sides of the Atlantic affirm that their movement shares a political agenda with feminism, inasmuch as to destabilize narrative relations between dominant and subordinate, container and contained, is also to destabilize the social and cultural relations of dominance and containment by which the

conventionally masculine subsumes and envelops the conventionally feminine" (*The Other Side of the Story*, p. 16). Hite's reference to postmodernism as a "movement" is problematic, however, given postmodernism's resistance to categorization.

72. Huyssen, "Mapping the Postmodern," pp. 182, 198–99.

73. One theoretical problem with Owens's essay, however, is that it collapses "feminists" and "women." It should also be mentioned that this essay focuses specifically on the visual arts ("The Discourse of Others," pp. 61–62).

74. These are some additional examples: Arac in his introduction to *Postmodernism and Politics* (xi); Hassan in "Postface 1982" (271); Foster in *The Anti-Aesthetic* (xv); Fiedler in "The New Mutants."

75. This is not true of the postmodernist debate within all disciplines. In the field of art, for example, women artists are at the forefront of those recognized as postmodern and are often used as examples within critical writing focusing on postmodern art. Nevertheless, as Wolff asserts, overall "the prominent names in postmodern art and literature are mainly those of men. The institutions of cultural production ... continue their age-old habit of writing women out of the account" (*Feminine Sentences*, p. 6). Although Waugh and Hutcheon are examples of critics who have begun to engage the link between feminism and postmodernism within the realm of literature, neither makes much use of feminist fiction as examples of postmodern fiction. While Waugh makes a firm distinction between postmodern and women's fiction, Hutcheon focuses almost exclusively on postmodernism, with relatively few examples of fiction by women or of feminist fiction. In *Special Delivery: Epistolary Modes in Modern Fiction,* Linda Kauffman connects recent fiction by women writers with postmodernism, but her discussion of postmodernism explores not its relationship with feminism but rather its connection with epistolary modes.

76. In addition, McHale's definition and separation of modernist poetics as epistemological and postmodernist poetics as ontological, the main thrust of his argument, is too rigid of a distinction (*Postmodernist Fiction,* p. 90).

77. All of these critiques also apply to McHale's more recent book, *Constructing Postmodernism* (1992), although his discussion is at times extremely useful, as I pointed out earlier in this chapter.

78. While Hutcheon as a critic of postmodernism cites more examples of postmodernist fiction written by women or feminist in impulse than does

McHale, the majority of her in-depth examples are nevertheless texts that
are written by men and texts that are not feminist. Two other recent books
on postmodern fiction, Lee's *Realism and Power* and Alexander's *Flights
from Realism,* similarly make few mentions of fiction written by women or
of feminist fiction.

79. See Hassan's "Toward a Concept of Postmodernism" and
"Pluralism in Postmodern Perspective" for discussions of postmodernism's
deconstructive and reconstructive tendencies.

80. Jameson, "The Politics of Theory," pp. 63, 65.

81. Jardine, *Gynesis,* pp. 57–60.

82. Hauser, *Mannerism,* pp. 3, 29–30, 356, 4. Hauser's book provides
a lengthy discussion of mannerism, its history, and its parallels with modernism.

83. Cixous has similar lists of oppositions in "Sorties," as does
Irigaray in *Speculum of the Other Woman.* Also see the work of Derrida and
Kristeva, among others.

84. From a discussion of Irigaray's *Speculum of the Other Woman* in
Felman's "Women and Madness: The Critical Phallacy" (3).

85. In more general terms, Hutcheon similarly argues that "postmodern discourses ... do not deny the individual, but they do 'situate' her/him"
(*A Poetics of Postmodernism,* p. 46).

86. Derrida, "Structure, Sign, and Play," p. 271. Although poststructuralist deconstruction is not equivalent to postmodernism, Derrida's
approach to the subject is compatible with that of postmodern theories.

87. Weedon, *Feminist Practice,* p. 125.

88. Waugh, *Feminine Fictions,* p. 210.

89. I am thus in agreement with Paul Smith's argument in
Discerning the Subject, in which he claims that "current conceptions of the
'subject' have tended to produce a purely *theoretical* 'subject,' removed
almost entirely from the political and ethical realities in which human
agents actually live" (xxix) but that "the 'subject' which feminism speaks for
and about is not an abstract or cerned entity" (xxxii).

90. Johnston, "Ideology, Representation, Schizophrenia," p. 87.
Similarly, Weedon suggests that subjectivity is always "in process, constant-
ly being reconstituted in discourse every time we think or speak" (Feminist
Practice, p. 33), Kaplan discusses the "process toward subjectivity"

("Feminism/Oedipus/Postmodernism, p. 34), and Belsey argues that "the possibility of transformation" lies in the fact that the subject is "perpetually in the process of construction" ("Constructing the Subject," p. 597).

91. Wood and Zurcher, *The Development of a Postmodern Self,* p. 125. The problem with Wood's and Zurcher's discussion, however, is that it leaves out political and historical dimensions.

92. Kaplan, "Feminism/Oedipus/Postmodernism," p. 43.

93. Weedon, *Feminist Practice,* p. 95. Similarly, Wolff argues that "Agents are therefore 'free' not in the sense of being undetermined, but in their ability to make situated choices and perform situated practices" (*The Social Production of Art*, p. 24); and Butler asserts that "the reconceptualization of identity as an *effect,* that is, as *produced* or *generated*, opens up possibilities of 'agency' that are insidiously foreclosed by positions that take identity categories as foundational and fixed" (*Gender Trouble,* p. 147).

94. Weedon argues that "forms of subjectivity which challenge the power of the dominant discourse at any particular time are carefully policed. Often they are marginalized as mad or criminal" (*Feminist Practice,* p. 91). However, Weedon's discussion focuses on *discourse,* since her topic is poststructuralism. Postmodern theories, on the other hand, have less of a tendency to reduce power relations to the realm of discourse, with the exception of certain strands of highly esoteric or theoretical postmodern theories.

95. Mouffe, "Feminism, Citizenship and Radical Democratic Politics," pp. 371–72, 381.

96. Feminists' fears are exacerbated by such critics as Marilouise and Arthur Kroker, who argue that "all the old (patriarchal) signs of cultural authority collapse in the direction of androgyny" within "the world of postmodernism" (*Feminism Now*, p. 5).

97. Barthes, *Writing Degree Zero,* p. 68. Although Barthes is speaking specifically about Realism, his remarks are applicable to modernism as well.

98. Waugh, *Metafiction,* p. 18. Although Waugh is discussing metafiction specifically, her argument is relevant to much postmodern fiction.

99. Wallis, "What's Wrong with this Picture?", pp. xiv–xv.

100. Wolff, *Feminine Sentences,* p. 62.

101. *Ibid.,* p. 28.

102. Linker, "Representation and Sexuality," p. 392.

103. Hutcheon, *A Poetics of Postmodernism,* p. 95.

104. Rimmon-Kenan, *Narrative Fiction*, pp. 2–3.

105. Jameson, *The Political Unconscious,* p. 35. Hutcheon similarly argues that "*history* does not exist except as a text," since the past's "accessibility to us now is entirely conditioned by textuality" (*A Poetics of Postmodernism,* p. 16).

106. The charge of ahistoricity is often levelled at postmodernism by its detractors. Hutcheon, however, goes to the opposite extreme by claiming that postmodernism is inherently historical and by rejecting ahistorical esoteric fiction as not postmodern (*A Poetics of Postmodernism*).

107. Hassan, "Pluralism in Postmodern Perspective," p. 20.

108. Carter's *Nights at the Circus* has not been as widely read or criticized as the other three novels, although her earlier rewritings of fairy tales are enjoying critical attention at the moment. A comparison of the analyses of the four novels in the conclusion of this study will attempt to offer an explanation of why Carter's novel has not met with as wide a readership as the other three.

Chapter 2: The Emergence of Disruptive Strategies in Women's Modernist Fiction

1. Huyssen, *After the Great Divide,* pp. 185–86, 189–90. Also see my discussion in Chapter 1. Unless otherwise noted, my references to *modernism* will refer to the institutionalized high modernism.

2. Ardis, *New Women,* p. 171.

3. For example, Kaplan claims that "In England during the first quarter of the twentieth century two movements reached their climax and converged. One was literary: the experimentation with modes of consciousness in the novel; the other was social: the feminist struggle for equality and independence" (*Feminine Consciousness*, p. 1).

4. Friedman, "Contexts and Continuities," pp. 3–4. Friedman is writing about twentieth-century experimental women writers in general, but her discussion parallels mine with the exception of her reference to women's experimental narratives as "feminine narrative." The designation "femi-

nine" is problematic in that it repeats or reinforces the traditional opposition between masculine and feminine.

5. This is not to say that disruptions of the Western tradition can be equated with feminism but rather that they can be co-opted to satisfy feminist aims. After all, much of modernist fiction does disrupt tradition and yet is misogynist.

6. Ardis, *New Women,* pp. 172, 3, 27. Ardis examines a number of New Woman novels such as Olive Schreiner's *The Story of an African Farm* (1883), Mona Caird's *The Wing of Azrael* (1889), Florence Dixie's *Gloriana* (1890), Thomas Hardy's *Tess of the D'Urbervilles* (1891) and *Jude the Obscure* (1896), George Gissing's *The Odd Women* (1893), Sarah Grand's *The Heavenly Twins* (1893), Dorothy Leighton's *As a Man Is Able* (1893), John Strange Winter's {Henrietta Stannard} *A Blameless Woman* (1894), Percival Pickering's *A Pliable Marriage* (1895), and Arabella Kenealy's *A Semi-Detached Marriage* (1899), among others.

7. I must note here that the term "modernism" has become a point of contention and that various critics are engaging in reevaluating it. In particular, critics are opening up and diversifying the category of modernism by bringing into it previously marginalized texts. However, an institutionalized version of high modernism as defined by the New Critics continues to dominate. Moreover, while the concept of high modernism is problematic in its exclusion of many modernist writers, it nevertheless points to certain characteristics of modernist writing that remain worth considering.

8. Because of the particular scope of my project, this discussion of women modernists will admittedly be a limited one that does not fully explore the volume of recent criticism on these various writers. My aim is a modest one: to briefly demonstrate some of the ways in which women modernists begin to challenge Western metaphysics as they work to represent a specifically female consciousness.

9. Hanscombe aptly argues that Richardson has a "bi-polar worldview, in which female consciousness is contradistinguished in nearly every particular from male consciousness" (*The Art of Life*, p. 34). It must also be noted that Richardson began writing *Pilgrimage* in 1913, publishing its first of thirteen books in 1915, and working on the novel until her death in 1957. The novel's last book was published posthumously in 1967.

10. Richardson, *Pilgrimage*, 4:122, 222, 298–99.

11. Richardson, *Pilgrimage*, 2:219–21, 131.

12. Hanscombe, *The Art of Life,* pp. 40, 42–43. Hanscombe further

notes that "Richardson regarded traditional language use as a predominantly male mode of expression, maintaining that men and women used two different languages," and saw "the stimulus to her own experimental technique as the polarity between male tradition and female consciousness" (39).

13. Richardson, *Pilgrimage*, 2:306.

14. Richardson, *Pilgrimage*, 3:254, 426, 463, 245-46, 504-05.

15. I have chosen to discuss one of Stein's early novels rather than one of her more experimental later texts, because the latter break more fully with modernism and thus are not as helpful to an examination of the bridges between modernism and postmodernism in women's fiction. Stein's radical experimentation with narrative and language has earned her the distinction not only of anticipating postmodern strategies but of being postmodern. All references to *Three Lives* will be included in the text itself.

16. Sinclair, *Mary Olivier,* pp. 123, 125, 201.

17. Although *HERmione* was written in 1927, it remained unpublished until 1981, twenty years after H.D.'s death in 1961. All references to *HERmione* will be included within the text itself.

18. DuPlessis argues that the novel explores "a bisexual love plot as another avenue to the critique of heterosexual romance" and presents "lesbian love" as "definitive in the formation of [Hermione's] identity" (*Writing beyond the Ending*, p. 71).

19. It should also be noted that Stein uses these techniques to a greater extent in her more overtly experimental fiction.

20. Although *Nights* was written in 1937, it remained unpublished until 1986, twenty-five years after H.D.'s death in 1961. All references to *Nights* will be included within the text itself.

21. Friedman, "Contexts and Continuities," p. 19.

22. Gerstenberger, "The Radical Narrative," p. 130.

23. Barnes, *Nightwood*, pp. 14, 31. All subsequent references to this novel will be included in the text itself.

24. Loy's *Insel* was written during the 1930s but was not published until 1991. I thank my colleague Linda Kinnahan, for pointing out the novel's existence to me, and the class discussions in the seminar we co-taught on the Women Modernists, for helping me think about this novel that was new to me. All references to *Insel* will be included in the text itself.

25. This is not to suggest that there are no strong critical discussions of these two novels. What I am suggesting, however is that the novels have received considerably less critical attention than many of Woolf's other texts. However, critics are currently reevaluating these novels, as evidenced by a number of recent articles focusing on these texts.

26. Woolf, "Mr. Bennett and Mrs. Brown," p. 28.

27. Woolf, *A Room of One's Own,* p. 4. All subsequent references to this book will be included in the text itself.

28. Woolf, *Three Guineas,* pp. 67, 5. Woolf's main argument focuses on the assertion that building women's colleges, promoting employment for women in the professions, and helping to prevent war are interrelated and thus inseparable causes that each deserve financial support. The first two activities are prominent liberal feminist topics. All subsequent references to this book will be included in the text itself.

29. I agree with Moi's assertion that Woolf "understood that the goal of the feminist struggle must precisely be to deconstruct the death-dealing binary oppositions of masculinity and femininity" (*Sexual/Textual Politics,* p. 13).

30. *Orlando's* use of fantasy as a vehicle to subvert the norms of Western culture anticipates in many ways Carter's *Nights at the Circus* (1984). For example, both novels stress the relative quality of clock-time.

31. Woolf, *Orlando,* p. 189. All subsequent references to this novel will be included in the text itself.

32. See Plumwood for a discussion of the problems with the concept of androgyny ("Women, Humanity and Nature," pp. 229–30).

33. This latter notion of the subject as centerless, unstable, and dispersed has generally been associated with postmodernism. A few other critics have discussed *Between the Acts* in terms of postmodernism but have not focused specifically on the issue of subjectivity. See, for example, the work of Marilyn Brownstein, Pamela Caughie, and Alan Wilde.

34. Woolf, *Between the Acts,* pp. 211, 58. All subsequent references to this novel will be included in the text itself.

35. In a similar vein, DuPlessis suggests that the novel's language "recasts the issue of dominant and muted, and the dialectic between them, by representing perpetual 'betweenness' itself" (*Writing beyond the Ending,* p. 176).

36. Brownstein, "Postmodern Language," p. 75. Brownstein refers to Woolf's *Between the Acts,* among other literary texts.

37. Joplin has argued more extensively that the novel links "patriarchy at home and its extreme form abroad, fascism" ("The Authority of Illusion," p. 210). Kaivola similarly suggests that the novel links "gender divisions" and "brutality, militarism, oppressive economic systems, and imperialism" (*All Contraries Confounded,* p. 50).

Chapter 3: Madness and Narrative Disruption in Doris Lessing's *The Golden Notebook*

1. Lessing, "A Small Personal Voice," p. 4.

2. Kauffman similarly argues that Lessing's novel "decenters such binary oppositions" as "the dichotomies between male/female, theory/fiction, or theory/practice" (*Special Delivery,* p. 133).

3. See Chapter 1 for a discussion of feminism and postmodernism and of the relationship between the two.

4. Hite, *The Other Side of the Story,* pp. 63, 2. Greene also notes in *Changing the Story* that Lessing's "novel combines Marxist exposure of the ways ideology is inscribed within literary forms with deconstructive critiques of an epistemology based on hierarchical oppositions, with a feminist analysis of the personal as political and of female identity as processive" (115). However, like Hite, Greene disassociates "feminist fiction" from "postmodern (i.e. male) writers" (1). In contrast, Kauffman discusses *The Golden Notebook* in terms of "postmodern fragmentation," although her emphasis is on epistolary modes (*Special Delivery,* p. xvi).

5. Lessing, "Introduction" to *The Golden Notebook,* p. viii–ix. Recently, critics such as Greene and Hite have been discussing the novel in terms of feminist fiction.

6. Cohen argues that rather than "a special pleading for women" the novel is "part of a larger plea, that humanity reexamine its direction" ("Out of the Chaos," p. 178). Rubenstein claims that, although "women occupy an important position" in Lessing's novel, there is no implication that "either her subjects or her audience are delimited by gender" (*The Novelistic Vision,* p. 5).

7. Drabble, "Doris Lessing," pp. 188–89. McCrindle also sees the

novel as "prophetic" and suggests that it "prefigures the women's movement" ("Reading *The Golden Notebook* in 1962," p. 54).

8. Lessing, "Introduction" to *The Golden Notebook*, p. ix. Indeed, as Knapp notes, the novel "spoke straight from the heart of the contemporary feminist climate in the early 1960s" (*"The Golden Notebook,"* p. 114).

9. Kauffman, *Special Delivery*, p. 161.

10. In *Money, Sex and Power,* Hartsock describes "a feminist standpoint" as a "vantage point on male supremacy ... that can ground a powerful critique of the phallocratic institutions and ideology that constitute the capitalist form of patriarchy" and that "can allow us to descend further into materiality to an epistemological level at which we can better understand both why patriarchal institutions and ideologies take such perverse and deadly forms and how both theory and practice can be redirected in more liberatory directions" (231).

11. Lessing, *The Golden Notebook,* p. 471. All subsequent references from this novel will appear within the text.

12. In much the same way, Hite suggests that since men "read 'free' as 'available' ... the relative independence of the protagonist emerges as merely another sort of constraint" (*The Other Side of the Story,* p. 61). Knapp's discussion also parallels mine when she asserts that Anna "is only superficially 'free'—that in fact she is bound by the old sexual and cultural norms" (*"The Golden Notebook,"* p. 113).

13. Kauffman, *Special Delivery,* p. 141.

14. McCormick is thus only partially correct when she argues that *"The Golden Notebook* teaches its readers about liberation through a character who is not liberated," since she does not account for the character Anna's attempts to liberate herself or for the fact that Anna is not just a character in the novel—Anna is also an author and editor ("What Happened to Anna Wulf," p. 62).

15. Sprague also notes that there are "many fictive Annas" in the novel and suggests that "Anna is a cosmos" ("Doubles Talk," pp. 45, 56). I agree with Moi's assertion that Lessing "radically undermine[s] the notion of the unitary self, the central concept of Western male humanism" in her rejection of "the fundamental need for the individual to adopt a unified, integrated self-identity" (*Sexual/Textual Politics,* p. 7). Hite goes even further, claiming that "Lessing in effect introduces one of the defining features of postmodernism, the decentered subject" ("(En)Gendering Metafiction," p. 484). Although I agree with Hite, I think it is more accurate to suggest that Lessing is moving *toward* a postmodern notion of the decentered subject.

Moreover, I argue that the novel gives rise to more than just "two distinct Annas who can be neither reduced nor subordinated to one another" (Hite, *The Other Side of the Story*, p. 80); rather, the novel gives rise to a multiplicity of Annas on various narrative levels.

16. I thus agree with Hite's assertion that "the problem with conceiving character in terms of preexisting forms is that such forms do not allow 'the future'—that is, anything genuinely new and unassimilated by the dominant culture—to be represented" (*The Other Side of the Story*, p. 65).

17. Lessing notes in her "Introduction" that *The Golden Notebook* gives "the same validity" to the perspectives of men and women (xi).

18. Greene, "Women and Men," pp. 280–83. Also see Greene's *Changing the Story* (113). Libby also suggests that in the novel "men and women are equally victimized" ("Sex and the New Woman," p. 111).

19. See Gilbert and Gubar's "The Queen's Looking Glass: Female Creativity, Male Images of Women, and the Metaphor of Literary Paternity" ("Chapter 1" of *The Madwoman in the Attic*).

20. Sprague argues that "The 'male' principle is therefore both male and not male. It is fundamentally without gender" ("Doubles Talk," p. 57).

21. For a good discussion of Lacan's conception of the human subject, see Ragland-Sullivan's *Jacques Lacan and the Philosophy of Psychoanalysis*.

22. There are critics, however, who have rejected the notion of wholeness as adequate to discussing the novel: Sprague in "Doubles Talk," Ezergailis in *Women Writers*, Schweickart in "Reading a Wordless Statement," Hite in *The Other Side of the Story*.

23. Cohen, "Out of the Chaos," p. 185.

24. Rubenstein, *The Novelistic Vision*, p. 108.

25. Draine, *Substance under Pressure*, p. 85.

26. Rigney, *Madness and Sexual Politics*, pp. 74–75.

27. Ezergailis argues that Lessing's novel views madness "as both the extreme representation of the split ['cultural schizophrenia'] and an indication of a cure" (*Women Writers*, p. 26). Showalter also suggests that the novel views "schizophrenia as an intelligible and potentially healing response to conflicting social demands" (*The Female Malady*, p. 238). As Kauffman notes, "Lessing is not romanticizing madness or idealizing schizophrenia" (*Special Delivery*, p. 141).

28. The work of Deleuze and Guattari attempts to show the relationship between capital and schizophrenia. For a discussion of the work of these two writers and of the postmodern subject as schizoid, see Johnston's "Ideology, Representation, Schizophrenia."

29. Felman, *Writing and Madness*, p. 12. Felman suggests that madness poses the question *"What does it mean to 'know'?"*

30. Greene, "Women and Men," p. 284.

31. Kauffman argues that Lessing's "novel demonstrates that the whole itself is a product, nothing more than a part alongside other parts, which it neither unifies nor totalizes" (*Special Delivery*, p. 172).

32. Hite states that "'Cracks' and 'gaps' thus function as elements of description, implying the existence of something utterly new and unrepresentable, at least within the realist tradition" (*The Other Side of the Story*, p. 92).

33. Greene also emphasizes that "Accessibility is a sine qua non for any writing concerned with social change." However, I disagree with Greene's argument that writers like Lessing "have strongly humanist values" and "rely on realism in a way that prohibits drastic ruptures of sequence or sentence, though they also interrogate the meanings of the conventions they enlist" (*Changing the Story*, pp. 3–4). I argue that Lessing's novel does subvert humanist values at the same time as it uses realist conventions to point out their limitations and to communicate with a large audience.

34. The term *metafiction* refers to self-referential fiction, to fiction that highlights its own status as fiction. Metafiction is created through the systematic use of self-reflexive structures, of representation within representation. See Waugh's *Metafiction* for a more extensive discussion of metafiction.

35. Greene, "Women and Men," p. 302.

36. Examples of this occur in Schweickart's "Reading a Wordless Statement," Sprague's "Doubles Talk," Howe's "*The Golden Notebook*," and Carey's "Art and Reality."

37. Hite also notes that Anna writes both "Free Women" and *The Golden Notebook (The Other Side of the Story*, pp. 96–97), as does Greene (*Changing the Story*, pp. 124, 127).

38. Huyssen, *After the Great Divide*, p. x. The book's third chapter, "Mass Culture as Woman: Modernism's Other," discusses this issue in

greater detail. Also see my discussion of high modernism and the women modernists in Chapter 2.

39. Other critics have made similar claims, although in the context of different arguments: DuPlessis (*Writing beyond the Ending,* p. 102), Fishburn ("*The Golden Notebook,*" p. 129), Hite (*The Other Side of the Story,* p. 68), Kauffman (*Special Delivery,* pp. 165, 170).

40. Along the same lines, DuPlessis argues that "The physical end of *The Golden Notebook* stands only to be eroded by the tidal rip of notebooks swelling around it" (*Writing beyond the Ending,* p. 101), Hite suggests that "the end of 'Free Women'" cannot be taken "for the conclusion of the entire narrative" (*The Other Side of the Story,* p. 61), and Hynes claims that *The Golden Notebook* rather than "Free Women" is the novel's last word ("The Construction of *The Golden Notebook,*" p. 105).

41. Hite asserts that "Neither ending ultimately contains the other unequivocally" ("(En)Gendering Metafiction," p. 485), that the novel "has no single 'real' ending" (*The Other Side of the Story,* p. 99). Lessing's novel can also be taken as an example of DuPlessis' argument that literary texts by twentieth-century women "incorporate a critical response both to the ending in death and to the ending in marriage, once obligatory goals for the female protagonist" (*Writing beyond the Ending,* p. 142).

42. In a similar vein, Hite notes that the novel puts forth the notion "that there is no truth apart from the telling, no real story, no authorized version, no vantage point that allows experience to be viewed as a whole," and that "Because there is ultimately no one 'correct' perspective, *The Golden Notebook* refuses to resolve into a single 'real' story" (*The Other Side of the Story,* p. 90, 101); and Tiger asserts that, through her "deconstructive form of writing," Lessing questions "the duplicities inherent in discourse" ("Illusions of Actuality," p. 102).

43. Greene suggests that Anna's recognition that all her versions of reality are untrue gives her "the power of renaming" (*Changing the Story,* p. 123).

44. Along similar lines, DuPlessis notes that Lessing's novel "is not severed from the personal or social needs that are its source" (*Writing beyond the Ending,* p. 103).

45. Greene argues that Anna's writer's block is "a personal, aesthetic, and political problem" ("Women and Men," p. 286).

46. Likewise, Howe asserts that the novel "grasps the connection between Anna Wulf's neuroses and the public disorders of the day" ("*The*

Golden Notebook," p. 178), and Kauffman notes that "Lessing consistently links psychic disintegration to social psychosis" (*Special Delivery,* p. 158).

47. In much the same way, Carey argues that in the novel Anna "begins to understand that in the 'naming game' she had broken life up into fragments" and that to "impose a name" is "to do something artificial" ("Art and Reality," p. 28). Moreover, Hite suggests that the novel presents the "tendency to use self-definition as a means of closing off possibility" (*The Other Side of the Story,* p. 74).

48. Gertrude Stein's writing is an exception, but in fact critics often discuss her work in terms of postmodernism.

49. Greene discusses this view of "interpretation as agency, as creative and culture building" (*Changing the Story,* p. 124).

50. Johnston, "Ideology, Representation, Schizophrenia," p. 87.

Chapter 4: Worlds in Confrontation:
Marge Piercy's *Woman on the Edge of Time*

1. Realist aesthetics depends on the rigid demarcation between reality and fiction and on the idea that literature reflects the experiences or thoughts of a distinct centered individual. See Belsey's *Critical Practice* for a good discussion of realist conventions. Also see my discussion of realist aesthetics in Chapter 1 of this book.

2. Barr and Smith, *Women and Utopia,* p. 1.

3. Barr, *Alien to Femininity,* p. xxi. Rosinski also uses the term "speculative fiction" in her book *Feminist Futures.*

4. Pearson, "Women's Fantasies," p. 50. However, her use of the term *patriarchy* is problematic since it places all forms of male dominance under a very specific and limited term—see Fox-Genovese's *Feminism without Illusions* (142-45).

5. Huckle, "Women in Utopias," p. 136.

6. Pearson, "Women's Fantasies," p. 50.

7. Keinhorst, "Emancipatory Projection," p. 91.

8. Huckle, "Women in Utopia," p. 129.

9. Russ, "Recent Feminist Utopias," p. 71.

10. McHale, *Postmodern Fiction,* pp. 59–60, 66.

11. Barr, "Feminist Fabulation," pp. 188–90. But her collapse of metafiction and postmodernism is problematic. See Waugh's *Metafiction* for a discussion of that term.

12. Pfaelzer, "Response," p. 194.

13. Kessler argues that Piercy's novel utilizes a notion of utopia as a "process of becoming—not a perfect or finished place" ("*Woman on the Edge of Time,*" p. 311). Pfaelzer notes that recent feminist utopias "reopen utopia as possibility" rather than "as final product, as system, as totality, as the conclusion of history" ("Response," p. 194).

14. Pfaelzer, "Response," p. 197. I should note here that Pfaelzer discusses feminist utopias in general, with their "multiple, fragmented, imperfect, and ordinary heroines," rather than Piercy's specific novel.

15. Piercy, *Woman on the Edge of Time,* p. 35. All subsequent references from this novel will be placed within the text.

16. Male inmates such as Skip also undergo brain implants. It is significant that Skip has also been marginalized by society for being homosexual; he has been labeled mad and institutionalized as a result of a suicide attempt. I would also like to note here that, while the novel exposes the ways in which Western institutions rob human beings of portions of themselves, the novel presents these selves as in process rather than as some static essence.

17. Hansen also notes the tensions between Connie's "local and specific behavior *as* a mother and the ideological and theoretical notions of what it means to (be a) mother" ("Mothers," p. 22).

18. Gardiner suggests that "The pimp and the mad doctor thus stand as the two exemplary villains in this society. Both profit from turning the private realms of sexuality and of mental fantasy into institutions of exploitation. Both wield socially sanctioned power over women's minds by controlling their bodies" ("Evil, Apocalypse, and Feminist Fiction," p. 75).

19. I thus agree with Pearson's suggestion that, because of "Its freedom from conventional ideas of reason and possibility," fantasy literature is able to "posit social institutions and cultural modes based on major changes in consciousness, in language and in ways of understanding 'reality'" ("The Utopian Novels," p. 84).

20. Examples include Annas in "New Worlds, New Words," Moylan in "Someday the Gross Repair Will Be Done," and Thielmann in *Marge Piercy's Women.*

21. This supports Pearson's claim that, in feminist utopias, "Lan-

guage is modified to reflect thinking processes beyond dualistic, linear patterns" ("The Utopian Novels," p. 86).

22. Wiemer suggests that, in Piercy's novel, "naming" is associated "with the discovery rather than the bestowal of identity" ("Foreign L'(anguish)," p. 168).

23. Firestone, *The Dialectic of Sex,* pp. 11–12.

24. Gardiner similarly notes that, "In order to emphasize the destructive potential of our current society, Piercy briefly elaborates a feminist dystopia that will come to pass if the needs of patriarchal corporations take precedence over human needs" ("Evil, Apocalypse, and Feminist Fiction," p. 75).

25. DuPlessis argues that, "If the future is no longer a resolved place, then in the same way, the past—history itself—no longer has fixity or authority" ("The Feminist Apologues," p. 2).

26. Rosinsky also notes that "an attempt to categorize these chapter-long, futuristic episodes as *either* madness or vision is distortingly irrelevant; these possibilities are complementary rather than mutually exclusive," because "Regardless of their origins, however, these visions or hallucinations depict society's impact on human potential in ways that make them effective narrative polemic" (*Feminist Futures,* p. 92).

27. In a similar vein, Rosinsky argues that the clinical reports, "which flatly contradict the previous 'realities' of this fiction, *require* evaluative choice from the reader" and that the reports "indicate that 'official' observers may be as biased, as narratorially unreliable as a potentially insane character" (*Feminist Futures,* p. 95). Hansen also notes that "The main story that precedes [the clinical reports], the bulk of the novel, indicts not Connie but, among other things, the crude and cruel ignorance of institutional psychiatry and social work" ("Mothers," p. 23).

28. Skip and Sybil, characters in the novel, are mental patients used in the experiment along with Connie.

29. DuPlessis, "The Feminist Apologues," p. 3. Gardiner also argues that "Connie's rebellion against the doctors is violent but individual and isolated; it cannot lead to the political revolution necessary to bring about the good future" ("Evil, Apocalypse, and Feminist Fiction," p. 75).

30. As Kessler argues, the novel's ending "becomes a call to us" to "accept our social obligation to stop such violation" (*"Woman on the Edge of Time,"* p. 315). Jones also notes that "the strength of reader involvement is

established by the frustration felt at the novel's ending, when Connie's narrative consciousness is replaced by the 'official' version of her complex self" ("Gilman," p. 125).

31. Pearson outlines the potential of a new or revised conception of time. She suggests that, "if time is relative and if space and time are a continuum, then it is possible that alternative futures and pasts do exist simultaneously with the present" ("The Utopian Novels," p. 87).

32. Kessler, "*Woman on the Edge of Time,*" p. 310.

33. Although Maciunas argues that "Piercy imagines a future whose grounding is in feminist postmodernism," she concentrates on Sandra Harding's theories about science, on "Harding's discussion of feminist epistemologies that are emerging as a response to sexist, classist and racist policies in science" ("Feminist Epistemology," pp. 253, 249).

Chapter 5: The Gap between Official History and Women's Histories: Margaret Atwood's *The Handmaid's Tale*

1. Rigney argues that "seldom have feminist novelists chosen the satire and irony of the dystopia, that genre of literature which refutes the escapism of fantasy and represents confrontation with a possible reality," and that Atwood's novel thus "provides a new element in feminist literature" ("Dystopia," pp. 143–44).

2. Examples include McCarthy's claim that, since she cannot "take the Moral Majority seriously, no shiver of recognition ensues" from her reading of the novel ([Book Review], p. 1), and Halliday's comments that the only thing "this book tell[s] us about the present" is that Atwood has "a great anxiety about conservatism, Christianity, and traditional female roles" and that the novel is filled with "cliches," such as "women being ground under the heels of a male world," used as if they were "some sort of truths" ("On Atwood," pp. 52–53).

3. In a similar vein, Cowart argues that "The reader who refuses to concede any real prophetic plausibility to the novel misses the contemporary actuality that fuels Atwood's speculation" (*History*, p. 109); and Murphy notes that the "dystopia provides a warning about the possibilities for a resurgence of such [patriarchal] oppression," by highlighting that in Gilead "only the relationship of relative power has changed" ("Reducing the Dystopian Distance," pp. 31, 33).

4. Atwood, *The Handmaid's Tale*, p. 379. All subsequent references from this novel will appear within the text. See Waugh's *Metafiction* for an in-depth discussion of metafiction.

5. Along the same lines, Freibert notes that *The Handmaid's Tale* "deconstructs Western phallocentrism"; however, her discussion focuses on the novel's exploration of elements of French feminist theory ("Control and Creativity," p. 280–81).

6. Other critics have made similar points, including Bergmann ("Teaching," p. 848), Davidson ("Future Tense," p. 113), Hammer ("The World," p. 46), and Keith ("Apocalyptic Imaginations," p. 125).

7. The reward is not merely one of position, however, since men have to get beyond the rank of Guardian before they are assigned a wife and allowed to engage in sexual procreative intercourse. The regulation of sexuality thus has everything to do with power, as I will discuss later in this chapter.

8. However, a few women fall within the cracks of the system, as in the case of those who function as prostitutes in a whorehouse that does not officially exist (see later discussion).

9. Hansen argues that "in the future world of the early Gilead era, mothering (and the institutions that control it, including marriage and domestic life) is women's *only* (illusory) power" ("Mothers Tomorrow," p. 28).

10. Rigney, *Margaret Atwood*, p. 115.

11. Rigney suggests that, through ceremonies such as the Salvagings and Particicutions, "collusion is insured; the individual is truly a part of the whole and shares responsibility for every aspect of the system, including the perpetration of atrocity" (*Margaret Atwood*, p. 114). It is noteworthy that Atwood has investigated this theme of the collusion of victims in all of her novels and that the consequences of such collusion become more devastating from novel to novel, reaching a high point in *Bodily Harm* and *The Handmaid's Tale* (and, indeed, continuing in her next two novels). Nonetheless, the story of Offred's life as a handmaid also embodies the capacity for individual survival in the face of inhumane circumstances. Stimpson asserts that the novel deals in part with "the meaning of Survival" ("Atwood Woman," p. 764). *The Handmaid's Tale*, in fact, subtly draws a parallel between Gilead and Nazi Germany (187–89). The narrator herself marvels that "Humanity is so adaptable" and finds it "Truly amazing, what people can get used to, as long as there are a few compensations" (349).

12. Sage, "Projections from a Messy Present," p. 307.

13. In much the same way, Rigney argues that in Atwood's novel, "as in the actual and current situation, some feminist groups exercise the same faulty judgement" as religious groups that censor books, "thereby forfeiting their own freedom" (*Margaret Atwood,* pp. 133–34), and Cowart asserts that "Atwood is aware that the suppression of pornography is a point on which fundamentalists and feminists can find common cause—but she makes painfully clear what kind of fire the feminist censor plays with" (*History,* p. 111). In more general terms, Freibert claims that "Atwood blames no one group, but indicts, by sheer exposure, those who espouse simplistic solutions that deny the rights and welfare of others" ("Control and Creativity," p. 284).

14. Rubenstein also notes that, in Gilead, "procreation and maternity are simultaneously idealized and dehumanized" and that handmaids are treated as "merely parts of bodies" ("Nature and Nurture," pp. 102, 104).

15. Hartsock, *Money, Sex, and Power*, p. 156.

16. In a similar vein, Wagner-Martin argues that Gilead is a "culture so frightened by normal sexuality that it codified and proscribed all such procreation, and created hierarchies of life and death around it" ("Epigraphs," p. 4).

17. Rigney, *Margaret Atwood,* p. 118.

18. Miner also asserts that "Offred realizes that this game [Scrabble] is forbidden sexual activity" ("'Trust Me,'" p. 148). Moreover, as Lacombe suggests, the word-game also "reinstates" her "into the symbolic order of language," denied to her by the official Gileadean regime, and thus gives her access to a degree of power ("The Writing on the Wall," p. 4).

19. Gilbert and Gubar link power and writing to male sexuality in "The Queen's Looking Glass: Female Creativity, Male Images of Women, and the Metaphor of Literary Paternity" (Chapter 1 of *The Madwoman in the Attic).*

20. The relationship between the narrator and the Commander is thus reminiscent of Hegel's master-slave dialectic.

21. Although some critics have argued that the narrator's name does appear in the text as "June," it remains unclear since the reference is fairly well masked. While the name "June" appears on the end of a list of names the handmaids exchange in the training center (5), assuming that "June" is the narrator's own name is plausible but grounded in nothing more than

guesswork. Indeed, the narrator could have left her own name out, or she could have fabricated pseudonyms for all the handmaids to protect their identities. As Givner notes, the list of names is an "indirect form of communication [which] suggests that while some names may be given, some may be lost; while some may be named some may be misnamed." Givner's discussion more specifically asserts that "In Atwood's work, names, faces and signatures, the very elements which suggest the referentiality of autobiography, become figures which undermine the referentiality they introduce" ("Names, Faces, and Signatures," pp. 58, 56). To return to my argument, *The Handmaid's Tale* conspicuously veils or leaves out the narrator's name. Moreover, critics' attempts to name the narrator are clearly caught up in the Western metaphysics that the novel is challenging. See my discussion of the novel's framing chapter for a more in-depth discussion.

22. Lacombe also points out these examples of the "falsification of Biblical texts and their eventual merger with the canon" ("The Writing on the Wall," p. 13), as does Cowart (*History,* p. 118).

23. This might also be a commentary on the present decline of literacy in the United States.

24. Likewise, Lacombe argues that "Offred's identity is indicated by her 'bloody nun' costume instead of by her real name" ("The Writing on the Wall," p. 7).

25. Rigney fails to note that the narrator's own version of her story is oral, rather than written, when she argues that, "For Atwood, writing itself becomes a political act" (*Margaret Atwood,* p. 111). I would argue that it is the telling of her story that is a political act rather than writing itself. In contrast to Rigney, Freibert points out that "Offred literally *tells* her story, recording it on tapes instead of writing it down" ("Control and Creativity," p. 286).

26. Lacombe asserts that "the paradox of state censorship" is that "reality is composed of official lies" ("The Writing on the Wall," p. 8).

27. Waugh, *Metafiction,* p. 7. Along the lines of my discussion, Caldwell notes that "Offred is a first-person narrator intensely aware that she is telling a story, one with a potential infinitude of permutations" ("Wells, Orwell, and Atwood," p. 341).

28. Waugh, *Metafiction,* pp. 106, 30–31.

29. Kauffman asserts that "Offred is overwhelmed by the incapacity of language to encompass experience or feeling; it is always approximate," and that Atwood's novel "purposefully blur[s] the boundaries between fiction and reality" (*Special Delivery,* pp. 228, 230).

30. In a related vein, Bergmann argues that "Offred survives through language" ("Teaching," p. 848); Freibert notes that, "Although Offred uses the oppressors language, she uses it to her advantage" as "a means of survival" ("Control and Creativity," p. 288); Reesman asserts that Offred "speaks herself into being" and that Atwood's novel demonstrates "a profound feminist commitment through language" ("Dark Knowledge," p. 6); and Rubenstein claims that Offred's "story is an act of self-generation" ("Nature and Nurture," p. 105).

31. Several critics seem to have missed the point of the last section and see the future world in which Pieixoto lives in a positive light. Rigney describes it as "a presumably better future in which women again participate as human beings" (*Margaret Atwood,* p. 119); Nischik claims that "the 'Historical Notes' might be seen as an optimistic coda to a pessimistic novel" ("Back to the Future," p. 140); Fitting argues that the novel presents the distant future as "another, more desirable society," so that the "framing device seems designed to counter the pessimistic impression that the central narrative leaves" ("The Turn from Utopia," p. 150); and Reesman asserts that "The reader is relieved to learn in this appendix that Gilead is eventually done away with in favor of an ethnically heterogenous and certainly more benign society" ("Dark Knowledge," p. 12). I strongly disagree with these readings of the "Historical Notes" segment.

32. A number of critics have made similar points, including Bergmann ("Teaching," p. 852), Caldwell ("Wells, Orwell, and Atwood," p. 341), Cowart (*History,* pp. 108–09), Freibert ("Control and Creativity," p. 289), Kauffman (*Special Delivery,* p. 227), and Murphy ("Reducing the Dystopian Distance," pp. 34–35).

33. Kauffman notes that "Offred's discourse is muted, mediated, and modified by the interventions of time and technology, and by a masculine interpretation appended to her own speech" *(Special Delivery,* p. 222), and Givner argues that the "Historical Notes" "parody the desire for historicity and authenticity uncontaminated by fictional elements" ("Names, Faces, and Signatures," p. 58). Moreover, Davidson's discussion parallels mine, when he points out that the "Retrospective analysis by a Cambridge don— male, of course—is ostensibly more authoritative than a participant woman's eyewitness account" and that the scholars never "acknowledge how much the very process of assembling a text (or writing the history of any age from its surviving traces) means *creating* a fiction" ("Future Tense," pp. 114, 155); however, Davidson does not address the text in terms of postmodernism.

34. As Davidson notes, Atwood's novel is on one level "an analysis of how patriarchal imperatives are encoded within the various intellectual

methods we bring to bear on history" ("Future Tense," p. 120).

35. Belsey, *Critical Practice,* p. 7.

36. Stimpson suggests that the "Historical Notes" section "does nothing to dispel the fear that pompous, sniggering academics will still be labeling reality in centuries to come" ("Atwood Woman," p. 766).

37. Kauffman also argues that Pieixoto "devalues the kind of information (intuitive, emotional, sensory) that she [the narrator] provides" (*Special Delivery,* p. 227).

38. In a similar vein, Davidson argues that, in Atwood's novel, "The grotesque transformation of women's bodies into passive receptacles for the perpetuation of the genes of the Regime's Commanders is itself grotesquely transmogrified, in the twenty-second century, into silly sexist jests" ("Future Tense," p. 116).

39. Many critics have noted the sexism inherent in Pieixoto's speech, which is difficult to miss. Moreover, Bergmann supports my argument with her claim that Pieixoto is intent on "verification" but "seems to refuse to read the document with any emotion whatsoever, distancing himself from the wrenching events as much as possible" ("Teaching," p. 853). Rubenstein also points out that Pieixoto "focuses less on the details of Offred's life than on the men who shaped it" ("Nature and Nurture," p. 112).

40. Givner notes "the instability of names," which "conveys the impossibility of tracing any originary, referential name" ("Names, Faces, and Signatures," p. 58). In addition, Hansen argues in a footnote that, ironically, the Gileadean "practice of naming a woman with an inflection of the patriarch's name ... recoils and erases the identity of the patriarch, however, in the future time, when what survives is the Handmaid's tale itself" ("Mothers Tomorrow," p. 42).

41. Malak, "Margaret Atwood's *The Handmaid's Tale,*" p. 15. Hansen also mentions the speaker's "apolitical stance" ("Mothers Tomorrow," p. 30), and Davidson argues that "the supposed objectivity" of Pieixoto's scholarship "is a chilling postscript to a story in which women ... have been totally *objectified*" ("Future Tense," pp. 114-15). I strongly disagree with Keith's assertion that "By the final chapter ... we are prepared to agree with a historian that 'we must be cautious about passing moral judgement upon the Gileadeans' [quoted from Atwood's novel]" ("Apocalyptic Imaginations," p. 126).

42. See McHale's *Postmodernist Fiction* for a discussion of how frame-breaking destabilizes ontology and thus "paradoxically *relativizes* reality" (197).

43. *Ibid.*, p. 90.

44. Armitage, "The Next Step," p. 4.

45. However, as Hutcheon succinctly argues, "History is not made obsolete" by postmodernist theory and fiction but rather is "being rethought—as a human construct." Postmodern theory and fiction do *not* deny that "the *past* existed" but rather assert that "its accessibility to us now is entirely conditioned by textuality" (*A Poetics of Postmodernism,* p. 16).

46. Kauffman claims that "The narrative we read is thus a reconstruction, an approximation, subject to numerous interventions, all of which undermine the voice(s) of authority, the validity of interpretation, and the notion of a center," and, indeed, asserts that "Postmodernism is stamped on [Atwood's] text." However, she does not address the issue of postmodernism in any detail, focusing her discussion on epistolarity (*Special Delivery,* pp. 226, 223). Keith notes that Atwood's novel "operates according to post-modernist and self-reflexive modes," but he does not pursue this line of discussion ("Apocalyptic Imaginations," p. 126).

47. Nischik similarly notes that "the events in the novel do not seem so fantastic any more once you start looking more closely—it's only their condensed and special combination which makes them appear outlandish at first sight" ("Back to the Future," p. 147).

48. Hansen also discusses Atwood's "pessimistic insistence on the ease with which feminist gains of the very recent past could be swept away [which] seems only more and more percipient and urgent as political events develop at the end of the 1980s" ("Mothers Tomorrow," p. 29).

49. Similarly, both Rigney and Nischik argue that the novel rejects any kind of absolutism or fanaticism.

Chapter 6: Fantasy and Carnivalization in Angela Carter's *Nights at the Circus*

1. In a related vein, Palmer locates "a key area of tension in Carter's writing" between "utopian elements" and a "strong emphasis on the analytic and the 'demythologising' [sic]" ("From 'Coded Mannequin' to Bird Woman," p. 179). I argue that the bringing together of these two impulses in *Nights at the Circus* creates not tension but rather a space where possibilities for change can be explored.

2. See "Chapter 1" for an in-depth discussion of feminism and post-modernism.

3. In one sense, then, Carter's novel is an example of what Lee describes as the tendency within British postmodern fiction to "challenge Realist conventions from within the very conventions they wish to subvert" (*Realism and Power,* p. xii). Lee does not discuss *Nights at the Circus* or how feminism and/or feminist fiction fits into her thesis.

4. Moi, "Postmodernist Theory: Feminist Postmodernism in the USA," pp. 36, 43.

5. Delphy, *Close to Home,* pp. 215, 211.

6. Carter, *Nights at the Circus,* p. 7. All subsequent references from this novel will be placed in the text itself.

7. Similarly, Robinson argues that Carter "disrupts an essentialist equation between biological sex and social gender" but, at the same time, "*foregrounds* gender as constitutive of subjectivity by tracing the processes by which 'official' women—that is, individuals sexed female—are socially and discursively constructed as Woman according to the needs of the dominant, 'official' sex, men" (*Engendering the Subject,* p. 77).

8. De Lauretis, *Alice Doesn't,* p. 7. Along the same line, Moi argues that "To name is to exercise power" and that although "Definitions may well be constraining: they are also enabling" ("Postmodern Theory," p. 37). Robinson notes that Fevvers "places Herself as the subject of her story" (*Engendering the Subject,* p. 23).

9. Schmidt, "The Journey of the Subject," p. 67. Siegel also notes that Fevvers is "hatched—in defiance of biological genre" ("Postmodern Women Novelists," p. 12).

10. For example, Hartsock argues in *Money, Sex and Power* that, within "masculinist ideology," "The body is both irrelevant and in opposition to the (real) self, an impediment to be overcome by the mind" (242), and that it is not surprising that the body and "material reality" are devalued by Western societies, since these are the realms with which women are in closer contact (235–36).

11. Although this interest in mirrors recalls mannerism, postmodern fiction more thoroughly problematizes the dichotomy between appearance and reality by demonstrating that reality is always already represented and thus cannot be disassociated from appearance. Fevvers's identity is one that she has created for herself and cannot be separated from what she appears to be.

12. Fevvers in this sense has more in common with Amazon warrior women than with traditional Western conceptions of women.

13. Robinson, *Engendering the Subject*, p. 77.

14. My argument thus differs from that of Robinson in *Engendering the Subject,* who argues that, "While Fevvers is placed as the object of various male gazes in the text, she simultaneously places herself as the subject of her story" (23). I am suggesting that Fevvers actively creates herself as subject *and* object, that she is not passively "placed as the object of various male gazes." Later in her discussion, however, Robinson seemingly contradicts her earlier analysis, when she suggests that "Fevvers takes full responsibility for engineering herself as spectacle and, thus, resists victimization" (125)—a formulation with which I thoroughly agree. In much the same way, Schmidt argues that "the miraculous Fevvers is the inventor of her own singularity for which she seeks acclaim" ("The Journey of the Subject," p. 72). As Siegel suggests, "Carter gives us woman as someone other than Other, someone who is not defined by and absorbed into the patriarchal power structure" ("Postmodern Women Novelists," p. 12).

15. Hartsock, "Foucault on Power: A Theory of Women?," pp. 170-72.

16. Finn, "Patriarchy and Pleasure," p. 91.

17. *Ibid.*, p. 89.

18. Barrett, *Women's Oppression Today*, pp. 42-43.

19. Delphy, *Close to Home,* pp. 217, 166.

20. FBI statistics on rape support the claim that women are victimized daily. For example, 1987 FBI statistics cited in *Crime in the United States* indicate that, in the United States alone, there is "one *Forcible rape* every six minutes" (6). The FBI reports define "forcible rape" as "the carnal knowledge of a female forcibly and against her will," which includes "Assaults or attempts to commit rape by force or threat of force" (13). These figures are necessarily conservative, since many rapes and attempted rapes go unreported.

21. In a similar vein, Hutcheon notes that Carter's novel "straddles the border between the imaginary/fantastic (with her winged woman protagonist) and the realistic/historical" (*A Poetics of Postmodernism,* p. 61), but she does not pursue this line of analysis.

22. Hartsock, *Money, Sex and Power,* p. 231.

23. Delphy, *Close to Home*, p. 59.

24. Barrett, *Women's Oppression Today*, p. 77. I am here using the

term *ideology* in the sense defined by Barrett, as "a generic term for the processes by which meaning is produced, challenged, reproduced, transformed" (97).

25. Carter, *The Sadeian Woman,* pp. 3, 9.

26. Atwood's *The Handmaid's Tale* similarly depicts the prostitutes working at the illegal hotel-turned-whorehouse as incorrigibles, many of whom had been professional women before the Gileadean regime took over.

27. This is particularly evident in attitudes and laws concerning women's reproductive capacities.

28. Bakhtin, *Problems of Dostoevsky's Poetics,* pp. 122, 107, 123, 157–58.

29. McHale, *Postmodernist Fiction,* pp. 172–74. However, I prefer to discuss postmodern impulses within fiction rather than postmodern fiction (see Chapter 1).

30. Bakhtin, *Problems of Dostoevsky's Poetics,* pp. 114–18.

31. Carter's clear theoretical awareness suggests that she knows Bakhtin's work and is using it for her own purposes. Palmer has, like myself, made the connection between Carter's *Nights at the Circus* and Bakhtin's concept of carnivalization. In a discussion aimed more specifically toward the novel's focus on "woman-identification and female collectivity," Palmer argues that Carter adapts carnivalistic perspectives to perform "an analysis of patriarchal culture and the representation of female community" ("From 'Coded Mannequin' to Bird Woman," pp. 200, 197).

32. In much the same way, the Amazon warrior woman has often been created as a figure that threatens the status quo.

33. Hutcheon also suggests in more general terms that in the fiction of writers such as Carter "subjectivity is represented as something in process, never as fixed and never as autonomous, outside history. It is always a gendered subjectivity, rooted also in class, race, ethnicity, and sexual orientation" (*The Politics of Postmodernism,* p. 39).

34. Although she does not explicitly assert that Fevvers creates herself as both subject and object simultaneously, Schmidt does note that "Fevvers does not simply become man's passive object, for her wings ensure that she herself constitutes a formidable subject which others must react to. But as the eye metaphor indicates, she does nevertheless need the reaction of others to have her own conception of herself confirmed" ("The Journey of the Subject," p. 68).

35. Hans and Lapouge, *Les femmes*, p. 24 (my translation).

36. Gubar argues that most feminists agree that "pornography represents male domination," even writers as dissimilar as "Millett and Carter" ("Representing Pornography," p. 730).

37. Carter, *The Sadeian Woman*, pp. 19–20.

38. Gubar, "Representing Pornography," p. 730.

39. Ragland-Sullivan, *Jacques Lacan*, p. 290.

40. Foucault, *Discipline and Punish*, pp. 248–50.

41. Much Marxist feminist analysis highlights the connection between women's reproductive capacities and women's oppression.

42. This contradicts charges that subversiveness is contained within the carnival and is thus not politically effective.

43. Palmer similarly argues that "Carter constructs a witty parallel between the subordinate position of the troupe of performing apes in the circus and the position of the women performers. Both are forced to endure frequent indignities and brutalities" and "both rebel" ("From 'Coded Mannequin' to Bird Woman," p. 199).

44. Jackson, *Fantasy*, pp. 4, 21. Jackson does not use the term *postmodernism* in her work; she uses the term *modern* to cover both modern and postmodern literary works.

45. McHale, *Postmodernist Fiction*, p. 75.

46. Jackson, *Fantasy*, pp. 42–43.

47. Woolf's *Orlando* is a good example of a novel that uses elements of the fantastic as a strategy to fulfill feminist aims and is thus a precursor of Carter's novel.

48. There is a strong parallel between Siberia in Carter's novel and the Zone in Pynchon's *Gravity's Rainbow*.

49. Barrett, *Women's Oppression Today*, p. 42.

50. In a related vein, Robinson argues that, near the end of the novel, "Lizzie, always the materialist, draws Fevvers back from this becoming Woman by pointing to the woman with a baby" (*Engendering the Subject*, p. 131). However, I find it problematic to hold on to the concept of "Woman," even if it is qualified by "becoming," and prefer to talk in terms of new female subjectivities that are always in process.

51. Bakhtin, *Problems of Dostoevsky's Poetics*, p. 127. Turner also links Fevvers' laughter at the end of the novel with Bakhtin's notion of ambivalent laughter, asserting that it "expresses a relationship to existence of all inclusive regeneration that is both mocking and triumphant" ("Subjects and Symbols," p. 57).

52. Bakhtin, *Problems of Dostoevsky's Poetics*, p. 164.

53. Atwood's *The Handmaid's Tale* also posits a connection between desire and subjecthood, but it does not investigate the link between desire and love.

Chapter 7: Feminist-Postmodern Fiction

1. Weedon, *Feminist Practice*, pp. 91, 95.

2. Carter's earlier rewritings of fairy tales are currently enjoying critical success, however, which might indicate that Carter is only just being *discovered* by a wider group of readers and critics in the United States.

3. See Waugh's *Metafiction* and Belsey's *Critical Practice* for a fuller discussion of how the conventions of realism function. Also see my discussion of the topic in Chapter 1.

4. McCaffery, *Postmodern Fiction*, pp. xxv–vi.

5. All three forms of politics are targeted, using a variety of disruptive strategies, in novels such as Morrison's *Beloved* and Walker's *The Color Purple*.

6. Lessing, *The Golden Notebook*, p. 467.

7. I must here credit Elizabeth Fox-Genovese for urging me to address more specifically the issue of collective values.

8. See Felski's *Beyond Feminist Aesthetics*, Hite's *The Other Side of the Story*, and Greene's *Changing the Story*.

BIBLIOGRAPHY

Adorno, Theodor. "Commitment." Trans. Francis McDonagh. In Bloch, 177–95.

Alexander, Marguerite. *Flights from Realism: Themes and Strategies in Postmodernist British and American Fiction.* London: Edward Arnold, 1990.

Annas, Pamela J. "New Worlds, New Words: Androgyny in Feminist Science Fiction." *Science Fiction Studies* 5 (1978): 143–56.

Arac, Jonathan. *Postmodernism and Politics.* Minneapolis: University of Minnesota Press, 1986.

Ardis, Ann L. *New Women, New Novels: Feminism and Early Modernism.* New Brunswick: Rutgers University Press, 1990.

Armitage, Susan. "The Next Step." *Frontiers* 7 (1983): 3–8.

Atwood, Margaret. *The Handmaid's Tale* (1985). New York: Ballantine, 1987.

_____. *The Robber Bride.* New York: Doubleday, 1993.

Bakhtin, Mikhail. *Problems of Dostoevsky's Poetics.* Trans. Caryl Emerson. Minneapolis: University of Minnesota Press, 1984.

Barnes, Djuna. *Nightwood.* New York: New Directions, 1961.

Barr, Marleen. *Alien to Femininity: Speculative Fiction and Feminist Theory.* New York: Greenwood, 1987.

_____. "Feminist Fabulation; or, Playing with Patriarchy vs. the Masculinization of Metafiction." *Women's Studies* 14 (1987): 187–91.

_____, ed. *Future Females: A Critical Anthology.* Bowling Green: Bowling Green State University Popular Press, 1981.

Barr, Marleen and Nicholas D. Smith, eds. *Women and Utopia: Critical Interpretations.* Lanham: University Press of America, 1983.

Barrett, Michèle. *Women's Oppression Today: Problems in Marxist Feminist Analysis.* London: Verso, 1980.

Barthes, Roland. *Writing Degree Zero and Elements of Semiology.* Trans. Annette Lavers and Colin Smith. Boston: Beacon, 1970.

Belsey, Catherine. *Critical Practice.* New York: Methuen, 1980.

_____. "Constructing the Subject: Deconstructing the Text" (1985). In Warhol, 593–609.

Bergmann, Harriet F. "'Teaching Them to Read': A Fishing Expedition in *The Handmaid's Tale.*" *College English* 51 (1989): 847–54.

258 BIBLIOGRAPHY

Bertens, Hans. "The Postmodern *Weltanschauung* and its Relation with Modernism: An Introductory Survey." In Fokkema, 9–52.

Bloch, Ernst, Georg Lukacs, Bertolt Brecht, Walter Benjamin, and Theodor Adorno. *Aesthetics and Politics*. Trans. ed. Ronald Taylor. London: NLB, 1977.

Brecht, Bertolt. "Popularity and Realism." Trans. Stuart Hood. In Bloch, 79–85.

Brownstein, Marilyn L. "Postmodern Language and the Perpetuation of Desire." *Twentieth Century Literature* 31 (1985): 73–88.

Butler, Judith. *Gender Trouble: Feminism and the Subversion of Identity*. New York: Routledge, 1990.

_____."Contingent Foundations: Feminism and the Question of 'Post-modernism.'" In Butler and Scott, 3–21.

Butler, Judith and Joan W. Scott, eds. *Feminists Theorize the Political*. New York: Routledge, 1992.

Cain, William E., ed. *Philosophical Approaches to Literature*. Cranbury: Bucknell University Press, 1984.

Caldwell, Larry W. "Wells, Orwell, and Atwood: (EPI)Logic and Eu/Utopia." *Extrapolation: A Journal of Science Fiction and Fantasy* 33 (1992): 333–45.

Calinescu, Matei. "Introductory Remarks: Postmodernism, the Mimetic and Theatrical Fallacies." In Calinescu and Fokkema, 3–16.

Calinescu, Matei and Douwe Fokkema, eds. *Exploring Postmodernism*. Philadelphia: John Benjamins, 1987.

Carey, John L. "Art and Reality in *The Golden Notebook*." In Pratt, 20–39.

Carter, Angela. *The Sadeian Woman: And the Ideology of Pornography*. New York: Pantheon, 1978.

_____. *The Bloody Chamber and Other Stories* (1979). New York: Penguin, 1981.

_____. *Nights at the Circus* (1984). New York: Penguin, 1986.

Caughie, Pamela L. *Virginia Woolf and Postmodernism: Literature in Quest and Question of Itself*. Urbana: University of Illinois Press, 1991.

Cixous, Hélène. "Sorties." In Marks, 90–98.

Cohen, Mary. "Out of the Chaos, a New Kind of Strength: Doris Lessing's *The Golden Notebook*." In Diamond, 178–93.

Coover, Robert. *The Public Burning*. New York: Viking, 1977.

Cornillon, Susan Koppelman. *Images of Women in Fiction: Feminist Perpectives*. Bowling Green: Bowling Green University Press, 1972.

Cowart, David. *History and the Contemporary Novel*. Carbondale: Southern Illinois University Press, 1989.

Crime in the United States: 1987 Uniform Crime Reports. Washington D.C.: Federal Bureau of Investigation, United States Department of Justice, 1987.

Daly, Brenda O. and Maureen T. Reddy. *Narrative Mothers: Theorizing Maternal Subjectivities.* Knoxville: University of Tennessee Press, 1991.

Davidson, Arnold E. "Future Tense: Making History in *The Handmaid's Tale.*" In VanSpanckeren, 113–21.

De Lauretis, Teresa. *Alice Doesn't: Feminism, Semiotics, Cinema.* Bloomington: Indiana University Press, 1984.

DeKoven, Marianne. *A Different Language: Gertrude Stein's Experimental Writing.* Madison: University of Wisconsin Press, 1983.

_____.*Rich and Strange: Gender, History, Modernism.* Princeton: Princeton University Press, 1991.

DeLillo, Don. *Libra.* New York: Viking, 1988.

Delphy, Christine. *Close to Home: A Materialist Analysis of Women's Oppression.* Trans. Diana Leonard. Amherst: The University of Massachusetts Press, 1984.

Derrida, Jacques. "Structure, Sign, and Play in the Discourse of the Human Sciences." In Macksey, 247–72.

Diamond, Arlyn and Lee R. Edwards, eds. *The Authority of Experience.* Amherst: The University of Massachusetts Press, 1977.

Docherty, Thomas, ed. *Postmodernism: A Reader.* New York: Columbia University Press, 1993.

Doctorow, E.L. *Ragtime.* New York: Random House, 1975.

Donovan, Josephine, ed. *Feminist Literary Criticism: Explorations in Theory.* Lexington: University Press of Kentucky, 1975.

Drabble, Margaret. "Doris Lessing: Cassandra in a World under Siege" (1972). In Sprague and Tiger, 183–91.

Draine, Betsy. *Substance under Pressure: Artistic Coherence and Evolving Form in the Novels of Doris Lessing.* Madison: University of Wisconsin Press, 1983.

DuPlessis, Rachel Blau. "The Feminist Apologues of Lessing, Piercy, and Russ." *Frontiers* 4 (1979): 1-8.

_____.*Writing beyond the Ending: Narrative Strategies of Twentieth-Century Women Writers.* Bloomington: Indiana University Press, 1985.

Eliot, T.S. "The Love Song of J. Alfred Prufrock" (1917). *Selected Poems.* New York: Harcourt, 1936.

Ezergailis, Inta. *Women Writers: The Divided Self.* Bonn, Germany: Bouvier Verlag Herbert Grundmann, 1982.

Felman, Shoshana. "Women and Madness: The Critical Phallacy." *Diacritics* 5 (1975): 2–10.

_____. *Writing and Madness.* Trans. Martha Noel Evans and the author. Ithaca: Cornell University Press, 1985.

Felski, Rita. *Beyond Feminist Aesthetics: Feminist Literature and Social Change.* Cambridge: Harvard University Press, 1989.

Fiedler, Leslie. "The New Mutants" (1965). In Fiedler, *The Collected Essays*, 379–400.

———. *The Collected Essays of Leslie Fiedler*. Vol. 2. New York: Stein and Day, 1971.

Finn, Geraldine. "Patriarchy and Pleasure: The Pornographic Eye/I." In Kroker, 81–95.

Firestone, Shulamith. *The Dialectic of Sex: The Case for Feminist Revolution*. New York: William Morrow, 1970.

Fishburn, Katherine. "*The Golden Notebook:* A Challenge to the Teaching Establishment." In Kaplan and Rose, 127–31.

Fitting, Peter. "The Turn from Utopia in Recent Feminist Fiction." In Jones and Goodwin, 141–58.

Fokkema, Douwe and Hans Bertens, eds. *Approaching Postmodernism*. Philadelphia: John Benjamins, 1986.

Foster, Hal. "Postmodernism: A Preface." In Foster, *The Anti-Aesthetic*, ix–xvi.

Foster, Hal, ed. *The Anti-Aesthetic: Essays on Postmodern Culture*. Townsend: Bay, 1983.

Foucault, Michel. *Madness and Civilization*. Trans. Richard Howard. New York: Pantheon, 1965.

———. *Discipline and Punish: The Birth of the Prison*. Trans. Alan Sheridan. New York: Pantheon, 1977.

Fowles, John. *The French Lieutenant's Woman* (1969). New York: Signet, 1970.

Fox-Genovese, Elizabeth. *Feminism without Illusion: A Critique of Individualism*. Chapel Hill: University of North Carolina Press, 1991.

Fraser, Nancy and Linda Nicholson. "Social Criticism without Philosophy: An Encounter between Feminism and Postmodernism" (1988). In Nicholson, 19–38.

Freibert, Lucy. "Control and Creativity: The Politics of Risk in Margaret Atwood's *The Handmaid's Tale*." In McCombs, 280–91.

Friedman, Ellen G. "Contexts and Continuities: An Introduction to Women's Experimental Fiction in English." In Friedman and Fuchs, 3–51.

Friedman, Ellen G. and Miriam Fuchs, eds. *Breaking the Sequence: Women's Experimental Fiction*. Princeton: Princeton University Press, 1989.

Fuss, Diana. *Essentially Speaking: Feminism, Nature & Difference*. New York: Routledge, 1989.

García Márquez, Gabriel. *One Hundred Years of Solitude*. Trans. Gregory Rabassa. New York: Avon, 1970.

Gardiner, Judith Kegan. "Evil, Apocalypse, and Feminist Fiction." *Frontiers* 7 (1983): 74–80.

Garner, Shirley Nelson, Claire Kahane, and Madelon Sprengnether, eds. *The (M)other Tongue.* Ithaca: Cornell University Press, 1985.

Gerstenberger, Donna. "The Radical Narrative of Djuna Barnes's *Nightwood.*" In Friedman and Fuchs, 129–39.

Gilbert, Sandra and Susan Gubar. *The Madwoman in the Attic: The Woman Writer and the Nineteenth-Century Literary Imagination.* New Haven: Yale University Press, 1979.

_____. *No Man's Land: The Place of the Woman Writer in the Twentieth Century.* 2 vols. New Haven: Yale University Press, 1988–89.

Givner, Jessie. "Names, Faces, and Signatures in Margaret Atwood's *Cat's Eye* and *The Handmaid's Tale.*" *Canadian Literature* 133 (Summer 1992): 56–75.

Greene, Gayle. "Women and Men in Doris Lessing's *The Golden Notebook:* Divided Selves." In Garner, 280–305.

_____. *Changing the Story: Feminist Fiction and Tradition.* Bloomington: Indiana University Press, 1991.

Gubar, Susan. "Representing Pornography: Feminism, Criticism, and Depictions of Female Violation." *Critical Inquiry* 13 (Summer 1987): 712–41.

H.D. *HERmione.* New York: New Directions, 1981.

_____. *Nights.* New York: New Directions, 1986.

Halliday, David. "On Atwood." *Waves* 15 (1987): 51–4.

Hammer, Stephanie Barbe. "The World As It Will Be? Female Satire and the Technology of Power in *The Handmaid's Tale.*" *Modern Language Studies* 20.2 (1990): 39–49.

Hans, Marie Françoise and Gilles Lapouge. *Les femmes, la pornographie, l'érotisme.* Paris, France: éditions du Seuil, 1978.

Hanscombe, Gillian E. *The Art of Life: Dorothy Richardson and the Development of Feminist Consciousness.* Athens: Ohio University Press, 1982.

Hansen, Elaine Tuttle. "Mothers Tomorrow and Mothers Yesterday, But Never Mothers Today: *Woman on the Edge of Time* and *The Handmaid's Tale.*" In Daly, 21–43.

Harari, Josue. "Preface" and "Critical Factions/Critical Fiction." In Harari, *Textual Strategies,* 9–14 and 17–92.

_____, ed. *Textual Strategies: Perspectives in Post-Structuralist Criticism.* Ithaca: Cornell University Press, 1979.

Hartsock, Nancy. *Money, Sex, and Power: Toward a Feminist Historical Materialism* (1983). Boston: Northeastern University Press, 1985.

_____. "Foucault on Power: A Theory of Women?" In Nicholson, 157–75.

Hassan, Ihab. "Postface 1982: Toward a Concept of Postmodernism." In *The Dismemberment of Orpheus,* 259–71. Madison: University of Wisconsin Press, 1982.

_____. *The Postmodern Turn: Essays in Postmodern Theory and Culture.* Columbus: Ohio State University Press, 1987.

_____. "Pluralism in Postmodern Perspective." In Calinescu and Fokkema, 17–39.

Hauser, Arnold. *Mannerism.* New York: Knopf, 1965.

Hite, Molly. *Ideas of Order in the Novels of Thomas Pynchon.* Columbus: Ohio State University Press, 1983.

_____. "(En)Gendering Metafiction: Doris Lessing's Rehearsals for *The Golden Notebook.*" *Modern Fiction Studies* 34 (1988): 483–500.

_____. *The Other Side of the Story: Structures and Strategies of Contemporary Feminist Narrative.* Ithaca: Cornell University Press, 1989.

Homans, Margaret, ed. *Virginia Woolf: A Collection of Critical Essays.* Englewood Cliffs: Prentice Hall, 1993.

Howe, Irving. "*The Golden Notebook:* Neither Compromise nor Happiness." In Sprague and Tiger, 177–81.

Huckle, Patricia. "Women in Utopia." In Sullivan, 115–36.

Hutcheon, Linda. *A Poetics of Postmodernism: History, Theory, Fiction.* New York: Routledge, 1988.

_____. *The Politics of Postmodernism.* New York: Routledge, 1989.

Huyssen, Andreas. "Mapping the Postmodern" (1984). In Huyssen, *After the Great Divide,* 179–221.

_____. *After the Great Divide: Modernism, Mass Culture, Postmodernism.* Bloomington: Indiana University Press, 1986.

Hynes, Joseph. "The Construction of *The Golden Notebook.*" *The Iowa Review* 4 (1973): 100–13.

Irigaray, Luce. *Speculum of the Other Woman.* Trans. Gillian C. Gill. New York: Cornell University Press, 1985.

Jackson, Rosemary. *Fantasy: The Literature of Subversion.* New York: Methuen, 1981.

Jameson, Fredric. "Reflections in Conclusion." In Bloch, 196–213.

_____. *The Political Unconscious: Narrative as a Socially Symbolic Act.* Ithaca: Cornell University Press, 1981.

_____. "The Politics of Theory: Ideological Positions in the Postmodernist Debate." *New German Critique* 33 (1984): 53–65.

_____. "Postmodernism, or The Cultural Logic of Late Capitalism." *New Left Review* 146 (Summer 1984): 53-92 (also reprinted in *Postmodernism, or, The Cultural Logic of Late Capitalism,* 1–54).

_____. *Postmodernism, or, The Cultural Logic of Late Capitalism.* Durham: Duke University Press, 1991.

Jardine, Alice A. *Gynesis: Configurations of Woman and Modernity.* Ithaca: Cornell University Press, 1985.

Johnston, John. "Ideology, Representation, Schizophrenia: Toward a Theory of the Postmodern Subject." In Shapiro, 67–95.

Jones, Libby Falk. "Gilman, Bradley, Piercy, and the Evolving Rhetoric of Feminist Utopias." In Jones and Goodwin, 116–29.

Jones, Libby Falk and Sarah Webster Goodwin, eds. *Feminism, Utopia, and Narrative.* Knoxville: University of Tennessee Press, 1990.

Joplin, Patricia Klindienst. "The Authority of Illusion: Feminism and Fascism in Virginia Woolf's *Between the Acts.*" In Homans, 210–26.

Kaivola, Karen. *All Contraries Confounded: The Lyrical Fiction of Virginia Woolf, Djuna Barnes, and Marguerite Duras.* Iowa City: University of Iowa Press, 1991.

Kaplan, Carey and Ellen Cronan Rose, eds. *Approaches to Teaching Lessing's "The Golden Notebook".* New York: MLA, 1989.

Kaplan, E. Ann. "Introduction" and "Feminism/Oedipus/Postmodernism: The Case of MTV." In Kaplan, *Postmodernism and Its Discontents,* 1–9 and 30–44.

_____, ed. *Postmodernism and Its Discontents.* New York: Verso, 1988.

Kaplan, Sydney Janet. *Feminine Consciousness in the Modern British Novel.* Urbana: University of Illinois Press, 1975.

Kauffman, Linda S. *Special Delivery: Epistolary Modes in Modern Fiction.* Chicago: University of Chicago Press, 1992.

Keinhorst, Annette. "Emancipatory Projection: An Introduction to Women's Critical Utopias." *Women's Studies* 14 (1987): 91–99.

Keith, W.J. "Apocalyptic Imaginations: Notes on Atwood's *The Handmaid's Tale* and Findley's *Not Wanted on the Voyage.*" *Essays on Canadian Writing* 35 (1987): 123–34.

Kessler, Carol Farley. "*Woman on the Edge of Time:* A Novel 'To Be of Use.'" *Extrapolation* 28 (1987): 310–18.

Kingston, Maxine Hong. *The Woman Warrior: Memoirs of a Girlhood Among Ghosts* (1975). New York: Vintage, 1977.

Knapp, Mona. "*The Golden Notebook:* A Feminist Context for the Classroom." In Kaplan and Rose, 108–14.

Kristeva, Julia. "Postmodernism?" *Bucknell Review* 25 (1980): 136–41.

Kroker, Marilouise and Arthur, eds. *Feminism Now: Theory and Practice.* Montreal, Canada: New World Perspectives, 1985.

Lacombe, Michele. "The Writing on the Wall: Amputated Speech in Margaret Atwood's *The Handmaid's Tale.*" *Wascana Review* 21 (1986): 3–20.

Lee, Alison. *Realism and Power: Postmodern British Fiction.* London: Routledge, 1990.

Lessing, Doris. "A Small Personal Voice" (1957). In Schlueter, 3–21.

_____. *The Golden Notebook* (1962). Reprint, with a 1972 introduction by Lessing. New York: Bantam, 1973.

_____. *The Four-Gated City* (1969). New York: Bantam, 1982.

Libby, Marion Vlastos. "Sex and the New Woman in *The Golden Notebook*." *The Iowa Review* 5 (1974): 106–20.

Linker, Kate. "Representation and Sexuality." In Wallis, *Art after Modernism*, 391–415.

Loy, Mina. *Insel*. Ed. Elizabeth Arnold. Santa Rosa: Black Sparrow, 1991.

Lyotard, Jean-Francois. *The Postmodern Condition: A Report on Knowledge*. Trans. Geoff Bennington and Brian Massumi. Minneapolis: University of Minnesota Press, 1984.

Maciunas, Billie. "Feminist Epistemology in Piercy's *Woman on the Edge of Time*." *Women's Studies: An Interdisciplinary Journal*. 20 (1992): 249–58.

Macksey, Richard and Eugenio Donato, eds. *The Structuralist Controversy*. Baltimore: Johns Hopkins University Press, 1972.

Malak, Amin. "Margaret Atwood's *The Handmaid's Tale* and the Dystopian Tradition." *Canadian Literature* 112 (1987): 9–16.

Marks, Elaine and Isabelle de Courtivron, eds. *New French Feminisms* New York: Schocken Books, 1981.

McCaffery, Larry, ed. *Postmodern Fiction: A Bibliographic Guide*. New York: Greenwood, 1986.

McCarthy, Mary. Review of *The Handmaid's Tale*, by Margaret Atwood. *New York Times Book Review* (9 February 1986): 1.

McCombs, Judith, ed. *Critical Essays on Margaret Atwood*. Boston: Hall, 1988.

McCormick, Kathleen. "What Happened to Anna Wulf: Naivety in *The Golden Notebook*." *Massachusetts Studies in English* 8 (1982): 56–62.

McCrindle, Jean. "Reading *The Golden Notebook* in 1962." In Taylor, 43–56.

McHale, Brian. *Postmodernist Fiction*. New York: Methuen, 1987.

_____. *Constructing Postmodernism*. New York: Routledge, 1992.

Michael, Magali Cornier. "The Political Paradox in Don DeLillo's *Libra*." *Critique: Studies in Contemporary Fiction* 35 (1994): 146–56.

_____. "Angela Carter's *Nights at the Circus:* An Engaged Feminism via Subversive Postmodern Strategies." *Contemporary Literature* 35 (1994): 492–521.

_____. "Woolf's *Between the Acts* and Lessing's *The Golden Notebook*: From Modern to Postmodern Subjectivity." In Saxton, 39–56.

Miner, Madonne. "'Trust Me': Reading the Romance Plot in Margaret Atwood's *The Handmaid's Tale*." *Twentieth Century Literature* 37 (1991): 148–68.

Moi, Toril. *Sexual/Textual Politics: Feminist Literary Theory*. New York: Methuen, 1985.

_____. "Postmodernist Theory: Feminist Postmodernism in the USA." In Zadworna-Fjellestad, 34–46.

Moore, Thomas. *The Style of Connectedness:* Gravity's Rainbow *and Thomas Pynchon.* Columbia: University of Missouri Press, 1987.

Morante, Elsa. *History: A Novel* (1974). Trans. William Weaver. New York: Knopf, 1977.

Morris, Meaghan. "Feminism, Reading, Postmodernism" (1988). In Docherty, 368–89.

Morrison, Toni. *Beloved* (1987). New York: Knopf, 1988.

Mouffe, Chantal. "Feminism, Citizenship, and Radical Democratic Politics." In Butler and Scott, 369–84.

Moylan, Thomas P. "Someday the Gross Repair Will Be Done: History and Utopia in Marge Piercy's *Woman on the Edge of Time.*" In Wolfe, 133–40.

Murphy, Patrick. "Reducing the Dystopian Distance: Pseudo-Documentary Framing in Near-Future Fiction." *Science Fiction Studies* 17 (1990): 25–40.

Nicholson, Linda, ed. *Feminism/Postmodernism.* New York: Routledge, 1990.

Nischik, Reingard M. "Back to the Future: Margaret Atwood's Anti-Utopian Vision in *The Handmaid's Tale.*" *Englisch Amerikanische Studien* 1 (1987): 139–48.

Owens, Craig. "The Discourse of Others: Feminists and Postmodernism." In Foster, *The Anti-Aesthetic,* 57–82.

Palmer, Paulina. "From 'Coded Mannequin' to Bird Woman: Angela Carter's Magic Flight." In Roe, 179–205.

Pearson, Carol. "Women's Fantasies and Feminist Utopias." *Frontiers* 11 (1977): 50–61.

_____. "The Utopian Novels of Dorothy Bryant, Mary Staton, and Marge Piercy." *Heresies* 4 (1981): 84–87.

Pfaelzer, Jean. "Response: What Happened to History?" In Jones and Goodwin, 191–200.

Piercy, Marge. *Woman on the Edge of Time.* New York: Ballantine, 1976.

Plumwood, Val. "Women, Humanity and Nature." In Sayers, 211–34.

Pratt, Annis and L.S. Dembo, eds. *Doris Lessing: Critical Studies.* Madison: University of Wisconsin Press, 1974.

Pynchon, Thomas. *Gravity's Rainbow* (1973). New York: Bantam, 1974.

Ragland-Sullivan, Ellie. *Jacques Lacan and the Philosophy of Psychoanalysis.* Urbana: University of Illinois Press, 1986.

Reesman, Jeanne Campbell. "Dark Knowledge in *The Handmaid's Tale.*" *College English Association—Critic* 53.3 (1990): 6–22.

Richardson, Dorothy. *Pilgrimage.* Vol. 1, *Pointed Roofs* (1915), *Backwater* (1916), and *Honeycomb* (1917). Vol. 2, *The Tunnel* and *Interim* (1919). Vol. 3, *Deadlock* (1921), *Revolving Lights* (1923), and *The Trap* (1925). New York: Knopf, 1938.

———. *Pilgrimage*. Vol. 4, *Oberland* (1927), *Dawn's Left Hand* (1931), *Clear Horizon* (1935), *Dimple Hill* (1938), and *March Moonlight*. London: Dent, 1967.

Rigney, Barbara Hill. *Madness and Sexual Politics in the Feminist Novel*. Madison: University of Wisconsin Press, 1978.

———. "Dystopia." *Canadian Literature* 111 (1986): 143–44.

———. *Margaret Atwood*. London: MacMillan Education, 1987.

Rimmon-Kenan, Shlomith. *Narrative Fiction: Contemporary Poetics*. New York: Methuen, 1983.

Robinson, Marilynne. *Housekeeping* (1980). New York: Bantam, 1982.

Robinson, Sally. *Engendering the Subject: Gender and Self-Representation in Contemporary Women's Fiction*. Albany: State University of New York Press, 1991.

Roe, Sue, ed. *Women Reading Women's Writing*. New York: St. Martin's, 1987.

Rosinski, Natalie M. *Feminist Futures: Contemporary Women's Speculative Fiction*. Ann Arbor: University of Michigan Research Press, 1984.

Ross, Andrew, ed. *Universal Abandon?: The Politics of Postmodernism*. Minneapolis: University of Minnesota Press, 1988.

Rubenstein, Roberta. *The Novelistic Vision of Doris Lessing: Breaking the Forms of Consciousness*. Urbana: University of Illinois Press, 1979.

———. "Nature and Nurture in Dystopia." In VanSpanckeren, 101–12.

Russ, Joanna. "Recent Feminist Utopias." In Barr, *Future Females*, 71–85.

Sage, Lorna. "Projections from a Messy Present." Review of *The Handmaid's Tale*, by Margaret Atwood. *Times Literary Supplement* (21 March 1986): 307.

Saxton, Ruth and Jean Tobin, eds. *Woolf and Lessing: Breaking the Mold*. New York: St. Martin's, 1994.

Sayers, Sean and Peter Osborne, eds. *Socialism, Feminism and Philosophy*. London: Routledge, 1990.

Schlueter, Paul, ed. *A Small Personal Voice: Essays, Reviews, Interviews*. New York: Knopf, 1974.

Schmidt, Ricarda. "The Journey of the Subject in Angela Carter's Fiction." *Textual Practice* 3 (Spring 1989): 56–75.

Schweickart, Patricio P. "Reading a Wordless Statement: The Structure of Doris Lessing's *The Golden Notebook*." *Modern Fiction Studies* 31 (1985): 263–79.

———. "Reading Ourselves: Toward a Feminist Theory of Reading" (1986). In Warhol, 525–50.

Scott, Joan W. "Experience." In Butler and Scott, 22–40.

Shapiro, Gary, ed. *After the Future: Postmodern Times and Places*. Albany: State University of New York Press, 1990.

Showalter, Elaine. *A Literature of Their Own: British Women Novelists from Bronte to Lessing*. Princeton: Princeton University Press, 1977.

―――. *The Female Malady*. New York: Pantheon, 1985.

―――. "A Criticism of Our Own: Autonomy and Assimilation in Afro-American and Feminist Literary Theory" (1989). In Warhol, 168-88.

Siegel, Carol. "Postmodern Women Novelists Review Victorian Male Masochism." *Genders* 11 (Fall 1991): 1–16.

Siegel, Mark Richard. *Pynchon: Creative Paranoia in* Gravity's Rainbow. Port Washington: Kennikat, 1978.

Sinclair, May. *Mary Olivier: A Life*. London: Lehmann, 1949.

Singer, Linda. "Feminism and Postmodernism." In Butler and Scott, 464–75.

Smith, Paul. *Discerning the Subject*. Minneapolis: University of Minnesota Press, 1988.

Spivak, Gayatri Chakravorty. *In Other Worlds: Essays in Cultural Politics*. New York: Routledge, 1988.

Sprague, Claire. "Doubles Talk in *The Golden Notebook*" (1982). In Sprague and Tiger, 44–60.

Sprague, Claire and Virginia Tiger, eds. *Critical Essays on Doris Lessing*. Boston: Hall, 1986.

Stimpson, Catherine R. "Atwood Woman." Review of *The Handmaid's Tale*, by MargaretAtwood. *The Nation* (31 May 1986): 764–67.

Sullivan, E.D.S., ed. *The Utopian Vision*. San Diego: San Diego University Press, 1983.

Taylor, Jenny, ed. *Notebooks/Memoirs/Archives: Reading and Rereading Doris Lessing*. Boston: Routledge, 1982.

Thielmann, Pia. *Marge Piercy's Women: Visions Captured and Subdued*. Frankfurt, Germany: Fischer, 1986.

Thomas, D.M. *The White Hotel* (1981). New York: Pocket Books, 1982.

Tiger, Virginia. "Illusions of Actuality: First-Person Pronoun in *The Golden Notebook*." In Kaplan and Rose, 101–07.

Turner, Rory P.B. "Subjects and Symbols: Transformations of Identity in *Nights at the Circus*." *Folklore Forum* 20 (1987): 39–60.

VanSpanckeren, Kathryn and Jan Garden Castro, eds. *Margaret Atwood: Vision and Form*. Carbondale: Southern Illinois University Press, 1988.

Wagner-Martin, Linda. "Epigraphs to Atwood's *The Handmaid's Tale*." *Notes on Contemporary Literature* 17 (1987): 4.

Walker, Alice. *The Color Purple* (1982). New York: Pocket Books, 1985.

Wallis, Brian. "What's Wrong with this Picture? An Introduction." In Wallis, *Art after Modernism*, xi–xviii.

―――, ed. *Art after Modernism: Rethinking Representation*. New York: New Museum of Contemporary Art, 1984.

Warhol, Robyn R. and Diane Price Herndl, eds. *Feminisms: An Anthology of Literary Theory and Criticism.* New Brunswick: Rutgers University Press, 1991.

Waugh, Patricia. *Metafiction: The Theory and Practice of Self-Conscious Fiction.* New York: Methuen, 1984.

_____. *Feminine Fictions: Revisiting the Postmodern.* New York: Routledge, 1989.

Weedon, Chris. *Feminist Practice and Poststructuralist Theory.* New York: Blackwell, 1987.

Weldon, Fay. *The Life and Loves of a She-Devil* (1983). New York: Ballantine, 1990.

Wiemer, Annagret J. "Foreign L'(anguish), Mother Tongue: Concepts of Language in Contemporary Feminist Science Fiction." *Women's Studies* 14 (1987): 187–91.

Wilde, Alan. "Touching Earth: Virginia Woolf and the Prose of the World." In Cain, 140–64.

Wolf, Christa. *Cassandra: A Novel and Four Essays* (1983). Trans. Jan Van Heurck. New York: Farrar, 1984.

Wolfe, Gary, ed. *Science Fiction Dialogues.* Chicago: Science Fiction Research Association, 1982.

Wolff, Janet. *The Social Production of Art.* New York: New York University Press, 1984.

_____. *Feminine Sentences: Essays on Women and Culture.* Berkeley: University of California Press, 1990.

Wood, Michael and Louis Zurcher Jr. *The Development of a Postmodern Self.* New York: Greenwood, 1988.

Woolf, Virginia. "Mr. Bennett and Mrs. Brown" (1924). In *The Hogarth Essays,* edited by Leonard and Virginia Woolf, 3–29. Freeport: Books for Libraries, 1970.

_____. *Mrs. Dalloway.* New York: Harcourt, 1925.

_____. *Orlando: A Biography.* New York: Harcourt, 1928.

_____. *A Room of One's Own.* New York: Harcourt, 1929.

_____. *The Waves.* New York: Harcourt, 1931.

_____. *Three Guineas.* New York: Harcourt, 1938.

_____. *Between the Acts.* New York: Harcourt, 1941.

Zadworna-Fjellestad, Danuta, ed. *Criticism in the Twilight Zone: Postmodern Perspectives on Literature and Politics.* Stockholm, Sweden: Almqvist & Wiksell International, 1990.

INDEX

Acker, Kathy, 6, 217
Adorno, Theodor, 8
aesthetics: and economics, 65; feminist, 5–7, 10, 24, 44, 221; humanist, 21–22; mannerist, 32, 252n. 11; and the material situations, 7–8, 55, 97, 101, 109–110; modernist, 37, 47–49, 96–97; patriarchal, 21, 62; and politics, 3–10, 37–38, 48, 55, 102, 133–134; postmodern, 5–8, 11, 17–19, 23, 27, 31–32, 37–38; and power relations, 51, 63, 66; realist, 9–10, 21, 37, 109–110, 242n. 1
agency, 2–4, 19, 34; and feminism, 10, 27, 172, 211; and postmodernism, 15
Alexander, Marguerite, 231n. 78
Annas, Pamela, 243n. 20
anti-referentiality, 17–18, 39, 42
Ardis, Ann, 48–49, 234n. 6
Armitage, Susan, 251n. 44
Atwood, Margaret, 9, 47, 171, 192; *Bodily Harm*, 246n. 11; *The Handmaid's Tale*, 44–45, 135–170, 174, 209–221; 254n. 26, 255n. 53; *The Robber Bride*, 36
audience, readers, 22, 42, 71; and experimentalism, 17; and political praxis, 6, 9–10, 104, 114, 132, 134, 136; and realism, 9–10, 172, 215–217; and subjectivity, 160
author, authorship, 22, 31; and humanism, 21, 86, 163; as male-centered, 177; and modernism, 49; questioning of, 59, 96, 106, 161, 168, 177, 213–214

Bakhtin, Mikhail, 29, 182, 206–207, 254n. 31
Barnes, Djuna, 49–50, 77; *Nightwood*, 59–61, 171
Barr, Marlene, 112, 242n. 3, 243n. 11
Barr, Marlene, and Nicholas Smith, 242n. 2
Barrett, Michèle, 7, 22, 178, 205, 224n. 12, 228n. 56, 253–254n. 24
Barthes, Roland, 37, 232n. 97
Baudrillard, Jean, 13
Belsey, Catherine, 9, 10, 26, 33, 163, 224n. 20, 232n. 90, 242n. 1, 256n. 3
Bergmann, Harriet, 246n. 6, 249nn. 30, 32, 250n. 39
Bertens, Hans, 16
binarism: and experimental aesthetics, 7, 38; and male dominance, 25, 57, 138, 228n. 58; and modernism, 47; and postmodern theories, 23, 25, 146; and power relations, 4, 38, 115; and Western metaphysics, 33, 35–37; and the women modernists, 49
Brecht, Bertolt, 8, 10, 224n. 23
Brooke-Rose, Christine, 6, 12, 28, 217
Brophy, Brigid, 14, 28; *In Transit*, 30
Brownstein, Marilyn, 236n. 33, 237n. 36
Burke, Carolyn, 48
Butler, Judith, 13, 33, 232n. 93

Caldwell, Larry, 248n. 27, 249n. 32
Calinescu, Matei, 225n. 27
Carey, John, 240n. 36, 242n. 47

269

carnivalization, carnivalesque, 181–183, 193–198, 200, 206–207, 255n. 42

Carter, Angela, 9, 28-29, 47; *Nights at the Circus,* 44–45, 61, 171–208, 209–221, 233n. 108, 236n. 30; *The Sadeian Woman,* 180, 181, 185, 186

Caughie, Pamela, 236n. 33

cause and effect logic, 2, 4

chaos, 4, 30, 197, 219, 221

characters, postmodern, 35, 43

Cixous, Hélène, 231n. 83

Cohen, Mary, 90, 237n. 6

coincidence, patterns of coincidences, 2–4

collusion, 82–83, 140–141, 149, 160, 246n. 11

Coover, Robert, *The Public Burning,* 18, 218–219

Cowart, David, 245n. 3, 247n. 13, 248n. 22, 249n. 32

Davidson, Arnold, 246n. 6, 249n. 33, 249–250n. 34, 250nn. 38, 41

deconstruction: and experimental aesthetics, 6; and feminism, 3, 45, 134, 172; and postmodern theories/aesthetics, 7, 11, 16, 27, 31

DeKoven, Marianne, 48

De Lauretis, Theresa, 33, 174

Deleuze, Gilles, and Felix Guattari, 240n. 28

DeLillo, Don, *Libra,* 1–4, 18–19, 39, 41–42, 44, 218–219

Delphy, Christine, 178, 252n. 5, 253n. 23

Derrida, Jacques, 33, 231nn. 83 & 86

desire: as disruptive, 53–54; as liberatory, 185, 189, 208; and love, 185, 191, 193; and postmodernism, 16; and power, 148–153, 193; and silence, 74. *See* love, subjectivity

difference, 25, 28, 30, 35-36, 66

discourse: and literary texts, 22; and postmodernism, 12, 42, 232n. 94; and power relations, 42

Doctorow, E.L., *Ragtime,* 18

Drabble, Margaret, 81

Draine, Betsy, 90

DuPlessis, Rachel Blau, 48, 132, 235n. 18, 236n. 35, 241n. 39, 40, 41, 44, 244n. 25

dystopia, dystopian fiction, 125, 135, 169, 244n. 24, 245n. 1

Engels, Frederick, 180

Eliot, T.S., 47, 98

Ellmann, Mary, 227n. 52

Ezergailis, Inta, 239nn. 22, 27

fantasy: as disruptive, 67, 77, 199, 236n. 30; and the material situation, 194, 197–198, 200–201

fascism, 3, 75, 237n. 37

Federman, Raymond, 16, 17

Felman, Shoshana, 93, 231n. 84, 240n. 29

Felski, Rita, 7, 24, 220, 223n. 2, 224n. 11, 224–225n. 25, 225n. 36, 256n. 8

feminist politics, 2-3, 6, 15, 21–23, 27, 30, 218, 228n. 59

feminist theory, and postmodernism, 1, 7, 14, 23–31, 43, 228n. 57, 228–229n. 60

feminist fiction, 29; and politics, 5–10, 29, 43; and postmodernism, 5, 19–20, 24, 44, 112, 209, 217–220, 227n. 51; and realism, 6, 8-10, 13, 24. *See* modernist fiction, postmodern fiction

Finn, Geraldine, 253nn. 16, 17

Firestone, Shulamith, 123

Fishburn, Katherine, 241n. 39

Fitting, Peter, 249n. 31

Foster, Hal, 13, 224n. 15

Foucault, Michel, 189

Fox-Genovese, Elizabeth, 24, 227n. 52, 242n. 4, 256n. 7

Fowles, John, *The French Lieutenant's Woman,* 18–19, 42

fragmentation: and aesthetics, 95, 102; of the subject, 71, 89

Frankfurt School, 8
Fraser, Nancy, and Linda Nicholson, 172, 228–229n. 60
freedom, as relative, 86, 143–144, 169
Freibert, Lucy, 246n. 5, 247n. 13, 248n. 25, 249nn. 30, 32
Friedman, Ellen, 48, 59, 233–234n. 4
Friedman, Susan Stanford, 48
Fuss, Diana, 33, 223n. 2

Gallop, Jane, 26
Gardiner, Judith, 243n. 18, 244nn. 24, 29
Gee, Maggie, 29
gender: disruptions of, 59, 67–69, 120–121, 176–177; and postmodernism, 228n. 57; as socially constructed, 25, 29, 30, 75; and Western thought, 23, 228n. 58
Gilbert, Sandra, and Susan Gubar, 22, 227nn. 52, 55, 239n. 19, 247n. 19
Givner, Jessie, 248n. 21, 249n. 33, 250n. 40
Grass, Gunter, 28
Greene, Gayle, 84–85, 94, 96, 220, 227n. 51, 237n. 4, 240n. 33, 241nn. 43, 45, 242n. 49, 256n. 8
Gubar, Susan, 186, 255n. 36. See Gilbert, Sandra

Habermas, Jurgen, 13
Halliday, David, 245n. 2
Hammer, Stephanie, 246n. 6
Hans, Marie-Françoise, and Gille Lapouge, 186
Hanscombe, Gillian, 234n. 9, 234–235n. 12
Hansen, Elaine, 243n. 17, 244n. 27, 246n. 9, 250nn. 40, 41, 251n. 48
Harari, Josue, 229n. 68
Harding, Sandra, 245n. 33
Hartsock, Nancy, 24, 148, 177, 179, 228n. 58, 238n. 10, 252n. 10
Hassan, Ihab, 11, 15–16, 26, 31, 42, 226n. 46, 231n. 79

Hauser, Arnold, 32, 231n. 82
Hawthorne, Nathaniel, The Scarlet Letter, 157
H.D., 49–50, 77; HERmione, 57–58, 235nn. 17, 18; Nights, 58–59
Hegel, G.W.F., 247n. 20
history: disruptions of, 41–43, 60, 164–170, 212, 244n. 25; and feminism, 42–43, 158; as male-centered, 164, 167; and postmodernism, 1, 17–19, 233n. 106, 251n. 45; reconstruction of, 146
Hite, Molly, 19, 21–22, 80, 220, 223n. 7, 229–230n. 71, 238n. 12, 238–239n. 15, 239nn. 16, 22, 240n. 32, 241nn. 39, 40, 41, 42, 242n. 47, 256n. 8
Howe, Irving, 240n. 36, 241–242n. 46
Huckle, Patricia, 242nn. 5, 8
Hutcheon, Linda, 4, 11, 16–17, 172, 223n. 8, 225n. 28, 226–227n. 47, 228nn. 57, 59, 229n. 60, 230n. 75, 230–231n. 78, 231n. 85, 233nn. 103, 106, 251n. 45, 253n. 21, 254n. 33
Huyssen, Andreas, 13, 17, 18, 27–28, 47, 97, 172, 226n. 41, 227n. 49, 229n. 68, 240–241n. 38
Hynes, Joseph, 241n. 40

identity: as cultural construction, 56, 156, 232n. 93; and feminism, 24–25; and material conditions, 91; as unstable, 32, 34–35, 59–61, 89-90, 137, 153, 175, 184, 195–196; and Western thought, 163. See self, subject
ideology, 224n. 12; and feminism, 7; and representation, 38; of the subject, 27
indeterminacy, 127, 167–168, 195, 199, 219; and identity, 153, 175, 204; and politics, 219; temporal, 203
interpretation, disruption of, 39–40, 106–107, 242n. 49
Irigaray, Luce, 26, 33, 231nn. 83, 84

Jackson, Rosemary, 199, 255n. 44
Jameson, Fredric, 3, 8, 13, 31, 172, 226n. 46, 229n. 68
Jardine, Alice, 26, 31–32, 229n. 67
Jehlen, Myra, 227n. 52
Johnston, John, 231n. 90, 240n. 28, 242n. 50
Jones, Libby, 244–245n. 30
Joplin, Patricia, 237n. 37
Joyce, James, 47

Kaivola, Karen, 237n. 37
Kaplan, E. Ann, 33, 34, 226n. 46, 231–232n. 90
Kaplan, Sydney Janet, 48, 233n. 3
Kauffman, Linda, 81-82, 83, 230n. 75, 237nn. 2, 4, 239n. 27, 240n. 31, 241n. 39, 242n. 46, 248n. 29, 249nn. 32, 33, 250n. 37, 251n. 46
Keinhorst, Annette, 242n. 7
Keith, W.J., 246n. 6, 250n. 41, 251n. 46
Kessler, Carol, 243n. 13, 244n. 30, 245n. 32
Kingston, Maxine Hong, 9; *The Woman Warrior*, 217
Knapp, Mona, 238nn. 8, 12
Kolodny, Annette, 227n. 52
Kristeva, Julia, 26, 229n. 67, 231n. 83
Kroker, Marilouise and Arthur, 232n. 96

Lacan, Jacques, 87–88, 187, 239n. 21
Lacombe, Michele, 247n. 18, 248nn. 22, 24, 26
language: instability of, 26, 39–40, 52, 103–105 121, 213; limits of, 54, 73, 105; as male centered, 51, 55, 121, 234–235n. 12; as material, 55, 58; and the material situation, 17, 30; and politics, 40; and power, 155–157, 160–161, 213. *See* subject
Lapouge, Gilles. *See* Hans, Marie-Françoise
laughter, as liberatory, 197, 206–207, 256n. 51
Lee, Alison, 231n. 78, 252n. 3

lesbianism, 189, 191–192
Lessing, Doris, 9, 47, 171, 192; *The Four-Gated City*, 57, 131; *The Golden Notebook*, 44–45, 57, 79-108, 130–131, 207, 209–221; "A Small Personal Voice," 79
Libby, Marion, 239n. 18
Linker, Kate, 38-39
love, as liberatory, 185, 189, 191, 193, 204–206, 208. *See* desire
Loy, Mina, 49–50, 77; *Insel*, 61-63, 235n. 24
Lyotard, Jean-Francois, 13

Maciunas, Billie, 245n. 33
madness: as constructed, 34, 56–57, 111, 131, 232n. 94; reconceptualization of, 57–58, 89–94, 130–131. *See* schizophrenia
Malak, Amin, 250n. 41
mannerism. *See* aesthetics
Márquez, García, 218
Marxist theory: and feminism, 171–172, 179–180, 184, 208, 255n. 41; and postmodernism, 1, 31, 172; and the Frankfurt School, 8
McCaffery, Larry, 18, 217–218, 226n. 41
McCarthy, Mary, 245n. 2
McCormick, Kathleen, 238n. 14
McCrindle, Jean, 237–238n. 7
McHale, Brian, 12, 28–30, 112, 182, 199, 225n. 30, 230nn. 76, 77, 250n. 42, 251n. 43
metafiction, 136, 173, 232n. 98, 240n. 34
Millett, Kate, 227n. 52
Miner, Madonne, 247n. 18
modernism, 234n. 7; and language, 104; and politics, 17, 47–48; and postmodernism, 16–17, 47–48, 226n. 46. *See* aesthetics, modernist fiction, self, subject
modernist fiction/art, 32, 98, 234n. 5; and feminism, 48, 227n. 51; by women, 45, 47–78; and postmod-

ernism, 16–17, 48. *See* aesthetics, modernism, narrative disruptions
Moers, Ellen, 227n. 52
Moi, Toril, 21, 26, 172, 227n. 52, 236n. 29, 238n. 15, 252n. 8
Moore, Thomas, 223n. 7
Morante, Else, 9; *History: A Novel,* 42–43
Morris, Meaghan, 13
Morrison, Toni, 9; *Beloved,* 42, 217, 256n. 5
mothers, mothering, 116–117, 122–124, 243n. 17, 246n. 9
Mouffe, Chantal, 13, 14, 33, 232n. 95
Moylan, Thomas, 243n. 20
Murphy, Patrick, 245n. 3, 249n. 32

names, naming: and objectification/containment, 55, 104, 153–155, 165, 174, 211; and power, 121–122, 252n. 8; refusal of, 163, 167
narrative disruptions, 40–43, 80, 95, 97–99, 133, 212; and the women modernists, 48, 50, 54, 59
New Woman novel, 48–49, 50, 234n. 6
Nicholson, Linda. *See* Fraser
Nischik, Reingard, 249n. 31, 251nn. 47, 49

oral histories, 159, 162, 164, 167, 174
Orwell, George, *1984,* 169
Other, object, 23, 87–88, 114–115, 153–155, 177–178
overdetermination, 4, 8, 31, 209, 218–219
Owens, Craig, 13, 28, 230n. 73

Palmer, Paulina, 251n. 1, 254n. 31, 255n. 43
Pearson, Carol, 242nn. 4, 6, 243n. 19, 243–244n. 21, 245n. 31
Pfaelzer, Jean, 243nn. 12, 13, 14
Picasso, Pablo, 71
Piercy, Marge, 9, 47, 171, 192; *Woman on the Edge of Time,* 44–45, 109–134, 135, 136, 207, 209–221

Plumwood, Val, 236n. 32
pornography: as critique, 186–187; and feminism, 144, 187, 247n. 13, 255n. 36; and male domination, 149, 186, 188
postmodern fiction, 12–13, 16–19, 32, 43, 227n. 50; and fantasy, 199; and feminism, 6, 8, 24, 28-31, 224n. 10, 230-231n. 78; and the material situation, 7–8; and politics, 1–5, 17, 19, 44, 218. *See* feminist fiction
postmodernity/postmodern condition, 7, 11
postmodern theory, 7, 11–13, 15–16, 26–27; and feminism, 28. *See* feminist theory, poststructuralism
poststructuralism, 14, 97, 220, 229n. 68; and feminism, 20–21, 25–26; and postmodernism, 24, 26–27, 32
Pound, Ezra, 47
prostitution, disruption of, 179–181, 183, 196
Pynchon, Thomas, 16; *Gravity's Rainbow,* 2, 4, 18, 218–219, 223n. 7, 255n. 48

Ragland-Sullivan, Ellie, 239n. 21, 255n. 39
reader. *See* audience
reality: and art, 8–9, 21–22, 32, 36–37, 228n. 56; as mediated/relative, 43, 70, 72, 100, 128–129, 157, 166–167, 199, 212; modernist notion of, 49
realism. *See* aesthetics, feminist fiction
reconstruction: and feminism, 3, 44–45, 134, 209, 214–215, 221; and postmodernism, 4, 16, 27, 31
Reesman, Jeanne, 249nn. 30, 31
representation, 31, 36–39; crisis in, 10, 43; and feminism, 9, 21, 38, 42; and the material situation, 17, 101, 107; and postmodernism, 37–38, 43, 61, 72, 99–104, 159, 176, 211–212, 228n. 59, 252n. 11
reproduction, and power relations, 114, 116, 122–124, 140, 145, 190–191, 255n. 41

Richardson, Dorothy, 49, 77; *Pilgrimage,* 50–52, 234n. 9, 234–235n. 12

Rigney, Barbara, 91, 140, 149, 245n. 1, 246n. 11, 247n. 13, 248n. 25, 249n. 31, 251n. 49

Robinson, Marilynne, 9; *Housekeeping,* 36, 217

Robinson, Sally, 176, 252nn. 7, 8, 253n. 14, 255n. 50

Rorty, Richard, 13

Rosinsky, Natalie, 242n. 3, 244nn. 26, 27

Ross, Andrew, 223n. 9

Rubenstein, Roberta, 90, 237n. 6, 247n. 14, 249n. 30, 250n. 39

Russ, Joanna, 242n. 9

Sage, Lorna, 144

schizophrenia, 239n. 27, 240n. 28. *See* madness

Schmidt, Ricarda, 175, 254n. 34

Schweikart, Patricio, 224n. 23, 239n. 22, 240n. 36

Scott, Joan, 21, 33

self: humanist/essential, 21, 24, 35, 53, 68, 88; modernist, 50, 57, 60; reconstruction of, 34, 36, 53, 184, 195–196, 201, 205, 243n. 16. *See* subject, identity

sexuality: as cultural construction, 22, 23, 29, 148; and desire, 144; and economics, 180–181; and power, 54, 126, 148–154, 178, 246n. 7; and reproduction, 122. *See* desire, pornography, subject, violence

Showalter, Elaine, 25, 227n. 52, 229n. 65, 239n. 27

Siegel, Carol, 252n. 9, 253n. 14

Siegel, Mark, 223n. 7

Sinclair, May, 49–50, 77; *Mary Olivier: A Life,* 56–57

Singer, Linda, 14, 15

Smith, Paul, 231n. 89

Spark, Muriel, 29

Spivak, Gayatri, 26

Sprague, Claire, 238n. 15, 239nn. 20, 22, 240n. 36

Stein, Gertrude, 29, 49–50, 77, 235nn. 15, 19, 242n. 48; *Three Lives,* 52–56

Stimpson, Catherine, 246n. 11, 250n. 36

stream-of-consciousness, 50, 56, 58, 77, 136

subject, subjectivity, 31, 33–36; death of, 15, 16, 17, 27; as centerless/dispersed, 70–71, 236n. 33; as constructed, 33, 55–56, 65–66, 73, 83–84, 184; and desire/sexuality, 153–154, 185, 208; female, 49, 53, 58, 66–67, 76–77, 79–80, 82, 92, 161, 208; and feminism, 10, 23–26, 33–36, 231n. 89; and language, 43, 155, 159–161, 213, 249n. 30; and the material situation, 82–84, 211; modernist, 35, 70–71, 76, 83–84; and power relations, 34, 63, 137, 148, 177, 232n. 94; in process/fluid, 34, 77, 92, 108, 125, 155, 169–170, 184–185, 193, 204, 208 231–232n. 90, 254n. 33, 255n. 50; reconceptualization of, 27, 34–36, 43, 84, 161, 177, 185, 206, 210–211, 213; and writing, 191. *See* identity, self

Sukenick, Ronald, 16, 17

surfiction, 17, 226–227n. 47

Thielmann, Pia, 243n. 20

Thomas, D.M., *The White Hotel,* 18, 19, 40–41

Tiger, Virginia, 241n. 42

time, disruptions of, 36, 67, 133, 135–136, 198–199, 202–203, 236n. 30, 245n. 31

truth, 31; and history, 41; as unstable, 37–38, 58, 60, 99–100, 157–158, 175

Turner, Rory, 256n. 51

underdetermination, 4, 8, 31, 209, 218–219

utopia, utopian fiction: and feminism, 5, 8, 109–113, 119, 134, 171, 191–192, 208, 218–221; and material existence, 205, 219

values, shared, 17, 219–220
violence: and narrative, 132–133; and power, 115, 132, 134, 178, 187–190; sexual, 74–75, 115–116, 143, 153
Vonnegut, Kurt, *Slaughterhouse-Five*, 18

Wagner-Martin, Linda, 247n. 16
Wallis, Brian, 37–38
Walker, Alice, 9; *The Color Purple*, 217, 256n. 5
Waugh, Patricia, 24, 33, 37, 230n. 75, 232n. 98, 240n. 34, 243n. 11, 246n. 4, 248nn. 27, 28, 256n. 3
Weedon, Chris, 26, 33, 34, 231n. 90, 232n. 94, 256n. 1

Weldon, Fay, 9; *The Life and Loves of a She-Devil*, 39, 217
Wiemer, Annagret, 244n. 22
Wilde, Alan, 236n. 33
Wittig, Monique, 28–29
Wolf, Christa, 9; *Cassandra*, 40, 43, 217
Wolff, Janet, 9, 15, 33, 38, 224n. 14, 225n. 29, 226n. 40, 230n. 75, 232n. 93
Wood, Michael, and Louis Zurcher, 34
Woolf, Leonard, 64
Woolf, Virginia, 49–50, 64, 77, 236n. 29; *Between the Acts*, 64, 67, 70–76, 119; "Mr. Bennett and Mrs. Brown," 64–65; *Mrs. Dalloway*, 87; *Orlando*, 64, 67–70, 171, 236n. 30, 255n. 47; *A Room of One's Own*, 65–66; *Three Guineas*, 65–67, 236n. 28; *The Waves*, 84
writing, 155–157, 168, 191, 248n. 25

Zurcher, Louis, Jr. *See* Wood, Michael

35870109